"Galatians and Romans have challenged and nurtured readers of Scripture for generations. To those who are familiar with Brendan Byrne's work, it will come as no surprise to find here an informed and informative guide to Paul's most challenging letters."

—Beverly Roberts Gaventa
Helen H. P. Manson Professor of
New Testament Literature and Exegesis
Princeton Theological Seminary, New Jersey

"Brendan Byrne has written a remarkably clear and persuasive interpretation of Galatians and Romans, two of Paul's most influential and controversial letters. He brings out both the similarities and the very real differences between the two letters and points to their significance for the latter church. I found his interpretations always insightful and helpful. He has done all of this in a way that is both well argued and easily accessible to a wider audience."

—Thomas H. Tobin, SJ
Professor of Theology
Loyola University Chicago

"Brendan Byrne brings wide learning, passion for Paul, and skill as a teacher to two of the most important documents in the Christian Bible. His clear and concise expositions can open these sometimes difficult Pauline texts to beginners in exegesis and theology, and provide a model of engaged and effective pedagogy. His glossary alone is one of the best introductions to Paul's theology that I know."

—Daniel J. Harrington, SJ
Professor of New Testament
Boston College School of Theology
and Ministry

Galatians and Romans

Brendan Byrne, SJ

LITURGICAL PRESS
Collegeville, Minnesota

www.litpress.org

Nihil Obstat: Reverend Robert Harren, *Censor deputatus*.

Imprimatur: ✛ Most Reverend John F. Kinney, J.C.D., D.D., Bishop of Saint Cloud, Minnesota. August 2, 2010.

Cover design by Ann Blattner. Image courtesy of Photos.com.

1   2   3   4   5   6   7   8   9

Library of Congress Cataloging-in-Publication Data

Byrne, Brendan (Brendan J.)
   Galatians and Romans / Brendan Byrne.
     p. cm.
   ISBN 978-0-8146-3324-3 — ISBN 978-0-8146-3937-5 (e-book)
      1. Bible. N.T. Galatians—Commentaries.   2. Bible. N.T.
   Romans—Commentaries.   I. Title.
   BS2685.53.B97 2010
   227'.1077—dc22   2010028895

Contents

Introduction

It is fitting to consider Paul's Letter to the Galatians and his Letter to the Romans together. This is so not only because they are similar in content but also because of the contribution that each has made to Christian life down the ages. Linking them in content is their common focus on the issue of whether right relationship with God ("righteousness") is attained through observance of the law of Moses or through faith. The precise terms in which Paul addressed that issue hardly bear on our concerns today. In fact, it was largely resolved well before the close of the first century AD. The theological depth, however, at which Paul addressed the issue in the two letters made a profound contribution to the forging of Christian identity especially when, along with the gospels and his remaining letters, they became part of the canon of Christian Scripture a century or so later on.

Above all, both letters stood at the center of the Reformation protest that rocked and eventually split the Christian Church in the sixteenth century. In fact, the beginning of the Reformation can with some justification be traced to Martin Luther's lectures on Romans (1515–16) and then Galatians (1517–18) at Wittenberg.

Thankfully, we live now at a time when the polemics of the sixteenth century have largely been put to rest. The contribution that Reformers such as Luther and Calvin made to the interpretation of the letters is now accepted within the Catholic tradition. Indeed the Second Vatican Council (1962–65) in many ways represented a recapturing on the part of the Catholic Church of a Pauline legacy that had largely become the prerogative of the churches of the Reformation.

While similar in content and influence on the Christian tradition, the two letters are very different in tone. Galatians is sharply polemical, Paul's anger frequently breaking through. Romans, by contrast, is measured, expansive, diplomatic—designed perhaps to correct an image of Paul created by the earlier letter. Where Galatians is one of the earliest of his surviving letters, Romans presents a mature understanding of the Gospel late in his apostolic career.

The two letters, then, make an interesting contrast while also shedding light on each other. It is helpful to consider them together but appropriate to begin with the earlier, shorter, and in some respects more engaging letter: Galatians.

All of Paul's letters, but these two in particular, throw up a great deal of Paul's distinctive theological terms and concepts. To assist the study of the letters a glossary of these terms and concepts gathers them together in an alphabetical list at the end of the book, with brief descriptions and references. Readers may find it helpful to consult this glossary when encountering an unfamiliar term not explained at that particular point in the running commentary.

Introduction to Galatians

Of all Paul's letters, Galatians provides by far the most information about Paul's own life, notably in the opening two chapters. This is one of its most interesting features. At the same time, while shedding much light on Paul himself, the letter leaves us in considerable ignorance regarding the people to whom it was written. Paul addresses his letter to "the churches of Galatia" (1:2), clearly meaning a number of communities of believers in a region identified as "Galatia." The problem is that at the time of Paul such a region could be understood in two distinct ways. In the early third century BC a Celtic people, known as the Galatai, invaded Asia Minor, and were, after a series of defeats by surrounding kingdoms, confined to a small area around the capital of present-day Turkey, Ankara (ancient Ancyra). In the late first century BC they were incorporated by the Romans into a much larger area to form the Roman province of "Galatia." The question is whether, when Paul wrote his letter, he was addressing the ethnic Galatians who lived in what was now their homeland in the northern regions of the Roman province, or whether he was addressing communities of believers who, with no necessary ethnic connection to the Galatians, simply lived within the boundaries of what was now "Galatia" in terms of the Roman province.

If the latter is the case, then it is possible to identify the recipients of the letter with the communities evangelized by Paul and Barnabas in what is conventionally termed his First Missionary Journey as described in Acts 13–14: that is, communities in the cities of Antioch in Pisidia, Derbe, Lystra, and Iconium (Konya). The problem is that Acts depicts Paul making converts in these cities from Gentiles who already had association with the Jewish synagogues, whereas the evidence of Paul's letter suggests that those to whom he was writing became believers directly from paganism. All in all, it is difficult to harmonize the evidence in Acts and Paul's letter in regard to the identity of the Galatians, and, in any case, precise identification has little bearing on its interpretation.

What is important is to recognize that the Galatians as addressed by Paul were converts from paganism living in central Asia Minor, who at a very vulnerable moment of Paul's life had shown him great kindness and received in return the gift of faith (4:13-14). The very special bond and sense of parental love in him (4:15-20) forged by this initial experience explains Paul's outrage that intruders who had subsequently come among his converts should sever the Galatians' allegiance to himself personally and to the Gospel as he had taught it.

When precisely the intrusion occurred and when and from where Paul composed his response is also uncertain. Acts tells of a long, almost three-year stay of Paul in Ephesus in the course of his Third Missionary Journey (19:1-41). It is likely that it was during this period that Paul faced both the difficulties to the west that prompted his correspondence with Corinth (1 and 2 Corinthians) and the difficulties to the east that prompted Galatians. This locates the composition of the letter some time in the early to mid-fifties AD but further precision is impossible.

What is more significant is the identity of the intruders and what they were saying about Paul and the inadequacy of his original formation of the Galatians in Christian faith and practice. As is the case with all Paul's letters, we have only one side of the "conversation." We have to reconstruct the situation that prompted the letter from what Paul says in it—especially by detecting arguments and accusations about himself made by the intruders that he seems at pains to rebut.

In his original stay among them Paul presumably had evangelized the non-Jewish (Gentile) Galatians according to his understanding of the Gospel. That is, he had not said anything to them about a need to take on the requirements of the Jewish law, especially the ritual requirements of circumcision, keeping the Sabbath, and various laws regarding food. They had to adopt the basic faith of Israel—the worship of the one true God—and live by the strict ethical precepts of the law. But they did not need to become Jews in order to be fully members of the end-time People of God, destined for salvation.

Some time after Paul went on his way, other Christian missionaries arrived in these communities in Galatia. Unlike Paul, they held that all believers, including those from the Gentile world, had to take on the practice of the law of Moses completely. Not content with implementing this policy in their own area—presumably Jerusalem and Judea—they actively sought to bring the Gentile communities converted on Paul's terms into conformity with it. In the early decades of the Christian movement it seems we have to reckon with a considerable variety of views in regard to the terms on which people of non-Jewish background (Gentiles) should be admitted to the community of believers. In relation to Judaism and the practice of the law there was a sliding scale, with these "intruders" at one extreme and Paul at the other. Where other leading figures such as James, the brother of the Lord, and Peter, stood is not entirely clear. In Acts, as well as in Galatians, both are represented as not requiring the imposition of circumcision on Gentile converts. Yet clearly by the time of the writing of Galatians, James, the leader in Jerusalem, remains very close to the Jewish heritage, while Peter's position would appear to be more complex and was perhaps shifting. If Paul's account in Galatians 2:11-14 is to be believed, after a clear adherence to the Pauline stance, Peter retreated to a more conservative position, closer to that of James.

While not necessarily directly inspired by James, the intruders represented the most rigorous position in regard to Gentile acceptance of the full yoke of the law. From the content of Galatians we can get some idea of how they were presenting their case. In the opening two chapters, Paul seems to be rebutting a contention that whatever apostolic status he has is secondary and subservient to that of the leading apostles, that he has spent time in Jerusalem being instructed by them, submitting to their direction and, in the matter of circumcision perhaps, even to their correction. Argument along these lines would explain Paul's insistence that his apostolic status stemmed directly from the risen Lord (1:1, 15-16) quite *independently* of the leading figures in Jerusalem. It would also account for his stress upon the formal *recognition* those same leading figures gave to his God-given responsibility for the Gentile apostolate: their public acknowledgment that the same Lord who called Peter to the evangelization of the Jews has bestowed on him a parallel—not dependent—calling in regard to the Gentiles (2:7-8).

The long discussion of Scripture (Old Testament) that occupies the central section of the letter (chaps. 3–4), with a particular focus on Abraham, suggests also that the intruders bolstered their case by scriptural argument. In particular, they would appear to have portrayed Abraham as at once the archetypal convert from paganism and the obedient fulfiller of the divine ordinance in regard to circumcision. Paul's lengthy "reclaiming" of Abraham as a figure of faith rather than obedience to law is clearly designed to address such a position.

Finally, it is likely that the intruders believed—even if they did not say so explicitly—that, without commitment to the law, recent converts from the Gentile world would lack effective motivation for living up to the strict ethical code required of the People of God. Hence Paul's insistence in the final section of the letter (chaps. 5–6) that freedom from the law does not mean license but is essentially expressed in love: that "the whole law is fulfilled in one statement, namely, 'You shall love your neighbor as yourself'" (5:14).

The foregoing may give the impression that Paul's Letter to the Galatians concerns an issue (freedom from the law) of little interest to readers of today. This would be unfortunate. The nerve point of Paul's objection to the Galatians' taking on the yoke of the law is his conviction that reliance on the law means nullifying or rendering otiose the supremely costly death of Christ upon the cross. When Paul says, "I have been crucified with Christ; . . . I live, no longer I, but Christ lives in me; insofar as I now live in the flesh, I live by faith in the Son of God who has loved me and given himself up for me" (Gal 2:19b-20), he is speaking not simply of himself. Every baptized believer should be able to take those words to himself or herself. Christ has loved me and given himself up for me. The freedom I now enjoy—from sin, law, and (eternal) death— is a freedom bought at supreme cost. To abandon or make light of it is to reject the love of Christ. No other letter of Paul puts the matter so starkly and so personally as this.

Paul's argument moves, then, not only from the thought of what Christ has done in the past but also from the present situation of believers. Baptism has created an ongoing union with the risen Lord in which former criteria of identity—ethnic, social, gender-determined—have lost relevance (3:26-28). The blessings of salvation, promised in the Scriptures to Abraham, are focused on Christ and come to believers in virtue of their union with him. Central to those blessings is the gift of the Spirit. The Spirit assures believers that Christ has already drawn them into the intimacy of his own filial relationship with God (4:6-7) and guarantees the hope of a fullness of salvation as an inheritance to come (5:5). In the place of the law the Spirit has also become both the guide and the energizing force of the new moral life where faith finds its essential expression in love (5:6). I have touched on a few of the rich theological seams mined by Paul in the course of his letter. It will be my task as interpreter to draw them out from beneath the surface of the text.

Whereas once Galatians stood at the nerve center of relations between Protestants and Catholics, there is some justification in seeing it now as standing at the nerve center of relations between Christians and Jews. It is possible to read Galatians in a way that is anti-Jewish, if not anti-Semitic. Such a reading, particularly in light of the Holocaust, is irresponsible and unethical as well as being, I believe, unfaithful to the text itself. Galatians does not record a division between Christians and Jews. Paul is contending in the letter not with Jews but with fellow Christians who have a different view of the terms on which those who respond positively to the Gospel from the Gentile world should become members of the community of faith. If, in the course of arguing strongly against imposition of the Jewish law upon such Gentiles, Paul makes negative statements about the law, it is this context that should be kept in mind when evaluating such statements in regard to Judaism. Galatians is not the text to go to when assessing the broader question of Paul's attitude to his ancestral people and their distinctive faith. That is something he takes up far more expressly and calmly in Romans, especially Romans 9–11.

Before taking up more detailed examination of the text, it will help to set out the basic structure of the letter. In his letters Paul adheres to the conventions of letter writing in the ancient world. Letters normally consisted of three sections: an introductory section, the main body of the letter, and a conclusion. The introduction itself usually contained three parts: an address naming the sender and recipients, a greeting, and an expression of hopes or thanksgiving for the health and well-being of the recipients. Paul normally turns this third part of the introduction into a thanksgiving prayer to God. The conclusion normally contains some indication of travel plans, greetings from others associated with the sender, and a final grace. This basic structure can be seen in Galatians, with the significant omission of the thanksgiving element in the introduction and the greetings in the conclusion.

OUTLINE OF GALATIANS

Introduction: 1:1-5:

Address and Greeting: 1:1-5

Body of the Letter: 1:6–6:10

Opening Astonished Protest: No "Other Gospel": 1:6-10

1. Paul's Apostolic Independence and Credibility: 1:11–2:21

The Divine Origin of Paul's Gospel: 1:11-12

Paul's Apostolic Call and Independence from Jerusalem: 1:13-24

Persecutor of the Church: 1:13-14

Encounter with God's Son and Calling: 1:15-16a

Paul's Early Years as a Believer: 1:16b-24

Paul's Letter to the Galatians

INTRODUCTION: 1:1-5

Address and Greeting: 1:1-5

> [1:1]Paul, an apostle not from human beings nor through a human being but through Jesus Christ and God the Father who raised him from the dead, [2]and all the brothers who are with me, to the churches of Galatia: [3]grace to you and peace from God our Father and the Lord Jesus Christ, [4]who gave himself for our sins that he might rescue us from the present evil age in accord with the will of our God and Father, [5]to whom be glory forever and ever. Amen.

Paul's letters normally open with an address, a greeting, and a thanksgiving prayer. Galatians is unique in the glaring absence of this third element. From what he has heard about the churches of Galatia Paul evidently feels—and signals by this omission—that he has nothing to be grateful for. Even the self-description in the address sounds a polemical note that will become insistent as the letter unfolds. Paul is an apostle, appointed not by human beings but by Jesus Christ and the Father who sent him and raised him from the dead. From the very start, then, Paul moves to counter any suggestion that he is not an apostle of equal rank and authority with others such as Peter and John.

Paul's problem was that there were divergent "definitions" of what it meant to be an apostle abroad in the early church. As far as he was concerned, there were only two criteria for this office: to have seen the risen Lord (that is, be a resurrection witness) and to have been commissioned by him to preach the Gospel and found churches. Another criterion, seen later in the Lukan literature (Acts 1:21-26; cf. Luke 6:13), was to have been a disciple of Jesus during his earthly life. This third criterion would exclude Paul from being an apostle of equal status with Peter and the rest of the Twelve. He could only be an apostle in a secondary sense, dependent on appointment to this office on the part of the original apostles chosen by Jesus. Hence his insistence that his apostleship in no sense flowed from human appointment but came to him directly from the risen Lord.

Paul includes in the senders of the letter "all the brothers who are with me" (v 2), a reference presumably to his coworkers in the mission. The strict translation "brothers" need not exclude women coworkers, since "brothers" was an inclusive term for members of the community of believers as the "family of God," and Paul elsewhere salutes several women as fellow workers (cf. Rom 16:1-7; Phil 4:2-3). The collective reference lends the sense that it is not simply Paul who has a problem with the communities in Galatia; he is calling them to account in the name of the wider mission.

The greeting or grace (v 3), while standard for a Pauline letter, concludes on a significant note. Christ "gave himself for our sins that he might rescue us from the present evil age in accord with the will of our God and Father" (v 4). As we have noted already, the sense of Christ's supremely costly self-gift on behalf of sinful human beings on the cross is the nerve point of Paul's rejection of any rival factor in the gaining of salvation—notably taking on the ritual requirements of the Jewish law (cf. esp. 2:19-20). To adopt such a path is to fly in the face of this divine act and render it otiose (2:21).

What Christ is rescuing us from is the "present evil age." This pessimistic judgment reflects the worldview of apocalyptic Judaism, which is the background to Paul's argument in the letter. In this perspective, which Paul shares with virtually all the New Testament writers, there is a profound pessimism in regard to the present state of affairs. The world as currently constituted is beyond repair. The faithful can only look to divine intervention, which will involve judgment and condemnation on the powers presently prevailing in the world, followed by a radical transformation on a truly cosmic scale. For Paul, and Christian believers generally, this divine intervention has already begun through the sending of the Son. Christ's obedience "to death" (Phil 2:8) on the cross, his resurrection and exaltation to God's right hand, have brought about the radical defeat of the powers opposed to God and the dawning of a new age attested by the Spirit. But this is only the beginning. Believers await the return of Christ to complete his messianic work. While bodily anchored in the present (evil) age, through the union with him brought about through faith and baptism, they share his entrance into the new age of the kingdom, enjoying a renewed relationship with God, attested by the gift of the Spirit. Hence Paul's distress at learning of the Galatians' temptation to place themselves back in a relationship with God belonging to the old era that they have radically outgrown: namely, life under the Jewish law.

BODY OF THE LETTER: 1:6–6:10

Opening Astonished Protest: No "Other Gospel": 1:6-10

> [6]I am amazed that you are so quickly forsaking the one who called you by [the] grace [of Christ] for a different gospel [7](not that there is another). But there are some who are disturbing you and wish to pervert the gospel of Christ. [8]But even if we or an angel from heaven should preach [to you] a gospel other than the one that we preached to you, let that one be accursed! [9]As we have said before, and now I say again, if anyone preaches to you a gospel other than the one that you received, let that one be accursed!
>
> [10]Am I now currying favor with human beings or God? Or am I seeking to please people? If I were still trying to please people, I would not be a slave of Christ.

In place of the customary thanksgiving, Paul sails straight into the main agenda of his letter with a strong expression of astonishment and reproach. How can the Galatians be forsaking so soon the one who called them by "[the] grace [of Christ] for a different gospel"? "The one who called them" refers not to Paul but to God. In forsaking the Gospel as he preached it to them, the Galatians are undermining and rebuffing the saving action of God in their regard. The move they are being tempted to make is no mere addition to or fulfillment of their original conversion. It is something that introduces—if that were possible—"another gospel," that would stand over against the Gospel of the God who has reached out to them in the grace of Christ.

This sense of God as a God of grace (*charis*) is the essential theological vision that stands behind the letter and Paul's writings as a whole. Perhaps we should linger here for a moment. The Greek word *charis* most basically denotes the charm or attractiveness of a person that spontaneously wins the favor of others. Reciprocally, then, it denotes the favor and goodwill created in the other person through such charm. More concretely *charis* can refer to a gift bestowed on a person as an expression of such favor. In the New Testament the Greek term picks up the sense, flowing from biblical (Old Testament) usage, of the favor of God bestowed on human beings, with or without their doing anything to merit it. For Paul the sense of unmerited divine favor predominates. He sees the entire sending and work of Christ as the spear point of an immense wave of God's grace flowing over a sinful world, seeking to reconcile it to its Creator (2 Cor 5:18–6:2; Rom 5:15). This is the heart of the Gospel that he preaches and that the Galatians have heard. There cannot be any "other gospel" (v 7)—especially one that involved taking on the yoke of the law—because that would purport to establish a relationship with God based on something other than grace.

In his strength of feeling about this Paul does not mince his words (vv 8-9). He calls down a curse (*anathema*) on any who might seek to proclaim an alternative gospel, including (hypothetically) even himself or an angel of God under its scope. A curse in the biblical sense assigns someone to divine destruction. The original call of the Galatians is a divine act that cannot be undone—not even by Paul himself. Those intruders now attempting to set it aside—and by implication the Galatians tempted to follow them—expose themselves to the destructive power of Paul's curse. We may not be too comfortable with such language. But we do not have to look far back from our own time to see that perversions of the Gospel, often with deadly implications in social terms, have not been confined to Paul's day.

Paul's protest climaxes (v 10) in a series of rhetorical questions that seem designed to counter the charges the intruders laid against him. Maybe Paul avoided mention of the obligation to take on the painful requirement of circumcision because what he was offering was a "soft selling" of the Gospel aimed at easy conversion rather than the requirements of God. Paul simply rejects such a charge outright. If he were seeking to please human beings rather than God, he would not be "a slave of Jesus Christ," bearing the scars that persecutions and labors have "branded" on his body to show to whom he belongs (6:17b). The apostolic life is no recipe for human approval.

1. Paul's Apostolic Independence and Credibility: 1:11–2:21

The Divine Origin of Paul's Gospel: 1:11-12

> [11]Now I want you to know, brothers, that the gospel preached by me is not of human origin. [12]For I did not receive it from a human being, nor was I taught it, but it came through a revelation of Jesus Christ.

Having gotten his anger out of his system for the time being, Paul addresses the Galatians more calmly. They are still his "brothers [and sisters]," fellow members of the "family" of God. He then goes straight to the point. The intruders presumably charged that the Gospel as he preached it lacked authority. Not being one of the original apostles, Paul has it "secondhand," as it were, and so is liable to correction or completion on the part of those who received it first. For Paul the divine origin of his Gospel stems from the fact that it came to him directly and immediately as "a revelation of Jesus Christ," that is, as a divine "uncovering" of the truth that Jesus of Nazareth, the crucified One, is indeed Messiah and Son of God (cf. 1:15-16; Rom 1:3-4). The autobiographical details in the remainder of this section (1:13–2:21) are all designed to establish this truth.

Paul's Apostolic Call and Independence from Jerusalem: 1:13-24

[13]For you heard of my former way of life in Judaism, how I persecuted the church of God beyond measure and tried to destroy it, [14]and progressed in Judaism beyond many of my contemporaries among my race, since I was even more a zealot for my ancestral traditions. [15]But when [God], who from my mother's womb had set me apart and called me through his grace, was pleased [16]to reveal his Son to me, so that I might proclaim him to the Gentiles, I did not immediately consult flesh and blood, [17]nor did I go up to Jerusalem to those who were apostles before me; rather, I went into Arabia and then returned to Damascus.

[18]Then after three years I went up to Jerusalem to confer with Cephas and remained with him for fifteen days. [19]But I did not see any other of the apostles, only James the brother of the Lord. [20](As to what I am writing to you, behold, before God, I am not lying.) [21]Then I went into the regions of Syria and Cilicia. [22]And I was unknown personally to the churches of Judea that are in Christ; [23]they only kept hearing that "the one who once was persecuting us is now preaching the faith he once tried to destroy." [24]So they glorified God because of me.

Persecutor of the Church: 1:13-14

We now enter upon a section of the letter that provides us with a good deal of information about Paul's early career. He does not provide this information for its own sake. It is selected and shaped for the sole purpose of establishing his apostolic credentials independent of the other apostolic authorities in Jerusalem. Hence Paul's insistence over and over again of how *little* contact he had with Jerusalem in the years immediately following his coming to faith in the risen Lord.

To make the point that his coming to faith and apostolic call involved a rupture in his life so great as to point inexorably to divine intervention rather than mere human transition, Paul sums up his preconversion life in Judaism. He was no likely candidate for conversion to faith in Jesus. On the contrary, as the Galatians well know, he was one of the most zealous young Pharisees of his age. In fact, his commitment to the traditions of his people drove him to become a persecutor of the church of God, seeking its destruction (also 1 Cor 15:9; Phil 3:5-6). It is not entirely clear what it was about the early believers in Jesus that so drew the ire of the young Jewish zealot. In any case, whatever the precise motive, the main point is clear: his life at the time was going in a direction diametrically opposite to that which might lead to conversion to Christ. If such a conversion was to take place—as indeed it did—it could only have been due to the intervention of God.

Encounter with God's Son and Calling: 1:15-16a

The actual description of this divine intervention is tucked away in the opening clause of a long sentence (vv 15-17), the main purpose of which is to assert Paul's absence from Jerusalem in the years immediately afterward. The language in which Paul describes his call ("from my mother's womb . . . set me apart") consciously echoes the call of prophetic figures in the Old Testament (Jer 1:4-5; Isa 49:1, 5-6). In line with these biblical figures, Paul sees himself as divinely chosen from the earliest moment of his existence for a saving role in regard to the nations of the world. While his persecuting career was at full cry, divine grace reached out to activate the vocation God had in store for him from the start, turning his life in a diametrically opposite direction.

The traditional understanding of Paul's conversion is largely determined by the three accounts of the event given in the book of Acts (9:1-19; 22:3-21; 26:9-18). These describe a visual experience on the road to Damascus where the risen Lord appears to Paul, identifies himself as "Jesus, whom you are persecuting" (9:5) and tells him to go into the city and await further instructions (subsequently completed by a disciple named Ananias). These later and more detailed accounts "unpack" with some plausibility the meeting that Paul describes so tersely here as God's being "pleased to reveal his Son to me." The crucified Nazarene, concerning whom claims were being made that up to now the zealous young Pharisee had regarded as blasphemy, was now revealed to him as not only Messiah of Israel but God's very own Son. The most profound comment on the experience is probably that given by Paul in a striking sentence in 2 Corinthians: "For God who said, 'Let light shine out of darkness' has shone in our hearts to bring to light the knowledge of the glory of God on the face of [Jesus] Christ" (4:6). In the "darkness" of his unbelief the Creator had said, "Let there be light" (Gen 1:3). So much of what Paul will write with such passion in the remainder of Galatians can be traced to the radical transformation in his life and understanding described here.

Besides referring to a revelation of God's Son "to" Paul (NAB), the Greek phrase (*en emoi*) could also have an instrumental sense echoing biblical (Hebrew) usage. The meaning would then be "reveal his Son *through* me," that is, as an instrument of the Gospel to the nations of the world. This sense prepares the way for the following purpose clause, "so that I might proclaim him to the Gentiles" (v 16b). We should probably recognize some intentional ambiguity in Paul's expression at this point. The total statement brings out the essential unity between his coming to faith in the crucified Messiah and his missionary vocation as apostle to the Gentiles.

Paul's Early Years as a Believer: 1:16b-24

The richly theological statements about Paul's call and mission (vv 15-16a) that are of such interest to us lead into what is most important for him: to insist on his independence from Jerusalem (vv 16b-24). He did not consult with any human being (literally, in biblical language, "flesh and blood"), nor go up to Jerusalem to confer with those who were apostles before him. Instead he went into Arabia, before returning to Damascus. By "Arabia" Paul could simply mean the region of the kingdom of Nabatea, which extended south and east of Damascus. In this case he would simply be indicating the beginning of his missionary career in the cities of this region. On the other hand, it could be that he is reporting on a period spent in the wilderness, in which, like his prophetic forerunner Elijah, he sought to come to terms with his prophetic mission (cf. 1 Kgs 19:1-18), before returning—again like Elijah—to Damascus.

Paul cannot deny, however, that there was one visit to Jerusalem, which included contact with at least two of the leading figures. But this occurred only "after three years" and, in Paul's carefully chosen language, involved a stay of fifteen days with Cephas (that is, Simon Peter) in order to "confer" with him (v 18). The Greek verb here translated "confer" has the sense of "visit with the purpose of finding out information." The information that Peter was uniquely equipped to provide had to do, surely, with the person of Jesus and all that he said and did during his earthly life. Though the pre-passion life and teaching of Jesus feature minimally in the letters of Paul, it is hard to believe that they lacked all interest for him. As the British scholar C. K. Barrett has drily observed, "They hardly spent two weeks talking about the weather!" The only other leading figure that Paul saw was James (v 19). This was not James, the son of Zebedee, one of the Twelve, but a member of Jesus' family ("the brother of the Lord"), who was eventually to replace Peter as leader of the community in Jerusalem. Aside from contact with these two figures, Paul insists with what is virtually an oath (v 20), that he saw none of the remaining apostles. The visit to Jerusalem was private and brief. It in no way involved his receiving commissioning or authorization from them.

Immediately afterward, Paul withdrew to the region of Damascus ("Syria") where he had experienced the call, and to Cilicia, his own native region (v 21). This brief reference is all we have to fill out more than a decade in Paul's life (around AD 40–49) about which we know very little. It was a time of missionary endeavor, since, as he himself tells us (vv 22-24), though his face was not known to the communities in Jerusalem, they "glorified God" because they were well aware that "the one who once was persecuting us is now preaching the faith he once tried to destroy." For Paul, however, the main point is his absence from Jerusalem throughout these years.

An Important Meeting in Jerusalem: 2:1-10

> 2:1Then after fourteen years I again went up to Jerusalem with Barnabas, taking Titus along also. 2I went up in accord with a revelation, and I presented to them the gospel that I preach to the Gentiles—but privately to those of repute—so that I might not be running, or have run, in vain. 3Moreover, not even Titus, who was with me, although he was a Greek, was compelled to be circumcised, 4but because of the false brothers secretly brought in, who slipped in to spy on our freedom that we have in Christ Jesus, that they might enslave us— 5to them we did not submit even for a moment, so that the truth of the gospel might remain intact for you. 6 But from those who were reputed to be important (what they once were makes

no difference to me; God shows no partiality)—those of repute made me add nothing. [7]On the contrary, when they saw that I had been entrusted with the gospel to the uncircumcised, just as Peter to the circumcised, [8]for the one who worked in Peter for an apostolate to the circumcised worked also in me for the Gentiles, [9]and when they recognized the grace bestowed upon me, James and Cephas and John, who were reputed to be pillars, gave me and Barnabas their right hands in partnership, that we should go to the Gentiles and they to the circumcised. [10]Only, we were to be mindful of the poor, which is the very thing I was eager to do.

Although the long period of Paul's evangelizing work in Syria and Cilicia remains obscure, it seems that during this time he was already fulfilling his distinctive call to be Apostle to the Gentiles, though this does not mean that he was not also proclaiming Messiah Jesus to Jews. Acts suggests that he was pursuing this missionary work very much as an emissary of the community of believers at Antioch, with a Jewish believer of Cypriot origin, Barnabas, performing something of the role of mentor to Paul (Acts 11:22-26).

At some stage, probably around the year AD 49, both apostles, Paul and Barnabas, sensed the need to have their missionary policy in regard to Gentile converts formally acknowledged by the leaders of the mother church in Jerusalem. This led to the significant meeting in Jerusalem that Paul describes at this point in Galatians (2:1-10). While there are some differences and discrepancies, the meeting in question is almost certainly the same as that described at greater length in Acts 15:1-29. The two accounts can be harmonized on the understanding that Luke, writing much later, has turned what was initially a rather private meeting between Paul and Barnabas and the three Jerusalem leaders (James, Peter ["Cephas"], John) into a large plenary gathering. Luke also adds to the agreement clauses in regard to food (Acts 15:19-20, 28-29) that seem to stem from a later meeting at which Paul was not present. What the two accounts are agreed on are the names of the leading figures involved (Paul and Barnabas, on the one hand; James and Peter [with the addition of John in Gal 2:9], on the other) and the fact that all agreed that converts from the Gentile world were not to be required to submit to circumcision.

It is this latter point that was, of course, most important for Paul. But it emerges in a rather oblique way in the rather tortuous account of the meeting that he now provides. Paul has to walk something of a tightrope here. He has to admit that, yes, eventually after a period of fourteen years (v 1), he did revisit Jerusalem. But this was not in response to a summons but rather as a result of a "revelation" (v 2). Quite aside from any human impetus, the same Lord who had called him to the apostolic task many years before was now impelling him, along with Barnabas, to go up to Jerusalem and lay before the leaders there the Gospel as he preached it among the Gentiles. Paul chooses his language ("lay before") carefully; he is not seeking approval or confirmation but rather recognition for the sake of the unity of the church.

Whether or not the issue of circumcision featured in this exposition of the Gospel we do not know. It was resolved, at least to Paul's satisfaction, in what occurred—or, rather, did not occur—in relation to Titus. Titus, who was later to play a significant role in Paul's relations with the community at Corinth, was a coworker of Paul of Gentile origin (literally "Greek" [v 3]) and as such uncircumcised. Paul seems to have brought him to Jerusalem as a test case. If Titus was not compelled to undergo circumcision, despite the presence and pressure of "false brethren" who in some underhand way had discovered his condition (literally "the freedom that we have in Christ Jesus" [v 4]), then this was tantamount to the leaders' acceptance of Paul's circumcision-free Gospel. Paul's "not yielding" for an instant to the demand that Titus be circumcised ensured that the "truth of the gospel" should stand for all Gentile believers, including the Galatians (v 5).

The remainder of the account (vv 6-10) bears on what was likely to have been the main agenda of the meeting: the recognition on the part of the leaders that Paul had received a mandate from the risen Lord to proclaim the Gospel to the Gentiles (literally "the uncircumcised") in parallel to the mandate that Peter had received from the same Lord in regard to the Jews. While clearly valuing the recognition he received, sealed by a handshake (literally "the right hands of partnership"), Paul speaks of the leaders—James, Cephas, and John—somewhat disparagingly ("who are reckoned to be pillars"). They are merely human figures; their approval does not mean much to him in view of the divine commissioning he already enjoys. The main point is that they recognized his distinctive gift (v 9) and did not add any further stipulation (v 6) to the Gospel as he preached it, in particular, anything in regard to circumcision.

One thing "the pillars" did ask of Paul and his coworkers was that they should "be mindful of the poor" (v 10a). "The poor" was an honorific title for the mother community of believers in Jerusalem. Paul is recalling here an agreement to raise a collection from his Gentile churches for the relief of this community, doubtless severely affected by the general economic hardship prevalent in Palestine at the time. As references in other letters show (1 Cor 16:1-4; Rom 15:25-28, 31; 2 Cor 8–9), Paul took this commitment very seriously. For him the collection was no mere relief measure but a key symbol of the unity of the overall church. Through it his Gentile churches acknowledged their debt in terms of spiritual blessings to the mother church in Jerusalem (Rom 15:27), while gracious acceptance of it on the part of that church would signal recognition of the Pauline communities as full partners and members of the one people of God.

But even this "clause" in regard to the collection, Paul is at pains to point out, was not something imposed on him. It was something he was always "eager" to do (v 10b). Once more, then, he has described a moment of significant contact with the church in Jerusalem. At the same time he has made clear that it was not approval or commissioning or delegation that he received but a recognition, solemnly sealed, of his God-given "gift" to proclaim the Gospel among the Gentiles, in the terms and conditions in which he and Barnabas had been proclaiming it hitherto.

Confrontation at Antioch: Paul Severely Rebukes Peter: 2:11-14:

[11]And when Cephas came to Antioch, I opposed him to his face because he clearly was wrong. [12]For, until some people came from James, he used to eat with the Gentiles; but when they came, he began to draw back and separated himself, because he was afraid of the circumcised. [13]And the rest of the Jews [also] acted hypocritically along with him, with the result that even Barnabas was carried away by their hypocrisy. [14]But when I saw that they were not on the right road in line with the truth of the gospel, I said to Cephas in front of all, "If you, though a Jew, are living like a Gentile and not like a Jew, how can you compel the Gentiles to live like Jews?"

The meeting in Jerusalem may have resolved the matter of circumcision. There were other prickly areas of relations between believers of Jewish and Gentile backgrounds that it did not address. For the benefit of his Galatian audience, and still in the interests of promoting his independence of human authority, Paul recalls an incident in Antioch in which he fell out sharply and bitterly with Peter (Cephas) over the issue of Gentile and Jewish believers sharing meals in common.

The meeting in Jerusalem had recognized separate and equal spheres of apostolate and mission: Peter to the Jews; Paul to the Gentiles (2:7-9). This neat division would have worked well in areas where communities of believers, Jewish and Gentile, were geographically separated, as presumably was the case in Palestine. Matters were not so easy when believers of diverse ethnic origin lived together in the same city, as was the case in Antioch. Here, by Paul's account (2:12), Jewish and Gentile members of the community met in common for shared meals (including, presumably, the Eucharist). Peter, when he left Jerusalem to join the community in Antioch, initially fell in with this local practice. When there came to the community "some people from James," he withdrew, as Paul says, "because he was afraid of the circumcised," to a separate table, taking with him all the other Jewish members of the community, including—to Paul's even greater dismay—his companion and erstwhile mentor Barnabas. For Paul this behavior amounted to "hypocrisy" (v 13) and to not being "on the right road in line with the truth of the gospel" (v 14), very serious accusations especially when delivered in the form of a public rebuke.

We have, of course, only Paul's side of the story. What might Peter have claimed in defense? What Paul saw as striking at the heart of the Gospel, Peter may have regarded as simply a strategic move for the sake of the unity of the church. Having come more recently from Jerusalem, he would be conscious of the difficult position of James who was trying to keep the overwhelmingly Jewish community of believers there in some sort of tolerable relationship with the wider Jewish populace, especially its leadership. Any suggestion that Jewish members of the community in Antioch were compromising the separation of Jews from Gentiles could make things very difficult for the vulnerable community in Jerusalem. When delegates came from James urging separation, it is understandable that Peter, like many in a leadership position, would align himself somewhere in the middle between the two factions, in an attempt to hold both wings of the church together.

Paul saw things very differently. For him "separate tables" compromised "the truth of the gospel," the same essential truth that had been at stake in the pressure to have Titus circumcised (2:3-5). Separate tables reerected the barrier between Jew and Gentile that the Gospel had overthrown (cf. later 3:26-28). It symbolically relegated believers of Gentile background to second-class status. It said to them, "If you want to really be members of the People of God, you must become fully Jews through circumcision and full observance of the ritual requirements of the law" (the "works of the law"). That is why Paul can characterize Peter's action as "compel[ling] the Gentiles to live like Jews" (v 14).

Paul's recalling here of an incident that ended up in his total isolation makes sense in view of his overriding purpose in this section of the letter, which is to establish his independence from the leading apostles. The intruders may have been telling the Galatians that Paul suffered a defeat in Antioch and submitted to the authority of Peter. Paul firmly rejects any hint of submission: he publicly called Peter to account in the name of the truth of the Gospel.

Justification through Christ Means No Going Back to the Law: 2:15-21

> [15]We, who are Jews by nature and not sinners from among the Gentiles, [16][yet] who know that a person is not justified by works of the law but through faith in Jesus Christ, even we have believed in Christ Jesus that we may be justified by faith in Christ and not by works of the law, because by works of the law no one will be justified. [17]But if, in seeking to be justified in Christ, we ourselves are found to be sinners, is Christ then a minister of sin? Of course not! [18]But if I am building up again those things that I tore down, then I show myself to be a transgressor. [19]For through the law I died to the law, that I might live for God. I have been crucified with Christ; [20]yet I live, no longer I, but Christ lives in me; insofar as I now live in the flesh, I live by faith in the Son of God who has loved me and given himself up for me. [21]I do not nullify the grace of God; for if justification comes through the law, then Christ died for nothing.

This passage is best understood as a continuation of Paul's remonstration to Peter during the confrontation at Antioch. He allows the Galatians to "overhear" his rehearsing for Peter's benefit what it meant, at radical depth, for Jews such as Peter and himself to become believers in Jesus.

Paul begins by first stating the conventional Jewish attitude to Gentiles that he and Peter would previously have held: "We . . . are Jews by nature and not sinners from among the Gentiles" (v 15). On this view, Jews are "holy" simply in virtue of belonging by birth to the People of God; through not belonging to that people, Gentiles are simply "sinners." The following sentence (v 16) describes the conversion that each had undergone: "knowing"—or having come to know—"that a person is not justified by works of the law but through faith in Jesus Christ, even we have believed in Christ Jesus that we may be justified by faith in Christ and not by works of the law." Within the worldview that Paul presupposes, justification is the verdict of acquittal or approbation that each Jewish person hopes to receive from God at the great judgment; it amounts to being declared righteous or in right relationship with God.

In conventional Jewish terms the faithful would hope to be declared righteous on the basis of their adherence to the law of Moses, that is, from doing "the works of the law." Paul reminds Peter that they have both undergone a conversion experience, a key aspect of which involved realizing that righteousness was not to be gained on such a basis—that, in fact, they were sinners, with a sinfulness that the law could not remedy. On the positive side, however, they could attain righteousness by putting their faith in Christ. More precisely, they could become righteous by allowing themselves to be drawn, through faith, into the saving act of Christ on the cross, in which God was graciously offering reconciliation to a world of sin. (Some interpreters see a reference here to Christ's own faithfulness, as well as to believers' faith "in" him.)

Paul clinches this conviction by a quotation from Psalm 143:2 (v 16e), before dealing with an objection that might be raised (v 17). To sweep away the validity of the law like this is to throw down the guarantee and marker of Israel's holiness; it is surely to reduce all to the status of "Gentile sinners," in which case—unthinkable though it might sound—Christ himself would be rendered in some sense a "minister of sin"! Paul allows the objection to surface only to brush it aside ("Of course not!"). He then goes over to the offensive as if to say, "I'll tell you what sin really is" (v 18). Sin—more correctly, "transgression"—is reerecting "what I have already torn down." What Paul and other Jewish Christians have "torn down" in coming to faith in Christ is the barrier between Jew and Gentile, between "holy nation" and unholy rest of the world that the law sought to preserve. To reinstitute "separate tables" was to fly in the face of the supremely costly divine act that had overthrown the barrier set up by the law.

Paul speaks here in the first person singular ("I") but really he means what he says to apply not only to himself but to all Jewish Christian believers, including Peter. If they truly understand the radicality of the Gospel in which they have believed, they must be able to say, as he continues:

> For through the law I died to the law, that I might live for God. I have been crucified with Christ; yet I live, no longer I, but Christ lives in me; insofar as I now live in the flesh, I live by faith in the Son of God who has loved me and given himself up for me. (vv 19-20)

Though applicable to all believers, these striking phrases take us into the heart of Paul's spirituality and his personal relationship to Christ. Paul is distinguishing two ways of being "alive," one belonging to the past, one belonging to the present. The old way, determined by the law, reflected the sharp distinctions between Jew and Gentile, between "holy nation" and "unholy rest (Gentiles)," that existence under the law upheld. Through the baptismal union with the crucified Christ, Paul—and every believer—has "died" to that old existence and to the distinctions that then mattered so much. The ego and the identity that rested so much on them have been crucified with Christ and in effect no longer exist. There is only Christ, in whom, as Paul will later maintain (3:26-28), there is no room for such distinctions. Whatever of "me" does continue to exist lives by virtue of the same union with Christ, whose costly love displayed in dying for me should now well up within me, determining my attitudes and behavior. Put another way, the union with the risen Lord means that he is constantly seeking to live out his self-sacrificing love in and through me. To seek to go back on all this by reerecting the barrier set in place by the law is to rebuff the grace of God. If righteousness comes through the law, then Christ died his supremely costly death in vain (v 21).

Whatever Peter made of this powerful remonstration on Paul's part we do not know. Certainly, it drew from Paul perhaps the most poignant and personal expression of his sense of Christ's love. There is surely a touch of mysticism in the "death" of the former "I," whose identity rested on external mark and status, and its "replacement" with a new identity resting totally on union with the crucified and risen Lord. As I remarked in the introduction, it is truly remarkable that the most personal expression of being loved by Christ in the New Testament is to be found in this passage, composed by one who—like us—never knew him in his earthly life.

The reversion to separate tables that for other leaders—Peter, Barnabas—was simply a pragmatic stratagem, impinged in Paul's view on the essence of the Gospel, which is focused on the death of Christ. It symbolized the divisions between human beings that Christ died to overthrow. It eroded faith's insight that God deals with human beings not on the basis that some are holy and some are not but solely on the basis of divine grace—grace that overcomes human sinfulness by enveloping it with love.

2. Arguments against the Position of the Intruders: 3:1–5:12

The Galatians' Experience of the Spirit: 3:1-5

³:¹O stupid Galatians! Who has bewitched you, before whose eyes Jesus Christ was publicly portrayed as crucified? ²I want to learn only this from you: did you receive the Spirit from works of the law,

or from faith in what you heard? [3]Are you so stupid? After beginning with the Spirit, are you now ending with the flesh? [4]Did you experience so many things in vain?—if indeed it was in vain. [5]Does, then, the one who supplies the Spirit to you and works mighty deeds among you do so from works of the law or from faith in what you heard?

Paul's concern up to this point has been to establish—or rather reestablish—his independent apostolic credentials and authority. Satisfied that he has achieved this, he now turns back to the Galatians. His strategy is first to appeal to experience and then to point out how that experience fulfills what Scripture had foretold regarding God's plan for the messianic age. So experience comes first and scriptural reflection follows—a model set for preachers, pastors, and spiritual directors for all time.

An opening discussion (v 1) shows again (cf. 1:6-9) the strength of Paul's frustration. It is as if the Galatians have had a spell cast over them that has taken away their freedom and good sense. Like an angry schoolmaster Paul interrogates them again and again about what they experienced when he first proclaimed the Gospel concerning the crucified Messiah (v 2; v 5). If at that time the Galatians experienced the Spirit, it was hardly a consequence of taking on the requirements of the Jewish law ("the works of the law"). Since it came to them precisely as non-Jews, as Gentiles, it must have come simply through the response of faith that they gave to the message. Why then (v 3), with acceptance by God (righteousness) guaranteed through the Spirit, are the Galatians now seeking to complete it with a rite (circumcision) that involves the "flesh" (*sarx*)? Paul speaks of "flesh" here in both a literal and a symbolic sense: literally, circumcision involves the cutting of human flesh; symbolically, it places a person back in an epoch of alienation from God now overtaken by the gift of the Spirit.

This is the first mention of the Spirit (*pneuma*) in the letter. For Paul the Spirit is essentially the felt experience of God's love (cf. Rom 5:5), the sure guarantee of right relationship with God and hence of justification already received. In the Spirit believers enjoy here and now the relationship with God that belongs to the final age. Hence the folly of seeking to go back "behind" that experience to an era that, as far as believers are concerned, belongs firmly in the past.

It is not entirely clear what is meant by the "mighty deeds" that God's supply of the Spirit has worked among the Galatians (v 5). The allusion could be to dramatic effects such as miracles or exorcisms accompanying Paul's ministry (cf. Rom 15:19; 1 Cor 2:4). But for him the experience of the Spirit consists above all in a sense of being grasped by God's love, bringing peace, freedom, and hope. Such effects can come through gentle, subtle intimations of the Spirit as well as through the more dramatic, such as speaking in tongues. The later Christian practice of the "discernment of spirits," as set out especially in the *Spiritual Exercises* of St. Ignatius Loyola, is testimony to this truth. Paul will, of course, have more to say on the "fruit of the Spirit" later in the letter (see 5:22-23).

Scripture Argument I: The Focus of the Promise to Abraham: 3:6-29

Gentiles Included in the Blessing of Abraham: 3:6-9

⁶Thus Abraham "believed God, and it was credited to him as righteousness."
⁷Realize then that it is those who have faith who are children of Abraham. ⁸Scripture, which saw in advance that God would justify the Gentiles by faith, foretold the good news to Abraham, saying, "Through you shall all the nations be blessed." ⁹Consequently, those who have faith are blessed along with Abraham who had faith.

It is likely that the intruders had bolstered their case through appeal to Scripture (Old Testament), specifically to Scripture's depiction of the figure of Abraham. What was not in dispute was the significance of Abraham in the Jewish tradition. As ancestor ("father") of the nation, he has a truly representative role: the stance he took before God, the choices he made and the promises he received remain determinative for the nation as a whole. Abraham defines the identity of the People of God. If his relationship to God was primarily determined by his obedience and submission to the command in respect to circumcision (Gen 17:9-14), then those features remain determinative for all time. If, on the contrary, as Paul will argue, Scripture shows him to have related to God primarily through grace and faith, then these will be the criteria for determining who are Abraham's true "children" (literally "seed"), heirs to the promise he received.

To establish the latter case Paul cites what is for him an all-important text from Genesis 15. In this passage Abraham complains to God that he continues to be childless in the sense of having no direct heir. God responds with a promise that he will indeed have a son and ultimately a progeny as numerous as the stars of heaven (15:1-5). The account continues, "Abraham put his faith in the LORD, who credited it to him as an act of righteousness" (v 6). The beauty of this text for Paul lies in its association of Abraham's "righteousness" simply with his faith in the divine promise. On the principle that the patriarch set a pattern for all his descendants,

Paul can then (v 7) go on to claim that it is believers who are his true children (literally "sons"). Moreover (v 8), precisely because Scripture "foresaw" that God would justify the nations ("Gentiles") through faith, it announced beforehand to Abraham: "Through you shall all the nations be blessed" (see Gen 12:3; 18:18). The blessing in question is justification and the gift of the Spirit that accompanies it. Hence Paul can conclude (v 9) that those who have faith are blessed along with Abraham who had faith. If the Galatians have been justified and received the Spirit, then, in conformity with the pattern set by God's dealing with Abraham, this must have been because of their faith. When Scripture indicated to Abraham the way in which justification would operate in the messianic age, it had Gentiles, like Paul's Galatian converts, specifically in view.

Christ Has Redeemed Us from the Law's Curse: 3:10-14

[10]For all who depend on works of the law are under a curse; for it is written, "Cursed be everyone who does not persevere in doing all the things written in the book of the law." [11]And that no one is justified before God by the law is clear, for "the one who is righteous by faith will live." [12]But the law does not depend on faith; rather, "the one who does these things will live by them." [13]Christ ransomed us from the curse of the law by becoming a curse for us, for it is written, "Cursed be everyone who hangs on a tree," [14]that the blessing of Abraham might be extended to the Gentiles through Christ Jesus, so that we might receive the promise of the Spirit through faith.

Having outlined the positive benefits the Gentiles derive from faith, Paul now puts before the Galatians the negative alternative: what lies before them if they embrace the way of the law (literally, if they proceed from "works of the law" [v 10]). To go this way involves coming under the operation of a curse, a grim conclusion Paul justifies by turning once again to Scripture (Old Testament). A text from Deuteronomy (27:36) pronounces a divine curse on anyone who does not keep all the precepts of the law. Paul arbitrarily expands the reference of the text to come away with an extremely rigorous view of the law hardly representative of Jewish understanding, then or now. His interpretation reflects the pessimism about human behavior that is part of his more general apocalyptic worldview. Since in this understanding the law requires perfect observance (repeated in 5:3), the proneness of human beings to sin means that all the law can do is to pronounce a curse; it may purport to give life (v 12, citing Lev 18:5) but will inevitably condemn.

In the same situation of sinfulness but in stark contrast, faith casts itself on the grace and mercy of God, a truth that for Paul finds scriptural validation in a text from the prophet Habakkuk 2:4: "the one who is righteous by faith will live" (v 11b). This prophetic text trumps for Paul the claims other texts make for the law (v 12). It is not that law is wrong; the curse is real. But as Paul goes on to insist (vv 13-14), Christ has redeemed us from the law's curse and brought in the era of faith. He is once more making the same basic point: Christ has rescued believers from the sphere of the law and its inevitable, death-dealing curse. How wrong to seek to go back "behind" this costly work of Christ, rendering it of no account (2:21).

The long sentence (vv 13-14) referring to this rescue mission contains one of the most striking statements of Christ's work of redemption. In the ancient world soldiers taken captive in war were inevitably sold into slavery. The only means by which families and friends could secure their release was by paying out the cost of their freedom. The Greek verb Paul uses here (*exagorazein*) refers to this practice and so has the basic sense of "liberate at a cost." In this case the cost incurred by Christ was that of taking and bearing in his own person the curse that the law was inflicting on humanity because of sin. Paul associates the law's curse with Christ by citing a text from Deuteronomy (21:23) that requires the removal before nightfall of the corpse of a criminal executed by being hanged from a tree; the corpse of one cursed by God must not be allowed to transfer the curse to the land. Paul carefully abridges the text to avoid any suggestion of Christ's being personally cursed, let alone cursed by God. Though personally sinless (cf. 2 Cor 5:21), Christ became a curse in the sense of entering deeply into the human situation of sin and bearing "on our behalf" the weight of the law's curse (cf. Rom 8:3-4; 15:3).

A twofold positive outcome flows from this redemptive act of Christ (v 14). It ensures, first, that the Gentiles receive the promise God made to Abraham in their regard and, second, that all, Jewish and Gentile believers together ("we"), receive the promised Spirit through faith. The promise God made to Abraham about the nations ("Gentiles") being blessed through him (Gen 12:3; 18:18; cited already in v 8) is fulfilled primarily in the gift of the Spirit, the guarantee of justification already received and the pledge of the fullness of salvation to come (5:5). As the focus of this promised gift and already its recipients, why would the Gentile Galatians seek to go back into the situation of slavery and curse, from which, at such cost, God has set them free?

The contrast Paul makes here between going the way of the law and the way of faith is not all that easy for us to enter into imaginatively today. There are perhaps times in our lives, however, when we feel drained and exhausted by a myriad of obligations pressing down on us and draining us of life. The obligations may seem to stem ultimately from God, and yet our inability to respond perfectly crushes the spirit, banishing joy. We feel trapped in a situation that Paul depicts even more dramatically in Romans 7:14-25. For him Christ has liberated us from seeking to relate to God in this ("law") way. The God of grace invites us to put our faith completely in the act of Christ, allowing our failure and weakness to be absorbed in his surpassing love. Divine love and grace, rather than external threat and sanction, can then shape the outward pattern of our life.

The Law Does Not Set aside the Promise: 3:15-18

¹⁵Brothers, in human terms I say that no one can annul or amend even a human will once ratified. ¹⁶Now the promises were made to Abraham and to his descendant. It does not say, "And to descendants," as referring to many, but as referring to one, "And to your descendant," who is Christ. ¹⁷This is what I mean: the law, which came four hundred and thirty years afterward, does not annul a covenant previously ratified by God, so as to cancel the promise. ¹⁸For if the inheritance comes from the law, it is no longer from a promise; but God bestowed it on Abraham through a promise.

Paul now adopts a more moderate tone, addressing the Galatians as "brothers [and sisters]." Still countering the claims of the intruders, he takes up an image from human affairs to put the law in its place and reduce its significance in the scheme of salvation. The image is that of a will or testament. Paul applies this to the promise God made to Abraham "and to his descendant[s]" that they should inherit the land (Gen 13:15; 17:8; cf. 24:7). In the original text the "land" in question was the land of Canaan. In the Jewish tradition presupposed by Paul the "promised land" had expanded to include not only the entire world (cf. Rom 4:13 ["inherit the world"]) but all the blessings of salvation. Hence the crucial necessity, shared by Paul and his opponents, of being "seed" or descendants of Abraham; only as such could they become heirs of the all-important promise. Where Paul differed with those troubling his Gentile converts in Galatia concerned the terms through which one became "seed of Abraham": through faith or through entrance into the realm and requirements of the law?

In a curious piece of scriptural interpretation Paul argues that, just as one cannot set aside a human will or add fresh clauses to what the testator has written, so the law (of Moses), coming on the scene some hundreds of years later than the promise (Paul says "430" [v 17]), cannot set aside or add to the original promise God made to Abraham. The promise drew a straight line between Abraham and his "descendant." The Greek word translated "descendant" (*sperma*) is singular in form, though predominantly collective in meaning (as is also the Hebrew *zera*ʿ lying behind the Greek translation of the Old Testament [the Septuagint: LXX]). Paul, however, exploits the singular form to find in the promise a narrow focus on a sole descendant, Christ, rather than a reference to a multitude of descendants, namely, the Israelites who received the law at the hands of Moses on Sinai. God graciously bestowed (*kecharistai*) the promise on Abraham and his "descendant" (v 18). Granted this narrow and singular focus on Christ, the sole way for others to come under its scope will not be through the law, as the Galatians are being persuaded to believe, but through the kind of "entrance into" Christ brought about by faith and baptism. Paul will discuss this "entrance" in due course (vv 26-29). For the present he devotes some space to explaining the nature and purpose of the law in the scheme of salvation.

The Law's Temporary Role: 3:19-25

[19]Why, then, the law? It was added for transgressions, until the descendant came to whom the promise had been made; it was promulgated by angels at the hand of a mediator. [20]Now there is no mediator when only one party is involved, and God is one. [21]Is the law then opposed to the promises [of God]? Of course not! For if a law had been given that could bring life, then righteousness would in reality come from the law. [22]But scripture confined all things under the power of sin, that through faith in Jesus Christ the promise might be given to those who believe.

[23]Before faith came, we were held in custody under law, confined for the faith that was to be revealed. [24]Consequently, the law was our disciplinarian for Christ, that we might be justified by faith. [25]But now that faith has come, we are no longer under a disciplinarian.

Paul has defended the primacy of the promise over the law. But the law is in some sense derived from God. A place must be found for it in the scheme of salvation. So Paul asks, "Why, then, the law?" (v 19a) and then in four short phrases manages to distance the law as far as possible from God. Whereas God "[graciously] bestowed" the promise directly on Abraham (v 18), the giving of the law came through two levels of mediation. The fact that a mediator (Moses) was necessary shows that it did not stem directly from God (v 20) but from angels. It was, moreover, a temporary dispensation, lasting only until the coming of the "descendant" (Christ) who was the true focus of the promise.

The law does not stand in opposition or rivalry to the promise—a suggestion Paul raises and swiftly dismisses (v 21a). Unlike the promise, the law was never intended to give life (v 21b). On the contrary, as "scripture" (Paul often writes interchangeably of "the law" and "scripture" [*graphē*]), it had the role of "confin[ing] all" (that is, Jews as well as Gentiles) under sin in order that the promise (and the "inheritance" it held out) might be given on a completely different basis: namely, faith (v 22). The law ("scripture") was given to bring home to the Jews that they, no less than the Gentiles, were bound up in a human solidarity in sin that was truly universal and knew no exceptions. This was the precise point Paul made in 2:15-16 when recalling what it meant for Jews such as Peter and himself to abandon the law as a source of right relationship with God and put their faith in the redemptive work of Jesus. The law's negative role, however, was all directed to a positive purpose: so that Jews, along with Gentiles, might come under the saving scope of the promise on the basis that God always intended, namely, faith—believers' faith in Jesus Christ or, as some interpreters would have it, the faithfulness of Jesus himself.

To drive home the point Paul reaches for a further image (vv 23-25). The law functioned for Israel much like a *paidagōgos* (NAB: "disciplinarian"), the household slave, whose task it was to escort children to school under close control. The image is not positive: ancient literature is replete with reports about the boorishness and brutality of the slaves assigned to be *paidagōgoi*. What Paul draws from the image is a sense of confinement, on the one hand, and of escort to a more positive outcome, on the other: in this case arrival at Christ and the obtaining of justification through faith in him. With the arrival of (the era of) faith, "we" (Jews) are no longer under such a "disciplinarian" (v 25). The law's irrelevance for Gentiles such as the Galatians should, then, be even more patent.

Sons and Daughters of God, Heirs of the Promise: 3:26-29

[26]For through faith you are all children of God in Christ Jesus. [27]For all of you who were baptized into Christ have clothed yourselves with Christ. [28]There is neither Jew nor Greek, there is neither slave

nor free person, there is not male and female; for you are all one in Christ Jesus. [29]And if you belong to Christ, then you are Abraham's descendant, heirs according to the promise.

Paul has shown the promise to be narrowly focused, without any interference from the law, on Abraham's sole descendant, Christ. He now explains how believers—and they alone—come under the scope of the promise and so become its "heirs" (v 29). This comes about through the union with Christ created through faith and baptism. Paul's reasoning here rests on his sense of the risen Lord as constituting a personal sphere of salvation "into" whom baptism has brought believers and "in" whom they now exist. They have "put on" Christ in much the same way as actors in ancient drama put on the costume of the character whose role they were to play. The all-enveloping nature of such a costume meant that the actors' individual features disappeared entirely beneath those of the character depicted by the costume (which had apertures for the eyes and mouth only). In very much the same way, ethnic, social, and gender distinctions that had meant so much in believers' preconversion life have now lost all significance as far as existence within the community of faith is concerned. "In Christ" there is

> neither Jew nor Greek, . . .
> neither slave nor free person, . . .
> not male and female. (v 28)

The slight variation in the third pair ("male *and* female") alludes to the creation account of Gen 1:26-28 ("male and female he created them"). It suggests that behind the formula as a whole lies Paul's sense of Christian life as a "new creation" (cf. Gal 6:15), a "fresh start" for humanity in the person of the "last Adam," Christ the risen Lord (1 Cor 15:45).

By invoking such a formula Paul does not mean that the old divisions are simply abolished: men remain men, women remain women; slaves are not necessarily immediately freed; nor can one simply put aside one's ethnic origin. The point is similar to that which he made to Peter in 2:15-16. In Christ these divisions have been radically overcome; the community should not live in a way that gives them significance. In a world in which the distinctions mean so much and cause so much suffering, the believing community should prefigure the new creation in which their significance will cease. To what extent Christians should seek to implement them in social structures beyond the community is not an issue Paul addressed; the miniscule numbers and vulnerable social situation of the early communities in the ancient world (cf. 1 Cor 1:26-29), along with the expectation of an early arrival of "the end" (Gal 1:4; 1 Thess 1:10), hardly made such a project feasible. But this does not mean that Paul's thinking cannot be "extended" in such a direction in the very different social and political contexts that exist today.

Paul's principal aim here, however, is to fasten upon the "oneness": "You are all one [person] in Christ Jesus" (v 28b). Making up "one [person]" in this sense, believers become "in Christ" the one "seed" or "descendant" of Abraham on whom the promise was focused. If they have received the Spirit—as indeed they have (3:1-5)—then this is because they are "heirs" of the promise made by God to Abraham "and to his [one] descendant," Christ. They have already come under the scope of the promise; there is no need to have anything to do with the (now irrelevant) law.

In reviewing Paul's argument in this way I have passed over a significant statement with which it began: "For through faith you are all children of God in Christ Jesus" or, more literally, "For you are all sons of God in Christ" (v 26). Paul is drawing here on a sense widespread in biblical and postbiblical Jewish literature of Israelites as "sons [and daughters]" or "children of God" (Deut 14:1; Exod 4:22-23; Hos 1:10; 11:1; Sir 36:17; etc.). This sense of a filial relationship to God is a privilege unique to Israel, a mark of distinction from all other peoples. In the later tradition it features particularly with respect to Israel of the end time, destined to inherit as God's "son" the blessings of the messianic age. When Paul, then, assures the Gentile believers in Galatia that, in Christ, they are all "sons [and daughters] of God" he is making clear that they not only are heirs of the promise but already enjoy the filial relationship with God that originally seemed to belong to Israel alone. Again the point is clear: if they already enjoy this status, why go back to a situation under the law that was never meant for them and that Israel itself should have outgrown?

No Longer Slaves: Children and Heirs through the Mission of the Son: 4:1-7

[4:1]I mean that as long as the heir is not of age, he is no different from a slave, although he is the owner of everything, [2]but he is under the supervision of guardians and administrators until the date set by his father. [3]In the same way we also, when we were not of age, were enslaved to the elemental powers of the world. [4]But when the fullness of time had come, God sent his Son, born of a woman, born under the law, [5]to ransom those under the law, so that we might receive adoption. [6]As proof that you are children, God sent the spirit of his

Son into our hearts, crying out, "Abba, Father!" [7]So you are no longer a slave but a child, and if a child then also an heir, through God.

With a fresh legal image Paul drives home his point that existence under the law belongs to a time of immaturity that believers have outgrown. Continuing the sense of "inheritance," the image envisages two stages of personal existence in which one can be an heir. A person can be designated an heir while still a child. While in prospect "owner of everything," during the time of immaturity the heir has in fact no disposition over the inheritance; it is all managed by guardians and administrators until he or she comes of age at the time appointed by the father (vv 1-2). During the period of immaturity, says Paul, the heir is no different from a slave. This is hardly true; the immature heir is unlikely to be treated like a slave by the overseers who know all along that they have been entrusted with the supervision of a child of the house. Paul, however, brings in the comparison with slavery because from now on in the letter the condition of slavery, so familiar in his context, will be the negative foil to the freedom attending the status of divine filiation (being God's "sons" and "daughters") that believers now enjoy (3:26).

Speaking in the first-person plural ("we" [v 3]), Paul seems to be relating the image of slave-like immaturity to the existence of Jews under the law. He does not, however, speak of a slavery "under the law" but "under the elemental powers of the world" (*ta stoicheia tou kosmou*), a mysterious reference that has long baffled interpreters. It seems best to see here a reference to spiritual or angelic forces who supervise Israel's life "under" the law and, in particular, note and "book up" for punishment all infringements of it (cf. Rom 8:38-39a). Paul speaks in this more general way because soon (v 9) he will propose that becoming subject to such forces, as the Galatians are minded to do through taking on the yoke of the law, would be tantamount to going back to the slavery that attended their former worship of idols. In this sense the "we" includes, at least potentially, the Gentile Galatians as well as Jews.

What has put the time of immaturity and slavery firmly in the past is the intervention of God: at the "fullness of time . . . God sent his Son, born of a woman, born under the law, to ransom those under the law, so that we might receive adoption" (vv 4-5). Once again (cf. 3:13-14) we have a richly theological statement of Christ's redemptive work. "Born of a woman" does not so much refer to Christ's birth from Mary but to his total entrance into and identification with the human condition, which, in its pre-redemption state, is one of slavery (cf. Phil 2:6-8). "Born under the law" specifies Christ's entrance into the subjection peculiar to Israel. Totally identified with the human and the Jewish plight in this way, Christ was in a position—through his unique obedience and righteousness (Phil 2:8; Rom 3:25; 8:3-4; 2 Cor 5:21)—to "ransom" those held in slavery and subjection "under the law" (v 5a): Jews in first instance but also—preemptively—any Gentiles who, like the Galatians, may be tempted to join their subjection.

The positive outcome, however, is that "we" (Jewish and Gentile believers) might receive the "adoption" (v 5b). In secular Greek usage "adoption" is a correct translation of the term *huiothesia*. Once again, however (cf. 3:26), I would suggest that Paul is working more from a biblical rather than secular background. He is contrasting the situation of a slave with the situation of those who are genuinely children of the house. Israel is God's son and heir. But Israel has undergone a period of immaturity under the law akin to slavery. In Paul's view Israel only truly comes into the status of sonship through the work of the One who is uniquely and personally God's Son. Through faith and baptism "into Christ" (3:26) all human beings, Gentiles as well as Jews, have access to this status. In a divine "interchange," the Son of God took on the slave situation of human beings in order that we might share the filial relationship with God that pertains primarily to him alone. He became what we were ("slaves") in order that we might become what he is: "sons" (and "daughters") of God (for the same "interchange" pattern see 2 Cor 5:21; 8:9; Gal 3:13-14).

Tangible evidence of this change from servile to filial status is provided by the Spirit (vv 6-7; cf. 3:2-5). God has sent the Spirit of the Son into our hearts crying out "Abba, Father" (v 6). *Abba* is one of only two Aramaic expressions (the other being *Maranatha* [1 Cor 16:22]) preserved in the Pauline writings of the Greek New Testament. It is the familiar address of the Jewish son or daughter to the male parent—expressive of a degree of intrafamily intimacy between the babyish "Daddy" and the more formal "Father." It seems that the early Christian community preserved the Aramaic form as a precious memory of the intimacy with which Jesus addressed God (cf. Mark 14:36), an intimacy that they felt themselves also drawn into, either at his instruction (the Lord's Prayer [Matt 6:9-15; Luke 6:2-4]) or, following his death and resurrection, as prompted by the Spirit (cf. also Rom 8:15).

Striking in both cases is the trinitarian shape of Paul's assertion here: God (the Father) sends the Spirit of the Son (v. 6). In stark contrast to the fear and distance of the past situation of slavery (cf. Rom 8:15), the cry prompted by the Spirit brings out intimacy with the divine that attends believers' new and present status. Through their existence "in Christ" they are caught up in the communion of love that is the Trinity. Hence Paul, speaking quite directly to each individual Galatian in the first-person singular, can draw his conclusion: "So you are no longer a slave but a child, and if a child then also an heir, through God" (v 7). Believers may not be already in full possession of the inheritance but as God's acknowledged sons and daughters, they are firmly set in line to inherit the promise. They do not have to "earn" their way to filial status and the inheritance by taking on the "works of the law" (2:16).

Why, Then, Return to Slavery? 4:8-11

> [8]At a time when you did not know God, you became slaves to things that by nature are not gods; [9]but now that you have come to know God, or rather to be known by God, how can you turn back again to the weak and destitute elemental powers? Do you want to be slaves to them all over again? [10]You are observing days, months, seasons, and years. [11]I am afraid on your account that perhaps I have labored for you in vain.

Paul once again (cf. 3:1-5) directly remonstrates with the Galatians. What they are tempted to take on (submission to the Jewish law) represents a reversion to the slavery of their former, preconversion existence, when they were enslaved to "things that by nature are not gods" (v 8). Now that they have come to "know" the true God—or, better, come to "be known" by God—why do they want to turn back to a similar condition of slavery? Paul exploits the biblical sense of "knowing," which, in reference to persons, goes beyond knowledge to include choice, experience, and intimacy. Not only have believers come to know God in this sense. More significant is the corresponding divine "knowing" of them: the gift of the Spirit (v 6) attests to God's acknowledging them as beloved sons and daughters. How futile, then, to want to turn back to a condition of slavery, involving service to "weak and destitute elemental powers" (v 9).

Here we meet again (cf. v 3) the mysterious reference to enslavement to "elemental powers [of the universe]," a condition that also involves "observing days, months, seasons, and years" (v 10). In mind here are the calendar observances of the Jewish law, obligatory for those who adopt circumcision. The Galatians' pagan past may well have involved worship of astral deities (sun, moon, stars) believed to regulate times and seasons. If so, Paul would then be equating the adoption of the Jewish law with a reversion to that pagan past. Both religious systems involve a "slavery" under elemental powers completely at odds with the freedom and dignity of belonging to the family of God. A concluding gasp of exasperation (v 11) expresses Paul's fear that his labors among the Galatians may have been all in vain.

The Galatians' Former Devotion to Paul: 4:12-20

> [12]I implore you, brothers, be as I am, because I have also become as you are. You did me no wrong; [13]you know that it was because of a physical illness that I originally preached the gospel to you, [14]and you did not show disdain or contempt because of the trial caused you by my physical condition, but rather you received me as an angel of God, as Christ Jesus. [15]Where now is that blessedness of yours? Indeed, I can testify to you that, if it had been possible, you would have torn out your eyes and given them to me. [16]So now have I become your enemy by telling you the truth? [17]They show interest in you, but not in a good way; they want to isolate you, so that you may show interest in them. [18]Now it is good to be shown interest for good reason at all times, and not only when I am with you. [19]My children, for whom I am again in labor until Christ be formed in you! [20]I would like to be with you now and to change my tone, for I am perplexed because of you.

The gasp of exasperation at the end of the previous section (v 11) introduces a more personal note. Leaving aside for the moment the argument from Scripture, Paul laments the injury the Galatians' falling away from the Gospel represents to their relationship with him. He implores the Galatians "be [or "become"] as I am, because I have also become as you are" (v 12ab). He has abandoned his Jewish way of life and "righteousness" under the law to live entirely by faith serving the Gospel to the Gentiles (2:19-20; 1 Cor 9:21; Phil 3:4-11). They, in turn, though tempted to adopt the Jewish law, are begged to adopt or remain in a similar commitment based solely on Christ.

Paul then recalls (vv 12c-15) the circumstances of his original preaching to the Galatians, reminding them in particular of the generosity with which they received him. What occasioned his sojourn in Galatia was an illness—one, it would seem, that made him at least for a time physically repulsive. The assertion that, "if it had been possible, you would have torn out your eyes and given them to me" (v 15b), suggests that it was some serious ailment of the eyes that made it impossible for Paul to continue his travels. Despite the "trial" (v 14) that his physical aspect represented for the Galatians, they did not reject him but received him as a genuine messenger (literally "angel") of God, ready to exchange for the gift of the Gospel something as precious as their own eyes. Where, then, he now asks (v 15a), has all this goodwill (literally, their regarding him as a "blessing") of theirs gone? Has he become their "enemy" simply because he was preaching "the truth" to them, that is, the Gospel as proclaimed and recognized by the church as a whole (cf. 2:5)?

Paul's thoughts then turn to the intruders (v 17), playing upon the multiple meanings of the Greek word *zēloun*, which range from the positive "show interest in," "court favor," "be zealous," to the negative "be jealous of." He points out that the intruders are courting the favor of the Galatians, but not in an honorable way. They are seeking to make the Galatians feel isolated (in their present law-free situation), in order that they will want to join the wider law-observant church. Paul concedes (v 18) that it is no bad thing (literally "good") for the community to be the object of interest from other Christian leaders when he is absent from them—but only if that interest is in a good cause, which is not the case here.

Finally (vv 19-20), Paul's feelings boil over in a mingling of love and exasperation. He suffered pain akin to childbirth when bringing the community in Galatia to birth. Does he now have to go through those pains again in order that Christ be formed in them? The sense is not so much that of individual believers becoming Christlike in their pattern of life but of the community as a whole becoming fully the Body of Christ, a corporate unity in which the risen Lord is present and active through the Spirit (1 Cor 12:12-13; Rom 12:4-5).

Scripture Argument 2: Allegory of Hagar and Sarah: 4:21-31

²¹Tell me, you who want to be under the law, do you not listen to the law? ²²For it is written that Abraham had two sons, one by the slave woman and the other by the freeborn woman. ²³The son of the slave woman was born naturally, the son of the freeborn through a promise. ²⁴Now this is an allegory. These women represent two covenants. One was from Mount Sinai, bearing children for slavery; this is Hagar. ²⁵Hagar represents Sinai, a mountain in Arabia; it corresponds to the present Jerusalem, for she is in slavery along with her children. ²⁶But the Jerusalem above is freeborn, and she is our mother. ²⁷For it is written:

"Rejoice, you barren one who bore no children;
     break forth and shout, you who were not in labor;
for more numerous are the children of the deserted one
     than of her who has a husband."
[28]Now you, brothers, like Isaac, are children of the promise. [29]But just as then the child of the flesh persecuted the child of the spirit, it is the same now. [30]But what does the scripture say?
     "Drive out the slave woman and her son!
        For the son of the slave woman shall not share the
            inheritance with the son"
of the freeborn. [31]Therefore, brothers, we are children not of the slave woman but of the freeborn woman.

After the personal appeal (4:12-20), Paul returns to an argument from Scripture—providing us, in so doing, with one the most obscure passages in all his letters. Exploiting the fact that the Greek word *nomos* can mean "law" both in the sense of legal code and "the Pentateuch" (or Scripture in general), he begins (v 21) by boldly claiming that those of the Galatians who "want to be under the law" (the Mosaic law) are not in fact listening to what the Law (the Pentateuch) is saying. The first part of his scriptural proof then draws from episodes in the story of Abraham in Genesis 16-21. So that Abraham would not remain childless, his wife Sarah, who was barren, urged him to have sexual relations with her slave girl Hagar. When Abraham does so, Hagar—to Sarah's great jealousy—gives birth to a son, Ishmael. Subsequently (Gen 21), in accordance with a divine promise, the formerly barren Sarah does provide Abraham with a son, Isaac. When Sarah sees Ishmael "playing" with her child, she urges her husband to send the slave girl and her son away, lest he deprive Isaac of his inheritance. Abraham does send her away, but not before being assured that, while his main line of descendants shall be named through Isaac, God will also make a nation out of Ishmael, who comes to live in the wilderness.

From this biblical tradition (vv 22-23) emerges a set of opposites that Paul proposes to interpret "allegorically." Allegorical interpretation involves seeing details in the narrative as disclosing deeper realities that are coming true in the writer's own time—in this case the messianic age now being realized in Christ. The opposites presently under consideration are two contrasting instances of motherhood: the slave girl Hagar's giving birth to Ishmael through a natural process (literally "according to the flesh") and the free woman Sarah's giving birth to Isaac through an exercise of divine power (overcoming barrenness) in fulfillment of a promise. In his allegorical interpretation, Paul refers the two instances of "mothering" to what he calls "two covenants" (v 24b). The first is the one promulgated on Mount Sinai. Through an ingenious—and to us quite arbitrary—word play (v 25a) he links this Sinai covenant to Hagar, the slave girl, and so deduces that what comes out of it, the Mosaic law, produces "descendants" destined for slavery. (Paul may associate Mount Sinai with Hagar because Sinai is located in Arabia [v 25a] and, through her son Ishmael, Hagar is the ancestor of the Arabians.) We would then expect Paul to go on and identify the second covenant as one linked to the free woman Sarah. Instead, he remarks further in regard to the first that it corresponds "to the present Jerusalem, [that] is in slavery along with her children" (v 25bc). He is locating, then, the enslaving first covenant at Jerusalem, the center of Judaism where that covenant is principally upheld and from where it is promulgated.

When at last (v 26) Paul identifies the second covenant, he does not mention Sarah by name but associates the covenant she, the free woman, represents with the "heavenly Jerusalem" (NAB: "the Jerusalem above"), the source of freedom and "our mother." The community of believers, made up of Jews and Gentiles, free from the slavery of the law, are already citizens or, more strictly within the present argument, "children" of this heavenly Jerusalem that is shortly to be revealed.

To support this interpretation of the tradition derived from "the law" (Genesis), Paul cites (v 27) a text from the Prophets (Isa 54). In its original setting the text in question, Isaiah 54:1, reassured Jerusalem, deserted and deprived of "her children" at the time of the exile, that she would soon have more children than a woman who had continually had a husband. Paul relates the two mothers alluded to in the Isaiah text to Hagar and Sarah, and to the two opposing covenants that they, respectively, represent. With the growth of the communities of believers in Christ, "our mother" ("Sarah," the "Jerusalem above") is no longer "barren" but can rejoice and exult in a multitude of "children"—more numerous, Paul implies, than the "children" of the slave girl, the present Jerusalem, center of the Mosaic law.

Whether by this "present Jerusalem" Paul means the whole of Judaism that has not come to faith in Jesus as Messiah or is referring more narrowly to the Jewish *Christian* mission, emanating from Jerusalem, the home base of the intruders into Galatia, is a matter of dispute. A similar juxtaposition of covenants in 2 Corinthians 3 does support the wider reference, leading to—at least in Galatians—a very negative view on Paul's part of that larger part of Israel that has not come to share his faith in Christ. But even if the reference is to a *Christian* mission emanating from Jerusalem, the negative view of the law as an enslaving system remains: with Judaism and the Mosaic law so intimately entwined, Judaism as a whole can hardly escape Paul's negative rating. In any case, we should not take this as Paul's last word on Israel. For that we should look to Romans 11:13-32, a passage where he may be intentionally modifying the harsh judgment found in Galatians. In the present context at any rate, Paul's allegory allows him to assure the Galatians (v 28) that they, in the line of Isaac, are "children of the promise," destined to come as free citizens into the inheritance promised to Abraham (cf. 3:29; Rom 9:7b-8).

Paul is not quite finished with the patriarchal traditions about the childhood of Ishmael and Isaac. Interpreting the motif of Ishmael's "playing" with the infant Isaac (Gen 21:9) as actually injuring or abusing the child, he interprets this (v 29) as a portent of the "persecution" that those committed to the imposition of the Mosaic law are currently inflicting on those descended from Isaac ("the child of the spirit"). Once again, it is not entirely clear whether Paul has in mind the harassment the intruders are inflicting on the Galatians or is thinking of more general Jewish persecution of those who believe in Christ (cf. 1 Thess 2:14-16). In any case, he finds in Sarah's demand to "Drive out the slave woman and her son," lest "the son of the slave woman . . . share the inheritance with the son" of the freeborn (Gen 21:10), a scriptural warrant for the policy that the Galatians themselves should adopt. Since they "are children not of the slave woman but of the freeborn woman" (v 31), they should "drive out" the intruders propagating the enslaving law-observant covenant.

Whatever we may think of Paul's argument in this passage, the conclusion arrived at is pronounced and clear. The message of Scripture (Old Testament), when read in the light of the Gospel, is one of freedom. The remainder of the letter concerns the preservation and living out of this freedom.

Do Not Be Moved from the Freedom Christ Has Won for You: 5:1-12

> [5:1]For freedom Christ set us free; so stand firm and do not submit again to the yoke of slavery.
>
> [2]It is I, Paul, who am telling you that if you have yourselves circumcised, Christ will be of no benefit to you. [3]Once again I declare to every man who has himself circumcised that he is bound to observe the entire law. [4]You are separated from Christ, you who are trying to be justified by law; you have fallen from grace. [5]For through the Spirit, by faith, we await the hope of righteousness. [6]For in Christ

Jesus, neither circumcision nor uncircumcision counts for anything, but only faith working through love.

⁷You were running well; who hindered you from following [the] truth? ⁸That enticement does not come from the one who called you. ⁹A little yeast leavens the whole batch of dough. ¹⁰I am confident of you in the Lord that you will not take a different view, and that the one who is troubling you will bear the condemnation, whoever he may be. ¹¹As for me, brothers, if I am still preaching circumcision, why am I still being persecuted? In that case, the stumbling block of the cross has been abolished. ¹²Would that those who are upsetting you might also castrate themselves!

The ringing command, "For freedom Christ set us free; so stand firm and do not submit again to the yoke of slavery" (5:1), could well stand as the climactic conclusion of the entire argument under way since the start of chapter 3. (For this reason several translations and commentaries associate it with what precedes, rather than with what follows.) On the other hand, it is also a fitting statement of theme for the rather disjointed series of commands, exhortations, and warnings that follow. Like repeated hammer blows, Paul drives home his injunction to stand firm in the freedom that Christ has won at such cost (5:2-12).

For the first time in the letter, we learn explicitly that the presenting issue is circumcision—though that has been implied ever since Paul mentioned Titus as a test case in 2:3-5. Paul warns about unfortunate consequences that flow from accepting circumcision (vv 2-4); then, by contrast, he points to the positive value of what, as believers, we already have: hope and love (vv 5-6); finally, with growing feeling, he excoriates the intruders and their attempts to win the community to their way of life (vv 6-12).

The consequence of having oneself circumcised, warns Paul, is that Christ ceases to be of any benefit. From living "in Christ," with all the familial intimacy with God (4:6-7) and loving divine favor ("grace" [5:4]) that it brings, circumcision means reverting to a condition where one must keep all the commandments of the law (cf. 3:10). Just as you can't have both Christ and the law (which is probably what the intruders were maintaining), neither can you pick and choose—smorgasbord fashion— among the law's commandments; it is a total package, a solemn commitment to a fully Jewish way of life.

Once again, we have to point out that Paul is maintaining here a view of life under the law that no devout Jew, then or now, would accept. For Jews, the Torah is not a heavy yoke but a way of life that preserves their relationship with God. When they sin or fail to keep this or that commandment, there is provision (especially on the Day of Atonement) for forgiveness and healing. Paul is, however, speaking to Gentiles, for whom the law was never meant. For them to take on the law through circumcision would mean reentering an old era now passing away, when "in Christ" they are already part of the dawning new creation (6:15).

Over against the way of the law, Paul gives two summaries of Christian life that sparkle like gems in the body of the letter (vv 5-6). The NAB translation of the first (v 5), "For through the Spirit, by faith, we await the hope of righteousness," could suggest that righteousness is the object of our hope. But for Paul, righteousness—the state of being in right relationship with God—is something that believers already enjoy; the present task is to preserve and live out the righteousness communicated as a gift. It is better to translate the final phrase: "the hope that springs from righteousness" or "the hope that rests upon righteousness." As in 4:6-7, the Spirit communicates the sense that we are not only God's children but also, as such, "heirs," confidently awaiting our "inheritance": the fullness of salvation still to come (cf. Rom 5:5; 8:9-11, 23-25; 2 Cor 1:22; 5:5). Secure in this hope communicated by the Spirit, we have no need whatsoever to seek any alternative source of righteousness—in particular, one based on the law.

The second summary (v 6) supports the first by recalling that believers have their current existence "in Christ." Just as "in Christ" the old distinctions that used to mean so much (Jew/Greek; slave/free; male/female) no longer have any significance (Gal 3:28), so now whether a person is circumcised makes no difference at all (cf. 1 Cor 7:17-24). The only thing that now counts is "faith working through love" or, to fill out this beautiful phrase more accurately, "faith making itself felt through love." In Paul's theology, faith, rather than "works" (the good that we do), is the absolute starting point of our relationship with the God of grace. But it is not quite true, as was maintained by some at the Reformation, that we are saved "by faith *alone*." The faith that, in response to God's grace, sets us in right relationship with God must be "lived out" in love if we are to preserve "the hope of righteousness"—as Paul will insist in the exhortation soon to follow (5:13–6:10). Before leaving these two summaries we might note how, taken together, they feature the full triad of Christian virtues according to Paul: faith, hope, and love (1 Cor 13:13; 1 Thess 1:3).

Now, in a more negative vein, Paul turns to the effect the intruders are having on the Galatians (vv 7-12). In terms of the athletic image that he often employs (1 Cor 9:24, 26; Gal 2:2; Phil 3:12-14), the Galatians, when he left them, were "running well." Who, he asks (v 7b), has now hindered them (literally "cut them off"—as one competitor cuts off another in a race) from following the "truth," that is, the Gospel as truly preached and lived out (Gal 2:5, 14)? The "enticement" addressed to them—in the shape of false and manipulative arguments—does not have its origins in the One who called them, that is, God (v 8). It comes from human considerations that can work subtly, yet powerfully, like the small amount of yeast that leavens a whole batch of dough (cf. 1 Cor 5:6).

In a climax (v 10), Paul expresses confidence that the Galatians will correctly conclude that the intruders, rather than himself, will be the ones (literally "the one," but Paul is using a generic singular) to bear the brunt of their condemnation—and by implication, their sentence of expulsion. Responding, it would seem, to a falsehood put about by the intruders to the effect that he himself is still preaching circumcision—even if for the present he omitted to require it of the Galatians—Paul protests (v 11a), "why am I still being persecuted?" The protest implies a time when Paul did in fact preach the necessity of circumcision. That time must have been before his conversion to Christ, when as a zealous young Jewish missionary he tried to win well-disposed Gentiles ("God-fearers") to become proselytes by taking on the full yoke of the law. But now it is precisely because he is refusing to impose circumcision on Gentile converts that he is himself suffering the persecution he once inflicted on others (cf. the reference to synagogue punishment "forty lashes minus one" in 2 Cor 11:24). If he still were preaching circumcision he would abolish the "stumbling block" that the proclamation of the cross of Christ constitutes for Jews (v 11b; cf. 1 Cor 1:23). Without this stumbling block, he would not be being persecuted, which is very much the case.

This thought of persecution, whether by Jews or by the false brethren represented by the intruders, leads Paul finally to blow his cool (v 12). The vigor of the language reflects the intense frustration he feels lest, in his absence, the community in Galatia be excised from the chain of Gentile churches owing allegiance to him. Would that those seeking that "cutting out" by urging a "cutting" rite (circumcision) would "cut" themselves out of the community instead!

3. Living out Christian Freedom in Love: 5:13–6:10

Love Is the Fulfillment of the Law: 5:13-15

> ¹³For you were called for freedom, brothers. But do not use this freedom as an opportunity for the flesh; rather, serve one another through love. ¹⁴For the whole law is fulfilled in one statement, namely, "You shall love your neighbor as yourself." ¹⁵But if you go on biting and devouring one another, beware that you are not consumed by one another.

So far in the letter Paul has stressed freedom. The Galatians have been set free by Christ and, at all costs, that is the state in which they ought remain. Now, while pursuing the topic of freedom, he adopts quite a different tack. In an exhortatory section, beginning now and lasting down to 6:10, he insists that freedom is not license to do whatever one pleases. On the contrary, Christian freedom is something that must be lived out in love. The change to exhortation to righteous living (in technical jargon "parenesis") at this point was doubtless a very necessary move for Paul to make. It is likely that the intruders stressed to the Galatians that they needed the moral guidance of the Jewish law if, as recent converts from the pagan world, they were to live out the strict pattern of life required of the People of God. If Paul is going to resist the imposition of the law successfully, he has to show that the Gospel of freedom as he proclaims it provides moral guidance and motivation to a degree comparable with, if not superior to, the law. What will run through the entire presentation is the absolute centrality of love (*agapē*), which he has already pointed to as faith expressing itself in action (5:6).

Paul grants that the Galatians were "called for freedom" (v 13a). But the Galatians are not to allow their freedom to be an opportunity for the flesh (v 13b). It is important to be clear about what Paul means by the term "flesh" (*sarx*). Though "flesh" is sometimes used by Paul in a neutral sense to indicate simply human origins or the physical aspect of human beings, more characteristically and especially in this part of the letter, Paul draws on a biblical (Old Testament) usage of "flesh" where it denotes the human person from the negative aspect of weakness and hostility to God, prone to mortality and sin. Characteristic of human beings as "flesh" is a radical inclination to live a life completely centered on self. Far from being confined to the purely sexual sphere, "sins of the flesh" can refer just as much to nonphysical vices such as false witness, slander, and backbiting—as would appear, from the context, to be the primary reference in Galatians.

At times, as here, Paul seems to picture "flesh" as a hostile power external to human beings that, in competition with the Spirit, is seeking to get a "base of operations" (the literal meaning of the word *aphormē* translated as "opportunity" in v 13b) in human beings, determining their behavior in a selfish direction, ruinous for peaceful life in community.

Over against this, in positive tone, Paul calls the community to "serve one another through love" (v 13c). The NAB translation actually masks the full force of his language, which literally calls upon them "to be *slaves* (*douleuete*)" of one another through love. It is highly—and intention-ally—paradoxical that, having all through the letter warned the Galatians not to enslave themselves by submitting to the Jewish law, Paul now urges them to a life of "slavery" through love. This sounds hopelessly provocative unless seen in the light of believers' union with Christ, who, in a free act of self-emptying love, embraced the "slave" existence of humankind in order to win it freedom (Phil 2:6-8; Gal 4:4-5). The love-inspired service as slaves that believers should exercise toward one another is nothing less than an extension in their lives of this redemptive love of Christ; because of their existence "in Christ" (3:26-28) it is in fact the love of the risen Lord continuing to well up within them, the supreme exercise of freedom through the Spirit (2 Cor 3:17).

Continuing the paradoxical note, Paul speaks (v 14) of "the whole law" being "fulfilled" in a single statement, namely, to "love your neigh-bor as yourself" (Lev 19:18). Previously, he had warned the Galatians that if they adopt circumcision they have to "do" the whole law, that is, fulfill each and every one of its multiple commands (5:3). He has also spent a lot of time insisting that the law is irrelevant, a thing of the past. Why now speak of its being "fulfilled"? The statement acknowledges that, though a thing of the past as a legal code, the law enshrined values that are lasting for human life. The problem with the law was that it expressed those values as external demands and prohibitions that did nothing to address the fundamental incapacity of human beings as "flesh" to carry them out. In his obedience "unto death" (Phil 2:8) Christ fulfilled all that the law required (Rom 8:4), unleashing through the Spirit a capacity within believers to live a life of love that simply gathers up and fulfills all commands and prohibitions of the law concerning one's neighbor. As Paul expresses the matter more extensively in Romans 13:8-10:

> [8]Owe nothing to anyone, except to love one another; for the one who loves another has fulfilled the law. [9]The commandments, "You shall not commit adultery; you shall not kill; you shall not steal; you shall

not covet," and whatever other commandment there may be, are summed up in this saying, [namely], "You shall love your neighbor as yourself" [Lev 19:18]. [10]Love does no evil to the neighbor; hence, love is the fulfillment of the law.

In seeing the law summed up in the words of Leviticus 19:18 in both these contexts, Paul is echoing Jesus' appeal to the same text when asked about the greatest commandment of the law (Matt 22:34-40; Mark 12:28-34; Luke 10:25-28; also Jas 2:8; Matt 19:19). When, through the Spirit, believers allow the unselfish love of Jesus to well up within them and find expression in service of the neighbor, all that the law required in this regard "is fulfilled" (the passive indicating the predominant role of God's grace).

After this sublime statement on love, a warning (v 15) brings us sharply down to earth. The image of "biting" and "devouring" one another suggests that not all the trouble in Galatia comes from outside (by the intruders). The Galatians are sharply at odds with one another— perhaps over the issues raised by the intruders, perhaps over more local issues of their own. Whatever these be, the admonition lays the ground for the instruction on the two ways—that of the flesh and that of the Spirit—that follows (5:16-26).

Live by the Spirit and Not by the Flesh: 5:16-26

[16]I say, then: live by the Spirit and you will certainly not gratify the desire of the flesh. [17]For the flesh has desires against the Spirit, and the Spirit against the flesh; these are opposed to each other, so that you may not do what you want. [18]But if you are guided by the Spirit, you are not under the law. [19]Now the works of the flesh are obvious: immorality, impurity, licentiousness, [20]idolatry, sorcery, hatreds, rivalry, jealousy, outbursts of fury, acts of selfishness, dissensions, factions, [21]occasions of envy, drinking bouts, orgies, and the like. I warn you, as I warned you before, that those who do such things will not inherit the kingdom of God. [22]In contrast, the fruit of the Spirit is love, joy, peace, patience, kindness, generosity, faithfulness, [23]gentleness, self-control. Against such there is no law. [24]Now those who belong to Christ [Jesus] have crucified their flesh with its passions and desires. [25]If we live in the Spirit, let us also follow the Spirit. [26]Let us not be conceited, provoking one another, envious of one another.

In approaching this very celebrated passage it is important to be clear about one thing from the start. The antithesis between "flesh" and "spirit" that Paul formulates here at length is not an anthropological one in the sense that "flesh" denotes the material element of the human person ("body") and "spirit" the immaterial or "soul." As I have already indicated, Paul's distinction reflects a biblical view where "flesh" (*sarx*) describes human existence from the aspect of its being hostile to God and other human beings because it is essentially turned in on self. "Spirit" (*pneuma*) denotes the life-giving power of God, at work in the "new creation" inaugurated by the Christ event. For Paul these two denote two determining spheres in which human beings can live and that radically influence—for ill and for good, respectively—behavior and ultimate destiny. To live "in the flesh" is like living among people in a boarding house, where suspicion, stealing, damage to property, violence, and abusive behavior of all kinds prevail. To live "in the Spirit" is like living in communities—for example, those founded by Jean Vanier—where charity and care for the most vulnerable are made central and determinative of every aspect of communal life.

As I have also pointed out, the Spirit in Paul is really the self-sacrificing love of Christ that he continues to breathe into the community in his ongoing life as risen Lord. If what characterizes human existence as "flesh" is a radical inclination to self-centeredness, one can readily understand why flesh and Spirit "are opposed to each other" (v 17c). Radical selfishness (flesh) is matched by radical unselfish love (Spirit). If, as seems likely, the intruders had warned the Galatians that they needed the law in order to check the impulses of the flesh, Paul's major concern in this passage is to maintain that that is precisely what they do not need. It was an unsuccessful remedy for the Jews in the past (3:22-24); it will not work for the Galatians now. The Spirit, on the other hand, is more than a match for all that the flesh in its various manifestations can throw up.

Hence Paul's confident exhortation: "live by the Spirit and you will certainly not gratify the desire of the flesh" (v 16). More than a match for the flesh, the presence of the Spirit will check the inclination to give in to each and every selfish desire (literally "doing whatever you want" [v 17d]). So Paul can conclude (v 18), "If you are [led (NAB's "guided" seems too weak)] by the Spirit, you are not [= "there is no need to be"] under the law." Once again, the passive form ("are led") expresses an important truth: the Spirit does not simply give guidance to believers; good works are entirely the result of divine grace being effective in human lives through the Spirit.

By way of illustration Paul offers two contrasting lists of the "works of the flesh" and "the fruit of the Spirit" (vv 19-23). Stating at the start that "the works of the flesh are *obvious*," he drives home the point that you don't need the law to tell you what is right and wrong. Look at outcomes! When the vices he is about to list are manifest, then clearly it is the flesh that has the upper hand; when the following qualities are evident, then equally clearly the influence of the Spirit is uppermost in community life. The list of fifteen works of the flesh follows a clear pattern. The first three items (immorality, impurity, licentiousness) do have reference to sexual behavior; the next two (idolatry and sorcery) bear upon relationship with God; then come eight dealing with human relationships (hatreds, rivalry, jealousy, outbursts of fury, acts of selfishness, dissensions, factions, occasions of envy), while the final pair (drinking bouts and orgies) deal with partying in a self-indulgent and sexually violent way. While the list begins and ends, then, with bad behavior of a sexual nature, the long central block listing offenses against community harmony suggest that in Paul's view it was in this area that "the flesh" could be most destructively at work among Galatians. He concludes by reminding the community (v 21b) that he has already warned them that those who practice such things will not "inherit the kingdom of God," a traditional expression of arrival at the blessings of salvation, more frequent in the gospels than the writings of Paul.

When it comes to listing outcomes on the positive side (vv 22-23a) Paul significantly speaks not of the "works" but of the "fruit" of the Spirit. This respects the truth I noted above: that the virtues that flourish in a Christian community are not ultimately the achievement of its members but the result or product of God's grace working through the Spirit. The Spirit works in a community like the sap that, rising in a tree, brings about a rich abundance of fruit. "Against such [things] there is no law" (v 23b) in the sense that, where such virtues prevail, the commandments of the law prohibiting offenses against the neighbor (Exod 20:13-17; Deut 5:17-21), being no longer needed, lose all relevance. In this sense, again, love is the "fulfillment of the law" (cf. Gal 5:14; Rom 13:8-10).

Reflecting the confidence in the power of the Spirit with which he began, Paul concludes with the rather startling assertion that those who belong to Christ have "crucified their flesh with its passions and desires" (v 24). United to Christ through baptism, believers experience his sacrificial love welling up within them in a fashion so antagonistic to the impulses of the flesh as to constitute its "crucifixion." The terminology is ironical: if manifestations of the flesh brought about Christ's crucifixion, believers can turn the tables on the flesh by allowing the power of the Spirit to determine the pattern of their lives. That is the essential burden of Paul's concluding exhortation (v 25) and warning (v 26).

Traditionally Paul's contrast between the works of the flesh and the fruit of the Spirit has been seen as providing a valuable template for the role and practice of discernment in Christian spiritual life. Such application has had the discernment of the Spirit's working in the individual believer primarily in view. This is quite valid, but we should not forget that what Paul had in mind was the flourishing of Christian life in community. Hence the predominance in both lists of vices and virtues that bear, respectively, on attitude and behavior toward one's neighbor. The lists are not, then, exhaustive. In regard to the individual, other "fruits" of the Spirit come into view as completions and refinements of what Paul has provided. The Rules for the Discernment of Spirits to be found in the *Spiritual Exercises* of St. Ignatius Loyola are one example of such refinements in the broader Christian tradition.

Bearing One Another's Burdens in Community Life: 6:1-10

⁶:¹Brothers, even if a person is caught in some transgression, you who are spiritual should correct that one in a gentle spirit, looking to yourself, so that you also may not be tempted. ²Bear one another's burdens, and so you will fulfill the law of Christ. ³For if anyone thinks he is something when he is nothing, he is deluding himself. ⁴Each one must examine his own work, and then he will have reason to boast with regard to himself alone, and not with regard to someone else; ⁵for each will bear his own load.

⁶One who is being instructed in the word should share all good things with his instructor. ⁷Make no mistake: God is not mocked, for a person will reap only what he sows, ⁸because the one who sows for his flesh will reap corruption from the flesh, but the one who sows for the spirit will reap eternal life from the spirit. ⁹Let us not grow tired of doing good, for in due time we shall reap our harvest, if we do not give up. ¹⁰So then, while we have the opportunity, let us do good to all, but especially to those who belong to the family of the faith.

Experienced pastor as he is, Paul knows that turning up the moral temperature in a community, as his exhortation (5:13-26) was designed to do, can result in some members becoming overbearing and judgmental. To nip such tendencies in the bud he insists that each one should look first to his or her own limitations, and, in regard to others, adopt a burden-lifting attitude rather than a judgmental one. This is the main thread running through the passage, which otherwise consists of a rather disconnected sequence of maxims, each giving practical expression to the love that fulfills the law.

There is a place for fraternal correction (v 1) in Christian community life. But it must be done with prior recognition that all human life is "burdened" in some way (v 5) and with a sense of one's own weakness and failings (v 4). The "spiritual" are not the morally superior but rather those whose attitude and behavior toward others is determined by the Spirit of Christ, who entered the human realm (Gal 4:4-5) to bear and remove its burden of sin (3:13). Bearing one another's burdens—helping each one to live with their weaknesses or applying a gentle remedy—members of the community "fulfill the law of Christ" (v 2) in that they allow Christ (2:20) to imprint the stamp of his own burden-bearing mission on their lives. Likewise, in a community there are different levels of maturity and experience of the faith. Some need to be instructed. Those who give instruction should act in the sympathetic spirit just outlined. Those who receive instruction, aware that this may take their instructors away from gainful employment, should be prepared offer them financial support ("share all good things" [v 6]).

A harvest image runs through a final section (vv 7-10), summoning members of the community, both on an individual (vv 7-8) and communal basis (vv 9-10), to live responsibly in view of the accountability incumbent on all. All will have to stand before the judgment seat of God to receive whatever "harvest" their pattern of life has "sown" (cf. 2 Cor 5:10). The one who through selfishness (or through taking on circumcision) "sows for his flesh will reap corruption" (v 8a): for them, that is, physical death will also mean eternal death, final separation from God. By the same token, the one who "sows for the spirit" will "reap" what the Spirit has to give: "eternal life" with God (v 8b; cf. Rom 8:10c). Present Christian life is demanding and in many respects burdensome. Within the perspective of faith, it is a time of "sowing" for a splendid "harvest" to come (cf. Ps 126:5-6).

It is interesting that Paul, who earlier had placed such emphasis on faith, can be equally insistent in a final exhortation (vv 9-10) on not growing tired in "doing good." Paul is not opposed to good works. They cannot earn God's favor and in this sense do not merit justification. But those justified through faith live out their new relationship with God ("righteousness") through good works that are the fruit of grace becoming effective in love (5:6, 14). Remarkably, the "good" in view here is directed not only to those who "belong to the family of the faith" but "to all" (v 10). As Christ gave himself up for all human beings without exception, so Christian love is not to be confined within the believing community but should extend to fellow citizens beyond its bounds. Within the wider civic society, the community of believers, as God's "family" or "household" (3:26; 4:6), should display before their fellow citizens the qualities of faith, hope, and love that flow from such kinship with God.

CONCLUDING POSTSCRIPT: 6:11-18

The Cross and the New Creation: 6:11-18

> [11]See with what large letters I am writing to you in my own hand! [12]It is those who want to make a good appearance in the flesh who are trying to compel you to have yourselves circumcised, only that they may not be persecuted for the cross of Christ. [13]Not even those having themselves circumcised observe the law themselves; they only want you to be circumcised so that they may boast of your flesh. [14]But may I never boast except in the cross of our Lord Jesus Christ, through which the world has been crucified to me, and I to the world. [15]For neither does circumcision mean anything, nor does uncircumcision, but only a new creation. [16]Peace and mercy be to all who follow this rule and to the Israel of God.
>
> [17]From now on, let no one make troubles for me; for I bear the marks of Jesus on my body.
>
> [18]The grace of our Lord Jesus Christ be with your spirit, brothers. Amen.

Paul concludes his letter with a postscript written in his own hand (v 11; cf. 1 Cor 16:21; Phlm 19; Col 4:18). The "large letters" reflect not so much awkwardness in writing as emphasis: what would correspond to raising one's voice at the end of a speech or using bold font in digital communication today. The postscript omits some features conventional in letters of the time, such as travel news and greetings. Apart from the concluding grace (v 18), it simply serves, in a tone of some exasperation, to drive home the main point: "Don't submit to circumcision!"

Repeating his warning to this effect, Paul plays on the double meaning of "flesh" (*sarx*). At one level circumcision involves an operation on the flesh in a simply physical sense. In a symbolic—and pejorative—sense it relocates those who submit to it away from the new world of the Spirit and back to the old era of weakness and hostility to God. The intruders who are pressuring the community in this direction are not operating out of the good Spirit but out of motives that are less than worthy:

the desire to make a good impression and to avoid persecution (vv 12-13). The mission of the intruders probably reflects pressure that the community of believers in Jerusalem, headed by James, was experiencing from the wider Jewish population. Jewish nationalism was on the rise in the years leading up to the revolt of AD 66. Such nationalism was wary of anything that weakened the sharp demarcation between Jews and Gentiles. To accept Gentiles as converts without requiring submission to the requirements of the law struck at that all-important distinction. The community of believers in Jesus, already suspect because of their messianic claims, would have laid themselves open to further suspicion and trouble when it became known that their fellows in Antioch and other places received Gentiles on terms (e.g., noncircumcision) that blurred identities. If such Gentiles could be persuaded to become full Jews, as proselytes, the grounds for persecution would be eliminated; in fact, the gaining of these new, full converts to Judaism, would be something about which to "boast" (v 13).

Seen in this way, the motives of the intruders are not worthy of condemnation out of hand. For Paul, however, circumcision is radically incompatible with the cross of Christ. It belongs to an era and a world that the cross is bringing to an end, a world that "crucifies" those who belong to Christ, as it crucified him (v 14). As such, Paul—and by implication all baptized believers—is "dead" as far as that world and the distinctions that meant anything in it (circumcision or the lack of it [literally "uncircumcision"]) are concerned (v 15a). They have entered and are already part of a "new creation" (v 15b), where "There is neither Jew nor Greek . . . slave nor free person . . . male and female," but where all are simply "one [person] in Christ" (Gal 3:28). The phrase "new creation" echoes the magnificent prophecy of Isaiah 65:17-25 telling of God's plan to make a new heaven and a new earth. This design is coming true through God's reconciling action in Christ, so that whoever is "in Christ" is "a new creation" (cf. 2 Cor 5:17). Paul's challenge to the Galatians, then, is this: "Do you want to remain within this new world into which faith and baptism have brought you? Or do you want to abandon it for a world of slavery, fear, and alienation from God, from which you have been rescued by the cross of Christ?"

At the close of these radical thoughts (v 16), Paul expresses a blessing (v 16). The tone is more conciliatory ("Peace and mercy") but the blessing is restricted to "all who follow this rule," that is, those whose lives are shaped by the Spirit. These constitute "the Israel of God": the community of believers, both Jewish and Gentile, called into being as the beachhead of the new creation. The intruders have doubtless maintained that the only Israel on which God's blessing falls is an Israel defined by ethnic origin, circumcision, and law. For Paul that definition has been overtaken by a new inclusive identity brought into being through Christ.

Understood in this way, Paul seems to be suggesting the simple replacement of "old" Israel by the church. But "Israel of God" is sufficiently vague and open-ended to resist the drawing of such a conclusion definitively. In Romans 11:25-32, perhaps in deliberate revision of what he states here, he will offer a far more nuanced view of the ultimate destiny of that "Israel" that has not come to faith in the crucified Christ ("For the gifts and call of God are irrevocable" [v 29]).

Before the concluding grace (v 18), in a slightly petulant outburst, Paul turns once more to himself (v 17). He already bears upon his body the marks (*stigmata*) left by his sufferings in the service of Christ (cf. 2 Cor 4:10; 6:4-10; 11:23-28). *Stigmata* are the marks of ownership branded on slaves in the ancient world. Paul bears such marks as badges of honor because they show him to be a true servant of Christ. But let the Galatians not add to them through the anxiety their behavior is provoking (cf. 2 Cor 11:28: "my anxiety for all the churches").

Without commendation of anyone or greetings, Paul concludes his letter with a brief formulation of the customary grace (v 18; cf. Rom 16:24; 1 Cor 16:23-24; 2 Cor 13:13; Phil 4:23; 1 Thess 5:28; Phlm 25; etc.). Only at the very end of the otherwise tense and querulous postscript is there a touch of relief and warmth as Paul addresses the Galatians as "brothers [*adelphoi*]." Coming before the final "Amen," the address contains hope that, for all the anxiety they have caused him, the Galatians will remain his brothers and sisters within the "family" of God.

Introduction to Romans

When we turn to Paul's letter to Rome after reading Galatians, we immediately sense that we are in a different world. The tone is so much more formal, more hesitant even. The apostle is writing to a community that he has not himself founded. Some of the members may be hostile to him, with a very unfavorable view of what they have heard about him and his way of preaching and living the Gospel. Paul writes to set the record straight, to give an accurate account of the Gospel as he proclaims and understands it, and to address false impressions that some in the community may hold concerning his views on various issues. He wants them to know, firsthand, as it were, what he really believes and, beyond this, to win them, if he can, to his vision of the Gospel and enlist their support for his future missionary plans.

The letter comes from a mature stage of Paul's apostolic career. He is writing from the Greek city of Corinth, where in the course of his Third Missionary Journey he has stopped to draw breath for some months before renewing his labors in new regions. As he himself notes toward its end, he feels that he has already completed all that he can accomplish in the eastern regions of the Roman Empire.

> For I will not dare to speak of anything except what Christ has accomplished through me to lead the Gentiles to obedience by word and deed, by the power of signs and wonders, by the power of the Spirit [of God], so that from Jerusalem all the way around to Illyricum I have finished preaching the gospel of Christ. (15:18-19)

With this sense of completion in regard to the east, his sights are now set on further missionary activity in the west, specifically in Spain. More immediately, he plans to go east to Jerusalem, bearing with him the collection he has raised from his Gentile communities for the church in Jerusalem. This money is not simply a measure of economic relief to a community going through hard times. It is a key symbol of the unity of the church, an acknowledgment on the part of the Gentile communities of the foundational role of the mother church in the city where the Gospel had its origin and from which it is spreading throughout the world.

Paul is anxious that his offering will be graciously and gratefully received in Jerusalem and asks his Roman audience to offer prayers to that end (15:30-31). His task in Jerusalem complete, his plan is to move on to Spain, stopping off in Rome on the way. The reason for the visit to Rome is unlikely to be mere convenience. To undertake a mission in a totally new area far afield, Paul needs a secure and supportive base. He needs to make sure of receiving a welcome from the Roman community so that he will quickly engage their support, in both human and economic terms, for his missionary enterprise in the west. Above all, as noted above, he needs to clear away any misunderstanding and disaffection from himself, and to assure the believers that his presence among them will not exacerbate divisions among themselves or threaten their vulnerable situation vis-à-vis the wider civic community.

To secure these aims Paul prefaces the announcement of his visit in the letter (15:24, 28) with an exposition of the Gospel and its practical consequences of such length and theological depth as to render Romans the most influential document in Christian theology. There are very few of the leading themes in theology that do not at some point receive an airing in the letter. It has at times been looked upon as a compendium of Christian theology, a description that its carefully structured and systematic content might seem to warrant. Nonetheless, we should keep in mind that Paul composed the letter for a particular aim and purpose connected with his visit. More than any other of his letters it has a timeless quality, but that does not mean that it should be removed entirely from its original setting and occasion.

In discussing the aim and purpose of the letter, I have focused primarily on Paul's need to write to Rome at this time in view of his own situation and plans for the future. Many scholars look also to the situation of the believers in Rome and ask whether there are not aspects of that situation that also prompted him to write as he did. Was there tension between believers of Jewish background and those who were converts from the Gentile world? Were there, as chapters 14–15 might particularly indicate, squabbles over the continuing relevance of the prescriptions of the Jewish law in regard to food? Paul does concede toward the end (15:15) that he has written "rather boldly" to the community and there are indeed passages where a strong tone of exhortation enters in (e.g., 6:12-14; 8:13). My overall sense, however, is that even such passages, rather than seeking to correct deviant behavior in the community, are designed instead to clarify and communicate an acceptable image of Paul. The exhortations are, in the end, rather general. There is no white-hot issue between Paul and the community as we have seen in the Letter to the Galatians, written several years before.

One issue, or, rather, complex of issues, that does bulk very large—because so central to Paul's apostolic life and mission—revolved around his attitude to his ancestral people, Israel, and to the place in the life of believers of the Jewish law. We have seen how central a role the latter issue played in Galatia, prompting the burning letter Paul composed and dispatched to the churches in that region. Overall, Galatians conveys the impression of a fairly unnuanced insistence on Paul's part of the replacement of the Mosaic law by the work of Christ; faith in that work is the sole factor in the gaining of the right standing before God ("righteousness") necessary for salvation. Where this leaves the bulk of Israel that has not come to faith, Paul does not discuss in Galatians, but an implication could be drawn that Paul, the believer in Christ, is now largely indifferent to his people's fate.

The community of believers in Rome most likely had arisen within the Jewish synagogues in the city. Many of its members, including even some converts from the Gentile world, probably retained strong sympathies and attachment to the Jewish heritage. If such people had actually read Galatians or got wind of it by rumor or report, it is easy to see that, particularly in regard to his apparent rejection of the Jewish law and indifference to Israel, their attitude toward Paul could be negative in the extreme. Such feelings would be exacerbated if they retained strong ties with the mother community in Jerusalem, a community that in all likelihood was still trying to reconcile its faith in Jesus as Messiah with continuing existence within the wider commonwealth of Israel.

All this would explain the great amount of space Paul devotes in his letter to Rome to the Jewish law, especially his lengthy explanation in the opening chapters of why its place in the scheme of salvation has been replaced by faith. While Paul will at times get carried away and a polemical tone will enter in, on the whole he strives to find a place for the law within the scheme of salvation. Likewise, he devotes a very distinctive section of the letter (chaps. 9–11) to a defense and exposition of his attitude to the bulk of Israel that has not come to faith in Jesus as Messiah, expressing a hope at the end that, in the unfathomable wisdom of God, "all Israel will be saved" (11:26).

Paul's exposition of the Gospel, then, addresses these two issues, deploying long discussions, with frequent appeal to Scripture (Old Testament), in chapters 1–4 and 9–11. Another major section, chapters 5–8, contains the material in the letter that readers today find most attractive. It proclaims the hope that springs from faith in the Gospel. This hope for salvation rests on the fact that the Spirit has replaced the law as the guiding principle and energizer of Christian life, allowing God's love to bring us to the fullness of salvation. A final major section, chapters 14:1–15:13, is devoted to living out the requirements of the Gospel in Christian community life, where love fulfills the multiple commandments of the law.

Within "frames" constituted by the introductory (1:1-17) and concluding sections (15:14–16:27), we can see the careful design of the body (1:18–15:13) of Paul's letter to Rome as follows:

OUTLINE OF ROMANS

Introduction: 1:1-17

Address and Greeting: 1:1-7

Thanksgiving: 1:8-15

Theme of the Letter: The Saving Power of the Gospel: 1:16-17

Body of the Letter: 1:18–15:13

1. God Restores Relationship with the World through *Faith*: 1:18–4:25.

No Alternative to Faith: 1:18–3:20

The Alienation of the Gentile World from God: 1:18-32

Those Who "Judge" Are Not Immune from the Wrath: 2:1-11

Possession of the Law and Circumcision Makes No Difference: 2:12-29

God's Faithfulness to Israel Stands: 3:1-8

Scripture Excludes Any Way of Righteousness Other than by Faith: 3:9-20

God's Righteousness Available in Christ through Faith: 3:21-31

The Revelation of God's Righteousness in Christ: 3:21-26

Conclusion: Faith Alone! 3:27-31

The "Mystery" of the Final Salvation of "All Israel":
11:25-32
Hymn to God's Inscrutable Wisdom: 11:33-36
4. Living Out the Gospel in *Love*: 12:1–15:13
Christian Life as "Rational Worship": 12:1-2
The Exercise of Different Gifts within the Community: 12:3-8
Love in Action within and beyond the Community: 12:9-21
Duties toward Civil Authorities: 13:1-7
Fulfilling the "Debt" of Love: 13:8-10
Living as People of the Day: 13:11-14
Tolerance in Christian Community Life: 14:1–15:13
The Tolerance Incumbent on All: 14:1-12
The Tolerance Asked Particularly of the Strong in Faith:
14:13-23
The Example of Christ: 15:1-6
Christ's "Acceptance as a Model for Community
Acceptance: 15:7-13

Conclusion: 15:15–16:27

Paul's Ministry of the Gospel to the Gentiles: 15:14-21
Paul's Travel Plans: Rome and then Spain: 15:22-33
Commendation of Phoebe and Greetings: 16:1-16
A Warning and Further Greetings: 16:17-23
Concluding Doxology: 16:25-27

Whether Paul explicitly intended it or not, we can note how the four major sections of the body reflect the pattern of faith, hope, and love, the triad of virtues characteristic of Christian life familiar from other places in his letters (the conclusion to the "Hymn to Love" in 1 Cor 13:13; the thanksgiving in 1 Thess 1:2-3). Keeping this overall pattern in mind will help us retain our bearings as we make the long journey through Romans.

Paul's Letter to the Romans

INTRODUCTION: 1:1-17

Address and Greeting: 1:1-7

> [1:1]Paul, a slave of Christ Jesus, called to be an apostle and set apart for the gospel of God, [2]which he promised previously through his prophets in the holy scriptures, [3]the gospel about his Son, descended from David according to the flesh, [4]but established as Son of God in power according to the spirit of holiness through resurrection from the dead, Jesus Christ our Lord. [5]Through him we have received the grace of apostleship, to bring about the obedience of faith, for the sake of his name, among all the Gentiles, [6]among whom are you also, who are called to belong to Jesus Christ; [7]to all the beloved of God in Rome, called to be holy. Grace to you and peace from God our Father and the Lord Jesus Christ.

As we noted when discussing the opening of the Letter to the Galatians, Paul normally conforms to ancient letter-writing practice when beginning a letter. Romans is no exception, featuring the three elements of address (vv 1-7a), greeting (v 7b), and prayer wish or thanksgiving (vv 8-15). The final elements tail off into a long sentence stating the theme of the letter as a whole (vv 16-17).

What is particularly striking when we consider the opening of Romans is the formality with which Paul introduces himself in the opening address. He is writing to a community that he has not himself founded. He probably suspects that at least some of those who will hear the letter do not have a good opinion of him and would be dubious about his entitlement to recognition as an apostle. So he sets out his apostolic credentials solemnly and at length. His opening self-description "slave of Christ Jesus" may seem rather extreme. "Slave" is, however, an accurate translation of the Greek word *doulos*. Paul is not afraid to express through this term his sense of being absolutely at the disposition of Jesus his Lord. The risen Lord has called him to be an apostle and, like the prophets of old (cf. Jer 1:5), "set [him] apart" for the task specific to apostles: the proclamation of the Gospel and the foundation of communities dedicated to living out the Gospel in faith, hope, and love.

The Gospel is first and foremost "the Gospel of God." It had been "promised beforehand" (literally "preannounced") by the prophets in the Holy Scriptures (Old Testament). But now it is focused on the person of Jesus Christ, the One in whom and through whom those promises of liberation proclaimed by the prophets are now coming true.

Employing what would appear to be a creedal formula used for catechetical purposes across the communities of believers (vv 3-4) Paul offers a "definition" of the Gospel now focused on Christ. The formula envisages Christ at two stages of his messianic career:

> . . . the gospel about his Son,
> *descended from David according to the flesh,* but
> *established as Son of God in power according to the spirit of holiness*
> through resurrection from the dead,
> Jesus Christ our Lord.

On the level of purely human descent Jesus was born of the "Seed of David." That is, in terms of his human origins ("according to the flesh") he fulfilled the messianic credential of belonging to the royal house of David, and was in this sense a "candidate" Messiah. The parallel statement refers to Jesus' existence in the order of the Spirit, that is, in the power of the new creation that has dawned in the world since his resurrection from the dead. In this order, the Son of David has been revealed as Son of God, clad with the power of the Spirit for the realization of God's plan of salvation for the world.

What the Gospel is proclaiming, then, is the "good news" that, following his resurrection from the dead, Jesus has been solemnly installed as Messiah and is at work through the Spirit to bring about the liberating reign of God in the world. In conventional Jewish messianic expectation the Messiah was simply a righteous king of David's line who would restore Israel to the glories of the kingdom of David and Solomon. In Christian understanding, as applied to Jesus and reflected in this short creed, the Messiah is God's instrument in a transcendent sense: as God's Son he enjoys a distinctive filial relationship with God; his messianic task outstrips the bounds of Israel to encompass, through the power of the Spirit, the entire world.

From the Messiah in this transcendent sense, Paul has received a unique vocation: the gift (*charis*) of apostleship with a specific reference to the nations of the world. Where other apostles will work specifically among the Jews, his task is to bring about among the nations ("Gentiles") what he terms "an obedience of faith" (v 5). This curious phrase has been variously explained. My sense is that Paul speaks of "obedience" in conscious allusion to the traditional understanding of Israel as the "obedient nation." Devout Jews recite every morning the Shema prayer (Deut 6:4-9), which summons them to listen to God, to love God, and to be obedient in carrying out the practice of the Mosaic law. (In Hebrew the verb *shmaᶜ* combines the meanings of "listen" and "obey.") Paul sees himself called to bring about among the nations of the world ("Gentiles") a similarly "obedient people," but obedient solely on the basis of faith.

Such is Paul's self-description as "Apostle to the Gentiles." There remains the other pole of the address, the audience of believers to whom he is writing in Rome. These too live "among the nations" and, like him, they have been "called"—not in the specific sense of being apostles but in the sense common to all believers of being the people called to belong to Christ (v 6), "beloved of God" and called to be holy (v 7a). It is easy to pass over these descriptions. But they contain a wonderfully rich theology of Christian identity, an identity that has been essentially recaptured in the Second Vatican Council's Constitution on the Church (*Lumen Gentium*) with its sense of the universal call to holiness. To the believers in Rome addressed in these terms, Paul expresses the grace formula that in Christian usage has taken over from the greeting of the conventional ancient letter: "Grace to you and peace from God our Father and the Lord Jesus Christ" (v 7b). The entire letter in many respects will simply "unpack" that divine intent of "favor" (*charis*) and "peace" toward the world.

Thanksgiving: 1:8-15

⁸First, I give thanks to my God through Jesus Christ for all of you, because your faith is heralded throughout the world. ⁹God is my witness, whom I serve with my spirit in proclaiming the gospel of his Son, that I remember you constantly, ¹⁰always asking in my prayers that somehow by God's will I may at last find my way clear to come to you. ¹¹For I long to see you, that I may share with you some spiritual gift so that you may be strengthened, ¹²that is, that you and I may be mutually encouraged by one another's faith, yours and mine. ¹³I do not want you to be unaware, brothers, that I often

planned to come to you, though I was prevented until now, that I might harvest some fruit among you, too, as among the rest of the Gentiles. [14]To Greeks and non-Greeks alike, to the wise and the ignorant, I am under obligation; [15]that is why I am eager to preach the gospel also to you in Rome.

Following his usual practice in letters to communities (save for Galatians, as we have seen), Paul converts the third introductory part of a Greek letter (the prayer wish) into a thanksgiving prayer. Strictly speaking, what he writes here is not so much a prayer directed to God but a *report to the community* about his constant thanks to God in their regard. This enables him (as is not infrequently the case with public prayer!) to get a few messages across to the community as well.

Beyond the rather extravagant compliment that the faith of the Roman community is "heralded throughout the world" (v 8), what Paul is really anxious to communicate is a sense that, though he has never visited Rome in person, they have been constantly in his thoughts and prayers. Many members of the community, perhaps a majority, are converts from the Gentile world. In this sense, as "called apostle to the Gentiles," he has a God-given responsibility in their regard and so his failure to visit them until now is something he has to explain. The matter is rather delicate because, as we know from the end of the letter, he's not now planning to visit them precisely for their own sake but to establish a base for his further mission work in Spain. (We all know that kind of embarrassment when, after a long absence, we're visiting a town where we've got old friends but are there for some purpose other than visiting them.) For the present, Paul keeps that news to himself. What he is trying to do at this point is to communicate a sense of his constant concern for the community despite his absence until now.

Paul does rather tie himself in knots in the following sentences as he seeks to explain what he would like to achieve were he at last able to visit the community. First, it is to share with them "some spiritual gift" for their strengthening (v 11). Then, perhaps feeling that he may have offended them by suggesting that the benefit is going to be all one way—from him as apostle to them as simple faithful—he quickly corrects this impression by speaking of mutual encouragement (v 12). The constant frustration of his long-standing plan to come to them should not be taken as a lack of desire to "harvest some fruit" (that is, win converts to the Gospel) among them "as among the rest of the Gentiles" (v 13). On the contrary, as called apostle, he feels keenly his God-given obligation in regard to all the Gentiles, whether they be Greeks (that is, people of the Hellenic culture pervasive in the Mediterranean world) or non-Greeks (literally "barbarians"), that is, people in the more remote regions whom the Greek-speakers might consider ignorant rather than educated (literally "wise"). Paul may already here have his Spanish mission in mind. Hence, despite his absence, his eagerness to preach the Gospel also in Rome (v 15).

This last statement, especially as formulated in the NAB translation above ("that is why I am eager"), is startling. The members of the Roman community whom he is addressing in the letter are already believers; they have heard and are living the Gospel. What would they make of a declaration by Paul that he is eager to "preach the gospel" to them as though they were as yet pagans? To give that impression would hardly be tactful. There is actually no main verb giving a precise time reference in the Greek of v 15 (no "is"; no "I am"). It is best to see here simply a restatement on Paul's part of his long-standing, albeit always frustrated, desire to preach the Gospel in Rome and win converts there as among the Gentiles elsewhere. His absence until now should not be taken as indicating any disinclination to visit them or, above all, any lack of confidence or fear about proclaiming the Gospel in the capital of the empire.

Theme of the Letter: The Saving Power of the Gospel: 1:16-17

> [16]For I am not ashamed of the gospel. It is the power of God for the salvation of everyone who believes: for Jew first, and then Greek. [17]For in it is revealed the righteousness of God from faith to faith; as it is written, "The one who is righteous by faith will live."

These two sentences stating the theme of the letter are packed with terms of such significance that we should linger here for a while and examine them at some depth.

Any hesitation Paul may have expressed in explaining his absence from Rome in the preceding sentences now slips away. He boldly expresses his absolute confidence in the Gospel. Though it has at its center One who underwent the most shameful death known in the ancient world, it is nonetheless "the power of God," leading to salvation for everyone who has faith. Let us take "salvation" first. This is a term we use a great deal in Christian discourse, especially in the liturgy. Most of us rarely stop to consider what it means beyond a vague sense of arriving ultimately where God wants us to be. In Paul's day "salvation" (*sōtēria*) or "being saved" had a definite meaning within the Jewish apocalyptic worldview that is the background to his thought. In that worldview the world in general was in a state of alienation from God, sunk in idolatry and captive to all manner of sin, while the faithful—especially those faithful to the observance of the law in Israel—suffered harassment and persecution at the hands of the wicked. What gave the faithful hope was an expectation that God would very soon intervene decisively on their behalf. At a great judgment God's "wrath" would fall destructively upon the wicked, while the faithful would be vindicated and rescued from this present (evil) time and brought into the blessed state that God had intended for human beings from the start.

All this may sound remote and alien to modern ears today. Nevertheless, as reading Romans will show, salvation in biblical terms is not simply "a pie in the sky when you die." Salvation in essence is the fulfillment of God's original and still valid design as set out in Genesis 1–2: the achievement of true humanity with the context of right relationship with God and a constructive attitude to the nonhuman created world that is the context for human life.

The Gospel is the "good news" that, with the resurrection of Jesus Christ and his "installation" as Messiah clad with the power of the Spirit (1:3-4), the saving intervention of God is well under way. The Gospel summons human beings to believe this message and so allow their lives to come under the scope of the transforming power that will rescue them from evil and set them on the road to salvation.

Where Paul parted company with more general Jewish expectation in regard to salvation had to do with the scope or breadth of the divine rescue mission. The Gospel was not just addressed to Jews piously keeping the law. It may have been addressed *first* to them but, beyond them, it was reaching out to the entire world. Though the world was alienated from God—Paul would even say at "enmity" (Rom 5:10) with God—God was in Christ graciously and freely offering reconciliation and peace. This is what the apostles, as servants of the Gospel, proclaimed:

> God was reconciling the world to himself in Christ, not counting their trespasses against them and entrusting to us the message of reconciliation. So we are ambassadors for Christ, as if God were appealing through us. We implore you on behalf of Christ, be reconciled to God. (2 Cor 5:19-20)

So the Gospel is the power of God leading to salvation for *everyone* who believes: "Jew first, and then Greek." ("Greek" here stands in the for the entire Gentile world; for stylistic reasons Paul uses the ethnic term to balance "Jew.")

The sole requirement on the human side is faith. Here, again, we have to pause to examine an all-important concept. In Paul's understanding faith involves both awareness and personal commitment. A person of faith understands God to be a God of grace above all and surrenders to that understanding in trust and obedience. Faith in this sense is the only appropriate response to the Gospel, which proclaims that God in Christ is reaching out to the alienated human world, graciously offering reconciliation and salvation.

For the present Paul simply makes this positive assertion about faith. Shortly, as in Galatians, he will set over against faith an inappropriate response to the Gospel: going the way of the Jewish law. To go that way would restrict salvation to Jews and to Gentiles prepared to convert to Judaism by taking on the full yoke of the law. Much of the early part of the letter will be taken up with this issue. For the time being, however, he is content simply to assert the universal saving scope of the Gospel on the basis of faith.

The second half of the theme statement (v 17) explains why the Gospel has this saving power. It is because it reveals to faith "the righteousness of God." "Righteousness" (Greek: *dikaiosynē*) is not a word we commonly use today—save in negative form to express the unattractive attitude "self-righteousness." The traditional Catholic translation of the Greek (through the Latin *iustitia*) has been "justice." "Justice" is not a particularly helpful translation, however, if what we have in mind is the everyday English sense where justice has to do with fairness, with equality of treatment, the fair distribution of rewards and penalties—what we would expect to receive in a proper legal process. Behind Paul's use of the Greek word *dikaiosynē* stands the use in the Hebrew Bible of the word group *tsedeq/tsedeqah*, where the essential idea is fidelity within a relationship. I am "righteous" when I am perceived by another party to have acted or be acting faithfully within the terms of our relationship. So "righteousness" does not refer to right behavior or morality in general. It has this specific note of right action within the terms of a relationship. A righteous judge, for example, might not be exemplary in other aspects of his personal life. Vis-à-vis the community for whom he is a judge, he is righteous if he discharges his judicial responsibilities fairly.

For Israel the most significant relationship was the covenant relationship with Yhwh. Within the terms of this relationship, Yhwh creates and nourishes the life of the people, giving growth and fertility through the cycle of the seasons. Israel also looked to Yʜwʜ for victory and rescue in times or war and other forms of distress. Yʜwʜ's saving action at such times was seen as a particular exercise of righteousness. On the human pole of the relationship, Yʜwʜ required righteousness from the people in two key areas in particular: loyalty in worship (no going after foreign gods) and social justice (especially nonexploitation and care for the vulnerable: the widow, the orphan, and the "stranger in the land").

Again and again, of course, Israel failed in one or both of these respects: on the human side, there was no righteousness. Then, as in many of the psalms, the people or the individual would confess their unrighteousness and look to God for forgiveness, healing, and renewal of life. We might think that Israel's failure in righteousness at such times would discharge Yʜwʜ from faithfulness to the divine side of the covenant. That was never the case. Again and again, Yʜwʜ would graciously intervene to rescue undeserving Israel and restore the relationship. Behind biblical "righteousness," then, is always the sense of God as a God of grace.

In the centuries just prior to the rise of Christianity, the "saving" sense of God's righteousness came to the fore. In fact, in the later prophetic books, such as Isaiah 40–66, and in many psalms, righteousness comes close to being synonymous with "salvation," a tradition flowing strongly through Paul. By the same token, on the human side of the equation, righteousness was seen more and more to consist in faithful observance of the law of Moses.

Returning then to our statement of theme, we can say that when Paul speaks of the Gospel as revealing God's righteousness he stands in line with this biblical tradition. God's intervention in Christ as proclaimed in the Gospel is a gracious rescue mission on God's part, one that reaches out not simply to Israel but to the world as a whole. In other words, God is showing righteousness not simply as covenant partner of Israel but as Creator bound in relationship to the entire world and seeking reconciliation and renewal of relationship with all prepared to respond in faith. This may well be the meaning of the rather cryptic phrase "from faith to faith": that is, from (God's) faith (= faithfulness) to human faith in response.

The phrase "righteousness of God," however, probably has reference not only to the faithfulness of God in God's self. As we noted above, a presupposition of the Gospel is the pervasive sinfulness and alienation of humankind apart from the grace of Christ. On the human side there is no righteousness whatsoever. If human beings are to be saved, it can only be through a righteousness that comes to them as pure gift from

God—a righteousness that, as Paul will later explain (3:21-26), comes to them through their union in faith and baptism with Christ. Thus "the righteousness of God" that renders the Gospel "the power of God [leading to] salvation" has also the sense of "the righteousness *from* God" graciously bestowed on believers in their union with Christ. As God's Son sent into the world for its salvation, he is the one truly righteous human being, who "did not know sin" (2 Cor 5:21). Through union with him believers, lacking all righteousness of their own, can enter into and begin to live out the righteousness that comes from God.

Our understanding of this area of Paul's theology can be helped if we keep in mind the classic parable of Jesus traditionally, though inadequately, known as "The Prodigal Son" (Luke 15:11-32). (A better description is "The Lost Son"; it is the father who is "prodigal," prodigal in grace.) The younger son has squandered all his patrimony and sunk into a life of debauchery and dehumanization. He thinks that he can never be received back as a son; as such, he has forfeited all "righteousness"; he might just be received back as a slave of the household; at least then he would get something to eat. That, however, is not the way the father in the parable sees or feels about the situation. For him, despite the young man's behavior, the father-son relationship is not broken. So we have a sense of the father constantly on the watch for the son's return. We learn of his rushing out to embrace the boy, his cutting off of the prepared spiel about being unworthy to be called a son and asking simply to be a servant, the commands to dress him in the best robe, the ring, the sandals, the feast: all symbols of a restoration of filial status going well beyond anything the son enjoyed before. (The older son's negative reaction we can leave aside for the moment.) All of this conveys something of Paul's sense of God as a God of pure grace who "clothes" sinful humanity with the righteousness of Christ, which is also "the righteousness of God." The only condition on the human side is faith: faith that believes that this is God's true character, a God of grace, to whom one can surrender one's life project in perfect trust and love.

There remains only for Paul to clinch his long statement of theme with a prophetic text (Hab 2:4). The great advantage of this text for Paul (see also Gal 3:11) is its linkage of "life" with "faith." Scripture (Old Testament) gives God's view of what was to prevail in the messianic era. Paul finds, then, in this text a divine indication that in the time of the Messiah it is those who become "right with God" (that is, have righteousness) through faith who will enjoy the "life" that is the essence of salvation. (I follow here the translation of this text as set out in the NAB.

Alternatively, the translation can run, "The righteous person lives by faith." This is slightly smoother in terms of syntax but the NAB translation better suits the run of Paul's argument at this point.)

BODY OF THE LETTER: 1:18–15:13

1. God Restores Relationship with the World through *Faith*: 1:18–4:25

No Alternative to Faith: 1:18–3:20

The Alienation of the Gentile World from God: 1:18-32

[18]The wrath of God is indeed being revealed from heaven against every impiety and wickedness of those who suppress the truth by their wickedness. [19]For what can be known about God is evident to them, because God made it evident to them. [20]Ever since the creation of the world, his invisible attributes of eternal power and divinity have been able to be understood and perceived in what he has made. As a result, they have no excuse; [21]for although they knew God they did not accord him glory as God or give him thanks. Instead, they became vain in their reasoning, and their senseless minds were darkened. [22]While claiming to be wise, they became fools [23]and exchanged the glory of the immortal God for the likeness of an image of mortal man or of birds or of four-legged animals or of snakes.

[24]Therefore, God handed them over to impurity through the lusts of their hearts for the mutual degradation of their bodies. [25]They exchanged the truth of God for a lie and revered and worshiped the creature rather than the creator, who is blessed forever. Amen. [26]Therefore, God handed them over to degrading passions. Their females exchanged natural relations for unnatural, [27]and the males likewise gave up natural relations with females and burned with lust for one another. Males did shameful things with males and thus received in their own persons the due penalty for their perversity. [28]And since they did not see fit to acknowledge God, God handed them over to their undiscerning mind to do what is improper. [29]They are filled with every form of wickedness, evil, greed, and malice; full of envy, murder, rivalry, treachery, and spite. They are gossips [30]and scandalmongers and they hate God. They are insolent, haughty, boastful, ingenious in their wickedness, and rebellious toward their parents. [31]They are senseless, faithless, heartless, ruthless. [32]Although

they know the just decree of God that all who practice such things deserve death, they not only do them but give approval to those who practice them.

At this point we come upon what is in many ways the most forbidding and least attractive part of Romans. So many readers who begin with the best intentions to study Paul are put off by what they read from 1:18–3:20. All seems to be sin, wrath, and menace as Paul describes the failure, first of the Gentile (1:18-32) and then the Jewish world (2:1–3:20) in regard to right relationship with God. Even readers who persevere with this section of the letter will probably not want to linger very long and it is not my intention to suggest they do so by going into it in any great depth. I think, however, it is important for an overall understanding of the letter that we do grasp two things in its regard: first, the reason that Paul has included this negative sequence; second, the distinctive literary or rhetorical form in which he has cast it. Appreciating both of these, and especially the second, is vital for interpretation and for ensuring that we do not come away from it with wrong or destructive messages.

As we have seen from the start, Paul's overall task in Romans is to present an accurate account of the Gospel as he preaches it, an inclusive gospel, reaching to all humanity and seeking a response in faith. It is through faith in God's redemptive action in Christ—and only through faith—that people find reconciliation with God and the hope of salvation that it offers. It is vital for Paul's purpose that he exclude any alternative means of achieving this reconciliation. In particular, it is vital that he rule out seeking to obtain it by going the way of the Jewish law. If salvation were tied to being righteous on the basis of observance of the law, that would mean its restriction to those who are Jews by birth and those non-Jews (Gentiles) who become converts to Judaism by taking on its ritual requirements (circumcision [for males]; Sabbath observance; food laws). Essential to Paul's understanding of the Gospel is the sense that God is summoning the nations of the world precisely as such, that is, *as Gentiles*, to membership alongside Israel of the People of God destined for salvation. To compel Gentiles to become Jews (by taking on circumcision and the law) runs contrary to this divine purpose, as Paul sees it. For Jews and Gentiles alike, the one essential response to the Gospel is faith. Hence Paul's task, before reasserting the centrality of faith (in 3:21-31), to clear away any suggestion that righteousness could come through practice of the law (what he calls in a technical phrase: "the works of the law"). This is what this whole negative section, 1:18–3:20, is all about.

To achieve this aim Paul adopts a rhetorical ploy familiar from other literature of his time—and indeed that he himself employs on a smaller scale in an extended response to Peter in his earlier letter to the Galatians (2:11-21). He sets up a kind of "straw man" dialogue or disputation with a Jewish teacher who represents the opposing view, namely, that righteousness is to be achieved on the basis of practice of the law. The problem is that he doesn't exactly signal that he is doing so. But most recent interpreters of Romans are agreed that this rhetorical dialogue is underway when, straight after speaking of the revelation of God's righteousness (1:17), he announces a quasi-parallel revelation of God's wrath (1:18).

Recognition that the dialogue with the Jewish teacher is already under way at 1:18 places the first section of the dialogue (1:18-32) in a category of its own. What we have here is a rhetorical trap that Paul sets up for the teacher to lull him into complacency so that all the more tellingly and powerfully he can launch against him the sustained accusation that makes up the whole of chapter 2. If we look closely at the structure and content of the passage we can see that it describes in a very formal way the human lapse into idolatry and the consequences of this in moral and social life. The opening verses (vv 18-20) set up a kind of "natural theology." They assert that human beings should be able to attain to knowledge of the existence and power of the unseen God through contemplation of the created world. This possibility renders the lapse into idolatry "inexcusable." Then follow parallel descriptions of the fall into idolatry in three waves running across the text (vv 21-23; vv 25-27; vv 28-31). Each pivots around the striking phrase "God handed them over to" and each concludes with a very negative description of the consequences in human life of this divine "handing over." The whole concludes (v 32) with a fearsome assertion that not only those who practice such vices but also those who approve them deserve to die.

What are we to make of this text and some of its specific content? First of all, we have to recognize that it bears striking resemblances to tracts against Gentile idolatry to be found in contemporary Jewish literature, notably the Wisdom of Solomon (chaps. 13–14). This suggests that Paul has not composed this piece specifically for his letter to Rome. Within the framework of the dialogue that he is setting up with the representative Jewish teacher, he is beguiling this figure with a conventional polemic tract against the idolatry of the Gentile world. He is not directly targeting the Gentile world and certainly not the Gentile believers in Rome. Rather, before springing his rhetorical trap (2:1), he induces his Jewish dialogue partner to sit back complacently at this point and say, "Yes, that's the Gentile world we all know."

Appreciating the rhetorical function of the piece in this way should point us to a correct interpretation of its many puzzling and off-putting aspects. Mention of the "wrath of God" takes us immediately into the world of Jewish apocalyptic discourse that is the background to the whole. In the Old Testament God's "wrath" was almost always directed against the nations that oppressed Israel, not against Israel itself. In respect to Israel the wrath functioned salvifically in the sense of putting down hostile powers. Here, reflecting conventional Jewish views, the tract sees the wrath already revealed in the multiple vices prevalent in the Gentile world. In response to that world's idolatry (its refusal to "know God") God has "handed over" the world to those vices as a kind of anticipation of a more radical destruction to come.

Among those vices listed, the controversial inclusion of—and indeed stress on—same-sex behavior (vv 26-27) again reflects conventional Jewish attitudes. These saw a close link between the idolatry and the sexual depravity of the Gentile world. In this context Paul's mention of such behavior is not surprising. As other passages of his letters make clear, he has a particularly high regard for human bodily life. Dishonoring one's body is a particularly gross manifestation of sin, since the body belongs to the Lord and is destined to share his risen life (1 Cor 6:12-20; 15:35-57). What is important to grasp, though, is that Paul is not here mentioning sexual behavior that he regards as deviant because he felt the Roman community stood in need of moral instruction or correction in this area. This is not the exhortatory section of the letter.

Aside from more passing allusions in vice lists in 1 Corinthians 6:9b-10 and 1 Timothy 1:9-10, this passage is the only clear reference to same-sex behavior in the New Testament. Its interpretation, from both an ethical and pastoral point of view, must be sensitive to both the context and specific rhetorical role it plays within the wider argument of Romans. In particular, we must reckon with a considerable gap between what is envisaged by this text from the ancient world and the personal situations addressed in moral and pastoral reflection today. What both the ancient literature in general and this text in particular have in mind is homosexual behavior on the part of those who have deliberately chosen to abandon what is considered to be the universal norm—heterosexual relations. The ancient world in general, and early Christian writers such as Paul, made no distinction between being of homosexual disposition as an abiding personal psychological orientation, the cause of which remains mysterious, and free choice on the part of heterosexual persons to engage in homosexual activity. Any modern moral assessment of the issue in which Scripture plays a part must clearly take this gap between ancient and modern thinking into consideration. The allusion to same-sex behavior is not there for its own sake but functions rhetorically as an element in the "trap" he is setting up for those (represented by the teacher) who condemn such behavior yet in some way (as he will explain in chap. 2) are guilty of misbehavior themselves and, in consequence, are hypocritical.

We have to reckon, then, with the fact that this passage, apart from its rather forbidding portrayal of God, can also function oppressively when applied without sensitivity to its context and rhetorical function. Even its suggestion that people should be able to "know God" from the created world will seem naïvely confident to many people today—though it was cited by the First Vatican Council (1870) in support of its teaching that God can be known by the natural light of human reasoning apart from scriptural revelation. Behind it all, however, is a sense stemming from the biblical tradition that human life flourishes when in vital relationship with God, while the absence or rejection of such relationship with the Creator has consequences detrimental on both an individual and social plane. As the letter proceeds, but especially in the latter part of chapter 8 and the beginning of chapter 12, we shall see the positive obverse of what Paul writes here in such a challenging way.

Those Who "Judge" Are Not Immune from the Wrath: 2:1-11

2:1Therefore, you are without excuse, every one of you who passes judgment. For by the standard by which you judge another you condemn yourself, since you, the judge, do the very same things. 2We know that the judgment of God on those who do such things is true. 3Do you suppose, then, you who judge those who engage in such things and yet do them yourself, that you will escape the judgment of God? 4Or do you hold his priceless kindness, forbearance, and patience in low esteem, unaware that the kindness of God would lead you to repentance? 5By your stubbornness and impenitent heart, you are storing up wrath for yourself for the day of wrath and revelation of the just judgment of God, 6who will repay everyone according to his works: 7eternal life to those who seek glory, honor, and immortality through perseverance in good works, 8but wrath and fury to those who selfishly disobey the truth and obey wickedness. 9Yes, affliction and distress will come upon every human being who does evil, Jew first and then Greek. [10]But there will be glory, honor, and peace for everyone who does good, Jew first and then Greek. [11]There is no partiality with God.

At this point Paul suddenly rounds on the dialogue partner he has set up and springs his rhetorical trap. The one who so confidently sits in judgment on the idolatry and depravity of the Gentile world in some sense "does the same" (v 1, v 3). If, as seems to be the case, Paul has a Jewish teacher in mind this accusation seems grossly unfair. How could such a teacher, presumably zealous for God, be captive to the kind of vices just listed as typical of the idolatrous Gentile world? What Paul is beginning here, however, is not a reasoned argument based on empirical observation but a prophetic accusation designed to erode confidence in a hope of right standing before God on any basis (especially the Jewish law) other than a response in faith to the Gospel. Paul places the teacher within the same theological framework (vision of God) that he had deployed when considering the idolatry of the Gentile world: a God summoning the world to judgment. This reflects the conventional understanding of Jewish apocalyptic, where judgment will be strictly according to works, with no partiality or special treatment. He places the teacher in that frame of reference and says, "Now, how do you stand?"

What we have to keep in mind is that neither this frame of reference nor the view of God that it projects corresponds to what ultimately emerges from the letter. It will in fact be countermanded or at least drastically revised very shortly when Paul returns to a positive statement of what the Gospel reveals in 3:21-26. Paul is actually entering here into the theological worldview of the teacher—possibly the worldview that he himself lived and worked out of during his persecuting years prior to his conversion to Christ and putting the teacher on trial, so to speak, within that rigorous frame of reference. Once again we have to be careful not to remove the passage from its context and apply it immediately and without qualification in theological, spiritual, or pastoral discourse. It is not that what it says is wrong: the principle of judgment according to works is valid. A wider reading of the letter, however, will soon show that God has not dealt with human beings on that basis alone, that in fact, in the face of human sin and failure in terms of that principle, God has intervened in Christ in a costly exercise of grace and love. It is very important when reading such texts as the present one, that we do not fail to keep that more gracious sense of the divine action very clearly in mind.

Possession of the Law and Circumcision Makes No Difference: 2:12-29

[12]All who sin outside the law will also perish without reference to it, and all who sin under the law will be judged in accordance with it. [13]For it is not those who hear the law who are just in the sight of God; rather, those who observe the law will be justified. [14]For when the Gentiles who do not have the law by nature observe the prescriptions of the law, they are a law for themselves even though they do not have the law. [15]They show that the demands of the law are written in their hearts, while their conscience also bears witness and their conflicting thoughts accuse or even defend them [16]on the day when, according to my gospel, God will judge people's hidden works through Christ Jesus.

[17]Now if you call yourself a Jew and rely on the law and boast of God [18]and know his will and are able to discern what is important since you are instructed from the law, [19]and if you are confident that you are a guide for the blind, and a light for those in darkness, [20]that you are a trainer of the foolish and teacher of the simple, because in the law you have the formulation of knowledge and truth— [21]then you who teach another, are you failing to teach yourself? You who preach against stealing, do you steal? [22]You who forbid adultery, do you commit adultery? You who detest idols, do you rob temples? [23]You who boast of the law, do you dishonor God by breaking the law? [24]For, as it is written, "Because of you the name of God is reviled among the Gentiles."

[25]Circumcision, to be sure, has value if you observe the law; but if you break the law, your circumcision has become uncircumcision. [26]Again, if an uncircumcised man keeps the precepts of the law, will he not be considered circumcised? [27]Indeed, those who are physically uncircumcised but carry out the law will pass judgment on you, with your written law and circumcision, who break the law. [28]One is not a Jew outwardly. True circumcision is not outward, in the flesh. [29]Rather, one is a Jew inwardly, and circumcision is of the heart, in the spirit, not the letter; his praise is not from human beings but from God.

Paul now begins to home in on the more specific point he wants to make. He moves to exclude once and for all any suggestion that possession of the law of Moses will give Jews protection against the operation of the divine wrath. Later he will make a similar point in regard to circumcision (2:25-29). Since, as he has already maintained, judgment will be according to a person's works, whether one possesses the law (as do

Jews) or do not possess it (as the Gentiles do not) ultimately makes no difference. The key thing is not simply to hear it but to carry out its commands. Moreover, he goes on (vv 14-15), whenever Gentiles, who do not possess the law, do "by nature" what the law commands, they show themselves to be in possession of the demands of the law "written in their hearts," with their conscience bearing witness either in accusation or defense.

This suggestion that Gentiles can know the Mosaic law "by nature" and carry out its moral precepts represents a severe relativization on Paul's part of its intrinsic value. In effect it renders its possession by Jews to be of no great advantage. And this is precisely the impression that Paul wants to convey.

While simply an element in his ongoing rhetorical accusation, the suggestion that human beings are capable of discerning moral values and precepts apart from positive revelation (in Scripture) is a place in Paul's writings where the influence of Stoic philosophy, mediated through his ancestral Hellenistic Judaism, can be detected. In parallel with the formulation of a natural theology in regard to knowledge of God in 1:19-20, we have here some scriptural foundation for the theory of natural law that was to be developed in the Christian tradition and that remains a significant element in Catholic moral theology to this day. Despite the generally negative tone of this entire sequence, the presence of such a motif at this point in Romans invites a reflection on the contemporary situation where Christian believers constitute only a small proportion of the population of the world and where millions live truly righteous lives, whether as committed adherents of another religion or as nonbelievers. In line with the teaching of Vatican II and much recent theology, it promotes a view of divine grace as ranging well beyond the bounds of explicit Christian faith.

In light of his assertion elsewhere of universal human sinfulness (3:23; 5:12), whether Paul really believed that, apart from Christian faith, any Gentiles did attain this "righteous" moral status, is much disputed. St. Augustine was of the view that Paul had righteous *believers* from the Gentile world rather than pagans in mind, a view that still has adherents today. In any case Paul's whole intent is to undercut any resting on the law on the part of the Jewish teacher, whom Paul now proceeds to attack in a manner that is much more intense and personal.

We may be shocked by the bitter and insulting tone of this following sequence (vv 17-24). It is in the literal and technical sense a diatribe, and as such not unusual in argumentative discourse in the ancient world.

Moreover, close inspection will reveal that it is rather artificially and cleverly contrived, building up a series of accusations in three sets of five: a fivefold list of Jewish privileges (vv 17-20); a corresponding five-fold list of the leadership roles that a pious Jew might hope to play on the basis of such privileges; finally, a fivefold set of accusations pointing to the gap between such roles and claims, on the one hand, and actual behavior, on the other. The accusations of hypocrisy are not dissimilar to Jesus' denunciations of the scribes and Pharisees in the Gospel of Matthew and, especially in view of the formal structure, probably reflect standard Christian polemic against representatives of the synagogue rather than something Paul has composed specifically for Romans. Some seem quite unreal—especially the suggestion that Jewish teachers of this kind would rob (pagan?) shrines and temples; some specific incident lost to us may be in view. Once again, however, we must insist that what Paul records here for his specific polemical purpose should not be taken as a genuine Christian indictment of Judaism as such, valid for all time.

The downgrading he has attempted in regard to possession of the Jewish law, Paul finally (vv 25-29) extends also to circumcision. Circum-cision commits the Jew to a life of observance of the law. Any "useful-ness" it has (in regard to salvation) is annulled where such observance is wanting. A long-standing biblical tradition had in fact insisted that physical circumcision be accompanied by the inward moral disposition dubbed "circumcision of heart" (Lev 26:41; Deut 10:16; 30:6; Jer 4:4; 9:26-26; Ezek 44:7, 9). Extending this principle, Paul maintains that the Gentile (literally "the uncircumcised man") who keeps the precepts of the law in this "inward" sense, which is what God really attends to, will be counted as circumcised and in fact qualified to sit in judgment on the circumcised Jew who fails in observance. Paul is in fact redefining Jewish identity when he insists (v 29) that "the real Jew" is not the person de-fined by outward marks such as physical circumcision but the one rec-ognized as such by God, whose "circumcision" is one wrought by the Spirit in the heart.

With this allusion to the work of the Spirit in the heart we seem to leave for a moment the purely intra-Jewish frame of reference in which the rhetorical accusation has until now been conducted and enter the Christian perspective. Paul does seem to identify the "true Jew" with the Christian believer, who through faith and baptism has entered the new era inaugurated by the resurrection of Christ, with the Spirit as transforming power (Rom 1:4; 2 Cor 3:17-18). In so doing he offers an anticipatory glimpse of what he will expound at length in chapters 5–8.

For the present we are left with what, taken in isolation, appears to be a highly negative portrayal of Jews and Judaism. This is not the last word on the topic in Romans, however, and we must keep in mind the rhetorical device he is employing and let the argument run its full course before drawing conclusions.

God's Faithfulness to Israel Stands: 3:1-8

> 3:1What advantage is there then in being a Jew? Or what is the value of circumcision? 2Much, in every respect. [For] in the first place, they were entrusted with the utterances of God. 3What if some were unfaithful? Will their infidelity nullify the fidelity of God? 4Of course not! God must be true, though every human being is a liar, as it is written:
> "That you may be justified in your words,
>   and conquer when you are judged."
> 5But if our wickedness provides proof of God's righteousness, what can we say? Is God unjust, humanly speaking, to inflict his wrath? 6Of course not! For how else is God to judge the world? 7But if God's truth redounds to his glory through my falsehood, why am I still being condemned as a sinner? 8And why not say—as we are accused and as some claim we say—that we should do evil that good may come of it? Their penalty is what they deserve.

At this point Paul at last seems to allow his Jewish dialogue partner to have a say. In classic question-and-answer diatribe mode, he puts on his lips a series of objections arising out of the severe undercutting of Jewish privileges and identity that the foregoing accusation has entailed. The objector understandably asks what advantage remains in being a Jew (v 1) and receives the rather lame response (v 2) that it was Jewish privilege to be entrusted with "the utterances of God," that is, the prophetic revelation about God's plans for the world in the messianic era. What is far more deeply at stake, however, is the faithfulness of God in God's self. What of all God's promises to Israel, what of God's stated plans for Israel, if all has been undercut and thwarted by Israel's failure? This basic issue is stated and restated several times in the course of the exchange, receiving responses (from Paul?) that seem arbitrary and are hardly adequate. The real value of the sequence for current interpretation, however, is the way in which it sets the phrase "God's righteousness" in parallel with similar expressions—"God's faithfulness," "God's truthfulness"—that disclose Paul's understanding of righteousness as continuous with its usage in the biblical and postbiblical Jewish tradition. God's righteousness is all about the divine faithfulness to the covenant partner, Israel.

The issue concerning God's faithfulness to Israel does not receive a satisfactory answer here. The whole exchange seems to run aground at v 8, with Paul protesting about the blasphemous nature of an accusation made by his adversaries that his thesis of God's grace addressing and triumphing in the context of universal human sinfulness amounts to making the end justify the means. The issue concerning Israel remains hanging in the air. Paul will return to deal with it at length in chapters 9–11. The issue concerning God's faithfulness will shortly receive a triumphant reassertion in 3:21-26. In the meantime Paul drives home his rhetorical accusation with a concentrated appeal to Scripture (3:9-20).

Scripture Excludes Any Way of Righteousness Other than by Faith: 3:9-20

⁹Well, then, are we better off? Not entirely, for we have already brought the charge against Jews and Greeks alike that they are all under the domination of sin, ¹⁰as it is written:
"There is no one just, not one,
    ¹¹there is no one who understands,
        there is no one who seeks God.
¹²All have gone astray; all alike are worthless;
        there is not one who does good,
            [there is not] even one.
¹³Their throats are open graves;
        they deceive with their tongues;
the venom of asps is on their lips;
    ¹⁴their mouths are full of bitter cursing.
¹⁵Their feet are quick to shed blood;
        ¹⁶ruin and misery are in their ways,
¹⁷and the way of peace they know not.
        ¹⁸There is no fear of God before their eyes."
¹⁹Now we know that what the law says is addressed to those under the law, so that every mouth may be silenced and the whole world stand accountable to God, ²⁰since no human being will be justified in his sight by observing the law; for through the law comes consciousness of sin.

This sequence, consisting largely of a chain of pessimistic phrases from the Psalms, probably wins the prize for the least attractive passage in the letter. Paul's use of Scripture here seems arbitrary in the extreme.

Within the mode of discourse that he has been employing since 1:18 it forms a fitting conclusion, not without parallel in other Jewish literature of the time, notably in the Dead Sea Scrolls from Qumran. Scripture gives God's view of the situation and God must be allowed to have the last and decisive word. With the culminating quotation of Psalm 143:2 in v 20 (though the phrase "by observing the law" is Paul's arbitrary addition) Paul clinches his overall thesis that the righteousness God requires of human beings cannot stem from observance of the law. This means that Jews along with Gentiles have no escape on that basis. "*Every* mouth" is to be "silenced" and "the *whole* world" is to stand "accountable [= "guilty"] to God" (v 19b). Jews have "no advantage" (v 9a) because *all*, Jews and Greeks, are "under the domination of sin" (v 9b).

With this last phrase we meet here (v 9) for the first time in the letter Paul's distinctive and sophisticated understanding of sin. Paul rarely thinks of sin in terms of individual acts of wrongdoing. He thinks of sin, which in many places we would do better to write as "Sin," as a kind of tyrant power or slave master that has got all humanity under its control. Rather than something calling for divine forgiveness (though that is presupposed), sin, for Paul, is a radical captivity from which human beings need to be set free. His belief that all, Jews as well as Gentiles, are bound together in this solidarity of sin is not so much an empirical judgment derived from observance of human behavior generally as a conviction stemming from coming to faith in the Gospel of the Crucified. If the cross of Jesus was the mode of the redemption that God saw the human race to require, what was the situation of humanity that called for so drastic a remedy? Paul's only response could be: a radical captivity to Sin. Paul sees in the psalm passages he quotes a divine confirmation of this view, one addressed, ironically, to Israel in first instance (v 19a). In the face of this captivity, the law is no help at all. It lends no capacity to carry out what it requires. On the contrary, it brings only a sense of helplessness, a heightened sense of being locked in "captivity to Sin," what Paul describes at the end (v 20b) as "a consciousness [= "experience"] of sin."

This brings us to the end of the long rhetorical accusation against the Jewish teacher that forms the negative background to the proclamation of righteousness by faith. Paul has allowed his Roman audience to "overhear" the dialogue he has set up in order to exclude any other way of righteousness, especially any lingering Jewish sense that righteousness could come by way of the Jewish law. It has all been very negative and, as I have insisted all through, it is misleading to single out and read as "Holy Scripture" any particular sections without awareness of the whole.

Above all, it is necessary to keep in mind that this negative affirmation, with its sense of a universal solidarity in sin, is only the background to a reassertion of a much more powerful human solidarity in grace that God is bringing about in the world through the work of Christ. It chimes in with the summary of Jesus' inaugural preaching of the Gospel: "The kingdom of God is at hand. *Repent*, and believe in the gospel" (Mark 1:14-15//Matt 4:17; emphasis added). The presupposition of the Gospel is conversion of heart, an honest deep-seated awareness of one's alienation from God and need for reconciliation and renewal of relationship that comes in Christ as a pure act of grace. What Paul has been about in this otherwise grim section of Romans is essentially an attempt to bring about that conversion of heart. Like the father's plea to the *older* brother in Luke's parable of the Lost Son (Luke 15:25-32), it has been an attempt to erode a clinging to any form of attaining right relationship with God other than through an abandonment in faith to grace.

God's Righteousness Available in Christ through Faith: 3:21-31

The Revelation of God's Righteousness in Christ: 3:21-26

[21]But now the righteousness of God has been manifested apart from the law, though testified to by the law and the prophets, [22]the righteousness of God through faith in Jesus Christ for all who believe. For there is no distinction; [23]all have sinned and are deprived of the glory of God. [24]They are justified freely by his grace through the redemption in Christ Jesus, [25]whom God set forth as an expiation, through faith, by his blood, to prove his righteousness because of the forgiveness of sins previously committed, [26]through the forbearance of God—to prove his righteousness in the present time, that he might be righteous and justify the one who has faith in Jesus.

This short passage has attracted more attention in the Christian tradition than almost any other in Paul. In particular, it has played a large part in explanations of Christ's work of redemption. Since some of those explanations are better founded in the text than others, it is important to see what the passage is *not* saying, as well as to note what Paul does seem to be affirming here.

In the preceding long exchange with the Jewish teacher (1:18–3:20), Paul has excluded any possibility of righteousness on the basis of observance of the Jewish law. That task complete, he now restates the positive theme of the letter: the universal availability of salvation on the basis of a righteousness ("the righteousness of God") available to human beings through faith. The all-important addition to the previous statement (1:16-17) is the inclusion of Christ's redemptive work as the focus of faith.

In the original Greek the passage consists of a single long and loosely constructed sentence, repetitive and overloaded with theological terms. Its complexity seems to be due to the fact that Paul has incorporated—though not digested very adequately into his syntax—a traditional Christian creedal formula portraying the death of Christ in sacrificial terms. Though not the main point of the passage, this reference to Christ's death has been the main focus of Christian theology. It has left a legacy requiring reexamination in the light of our wider understanding of Paul.

Leaving that aside for a moment, let us attend to some features in the passage. We note that it begins with a double announcement of the revelation (NAB: "manifestation") of "the righteousness of God" (vv 21-22). Discussing this phrase in the original statement of theme (1:17), I pointed out that it seems to be capable of a dual or "bipolar" reference: to refer to God's own righteousness and also to the righteousness that God bestows as a gift of pure grace on human beings who have no righteousness of their own. The initial statement here (v 21) seems to refer to God's righteousness in the first sense. In an earlier passage, 3:1-8, Paul had cited an objection to the effect that to claim that the Jewish world lacked righteousness just like the rest of humanity put in question God's own righteousness (fidelity) to Israel (v 5). Paul left the issue hanging there at the time. Now he returns to it triumphantly, with the assertion that, in the face of a human alienation from God that is truly universal (that is, inclusive of Jews as well as Gentiles [v 22d-23]), God is displaying "righteousness" (covenant fidelity) on an equally universal scale. God is displaying fidelity as covenant partner to Israel, while displaying the same fidelity as Creator to the entire world. In other words, Paul sees the covenant fidelity (righteousness) that binds God to Israel to be operative in Christ to the entire world.

The second reference to "God's righteousness" (v 22) would then refer to the effect of God's exercise of covenant faithfulness on the *human* side of the equation: to the *gift* of righteousness that God graciously bestows on human beings in the face of their lack of any righteousness of their own. The sole condition on their part is faith: that they believe and place their entire hope for relationship with God on this divine exercise of generosity and grace.

All this is "apart from the law" (v 21a). If the law had anything to do with it, the scope of God's action would be restricted to Israel, and, in any case, since "all have sinned and are deprived of the glory of God" (v 23), the law, which cannot deal with sin, would be useless. The only role the law can play in the new era is to act as witness. In the sense of Scripture (the Pentateuch), along with the Prophets, it bears witness to righteousness by faith. Paul will illustrate this witness when he reexamines Scripture's depiction of Abraham in the following chapter (4:1-25).

In the central part of the present text Paul describes God's gracious bestowal of righteousness on believers through the redemptive work of Christ (vv 24-25a). The language is primarily metaphorical. We should not seek to extract too much theological rigor from the images employed. "Justification" or "being justified" is an image taken from legal process. It has a role in Paul's theology since the apocalyptic frame of reference in which it is cast included, as we have seen, the expectation that God would soon institute a final judgment in which the wicked would be punished and the faithful vindicated. "Justification" refers to this last process: the vindication of the innocent, the declaration that they have been found to be "in the right" or "righteous." (In Greek, unlike English, the same basic word stem [*dik-*] serves for both "justification" and "righteousness.") For Paul, of course, since "all have sinned" (v 23a; 5:12d), there is no righteousness, no hope of justification at all. The Gospel proclaims, however, that in Christ God is graciously "justifying" (extending "righteousness") to human beings simply on the basis of faith. For believers the end-time verdict has been brought forward; as far as relations with God go, they have already passed through the judgment and entered into the new age with Christ.

"Justification" is hardly congenial or meaningful terminology for people today. In pastoral contexts it's best to ignore the legal origins of the image and think of it simply in relational terms. Justification refers to God's righting of relations, drawing alienated human beings back into right relationship. It is virtually the same as reconciliation, provided one understands that in the reconciling process the initiative comes entirely from the side of God.

Paul describes Christ's role as a "redemption." Here again the language was metaphorical before it entered into theology. The Greek word *apolytrōsis* refers to the liberation of those who had been enslaved after being taken prisoner in war. Relatives or friends could obtain their freedom through the payment of price. Paul, as we have seen, thinks of all human beings as enslaved under the power of the tyrant slave-master Sin (3:9). There is no suggestion that Christ paid a price *to* any agent—the Devil or even Sin personified. But the language of "redemption" conveys the sense of freedom achieved at a cost, the cost here being the suffering involved in his death on the cross.

We dive more deeply into this mystery with the following phrase: "whom God set forth as an expiation, through faith, by his blood" (v 25a). The Greek word translated here as "expiation," *hilastērion*, refers in secular Greek to the placation or propitiation of an angry human person or a god. If we read this meaning here and also understand "God's righteousness" as "God's justice" in the sense of the kind of justice handed out in a secular court of law, we soon emerge with an understanding of redemption that has been quite prevalent in the Christian tradition: Christ through his bloody and painful death assuages the anger of God at human sin; he "satisfies" the demands of divine justice so that forgiveness and justification can flow. The problem with this kind of theory (the satisfaction theory, associated in particular with St. Anselm of Canterbury) is that it drives a wedge between God (the Father) and the action of Christ. It communicates a sense of God as only grudgingly conceding forgiveness when the Son has painfully paid the penalty demanded by justice. It locks the divine action into a legal straightjacket that has more in common with medieval conceptions of relations between masters and servants than first-century biblical theology. Above all it neglects the fact that in Paul's expression it is God, not Christ, who is the primary agent ("whom God set forth"). The aim of the divine action is not to change an attitude in God. It is to change something on the human side: to transform human hostility and alienation into right relationship through a one-sided reaching out in grace.

Paul in fact is likely to be using the word *hilastērion*, not in its meaning in secular Greek, but in a metaphorical way derived from the biblical Day of Atonement ritual. In the Greek version of the Old Testament (Septuagint) *hilastērion* refers to the golden cover placed over the ark of the covenant in the innermost shrine of the temple, the holy of holies. It featured in the Day of Atonement ritual (Lev 16:15-16) in that the high priest sprinkled on it the blood of the goat slain as a sin offering on that day of forgiveness and reconciliation with God. It was not that the ritual "moved" God to effect forgiveness. The "flow" was all the other way: the ritual enacted in a tangible sacramental way God's gracious "wiping away" of the accumulated sins of the people, thereby restoring to full vigor the covenant relationship for the year to come. In connection with the ritual it is appropriate to speak of "expiation" in the sense that sin was wiped away (the underlying Hebrew verb *kipper* has this sense, as, e.g., when a lecturer wipes away writing on a whiteboard), but not in the sense that the deity was appeased or placated by the bloody aspect of the sacrifice. Such an idea was foreign to the Israelite idea of sacrifice, where the initiative always remained with God. In referring to Christ as *hilastērion* Paul aligns himself with an early Christian way of coming to terms with the mystery presented by the death of Christ. The shedding of Christ's blood on the cross led the early disciples to understand it in terms of the Day of Atonement imagery: to see it as the culminating Day of Atonement wiping away human sin. In this sense Christ "died for our sins" (1 Cor 15:3; Rom 4:25), died for their "removal."

Where the earliest tradition probably related this removal of sin simply to Israel, Paul saw the matter in more universal terms. In Christ's death God was not only enacting, as covenant partner, a climactic Day of Atonement on behalf of Israel. As universal Creator, God was enacting a Day of Atonement for the entire world. The perfect commentary is a passage from another letter of Paul that we have already seen:

> [18]And all this is from God, who has reconciled us to himself through Christ and given us the ministry of reconciliation, [19]namely, God was reconciling the world to himself in Christ, *not counting their trespasses against them* and entrusting to us the message of reconciliation. . . . [21]For our sake he made him to be sin who did not know sin, so that we might become the righteousness of God in him. (2 Cor 5:18-19, 21; emphasis added)

We note the final phrases. The effect of the divine action in Christ is not simply that we should become righteous but that we should attain this status in God's eyes through union with Christ, who in his person embodies the divine righteousness or fidelity in the world. What I have described as the two "poles" of Paul's sense of "the righteousness of God"—the divine and the human—come together in Christ.

In its final phrases (vv 25b-26) the passage relates this redemptive action of God to past and present respectively. It deals with all the human sins "previously committed," that is, in the human race before the coming of Christ, when God, displaying righteousness, tolerated sin "in forbearance" in view of the redemption to come. It also shows God to be righteous in the present time in that, through the worldwide proclamation of the Gospel, the nations of the world may come under the scope of the divine reconciliation and so find justification in Christ through faith.

The issue raised by the objector in 3:3-6—that Paul's thesis of Israel's sinfulness puts in question the righteousness of God—has now been laid to rest. In Christ God has dealt faithfully with Israel's sinfulness as God always did in the Day of Atonement ritual year by year. The new thing is that God, showing covenant fidelity as Creator, has graciously drawn the entire world into the atoning ritual hitherto confined to Israel alone. Hence Paul's stress at the beginning and end of the passage (vv 21-22 and vv 25b-26) on the "revelation" or "proof" of the righteousness of God.

As I said at the start, this passage has attracted immense theological attention because of the part played in the explanation of redemption by its references to Christ's death in sacrificial imagery. Paul, I suspect, would be surprised by that development and would remind us, I'm sure, not to wring too much theology in a rigorous systematic sense out of the images he used. Above all, I think he would say that the statements about Christ's death are not in fact the main point. The main point is the assertion that, in the face of universal human alienation from God and the impotence of the Jewish law to do anything about it, God in Christ has opened up to the entire world a new possibility of righteousness through *faith*. The consequences are drawn in the short passage that follows.

Conclusion: Faith Alone! 3:27-31

> [27]What occasion is there then for boasting? It is ruled out. On what principle, that of works? No, rather on the principle of faith. [28]For we consider that a person is justified by faith apart from works of the law. [29]Does God belong to Jews alone? Does he not belong to Gentiles, too? Yes, also to Gentiles, [30]for God is one and will justify the circumcised on the basis of faith and the uncircumcised through faith. [31]Are we then annulling the law by this faith? Of course not! On the contrary, we are supporting the law.

Reverting to back and forth exchange (diatribe), Paul draws the conclusion he has been driving since he first launched the dialogue with the Jewish teacher at 1:18. "Boasting" here does mean bragging about one's own achievements as it does for us today. In Paul's usage one "boasts" in that in which one places one's hope for acceptance by God, that is, for justification. The point is that God's intervention in Christ has excluded "boasting" as a source of confidence in anything other than faith—notably, one's performance ("works") of the Jewish law. That is why "a person is justified by faith apart from works of the law" (v 28). This last statement achieved notoriety when the sixteenth century Reformer Martin Luther added the word "alone" to faith, and "by faith alone" became a catch-cry of the Reformation. Though no word for "alone" stands in the Greek text, in *this* context Luther's addition is quite true to Paul's meaning. But in a broader perspective, while faith may be the beginning of the process of salvation, more is required: living out faith in obedience and love. Paul will attend to this expressly later (6:1–8:13).

The questions and responses about God in the second half of the passage (vv 29-30) reveal the depth of Paul's theological vision. If, as all Jews believe and affirm each day in the Shema prayer (Deut 6:4-9), there is only one God—God of the Gentiles as well as of Jews—God cannot have, as it were, two faces toward the world. There must be just one principle of divine acceptance (justification). Since the Gentiles do not have the law of Moses, that principle must be faith. Thus, in a bold theological stroke, from the very heart of the Jewish faith (its monotheistic belief in the "one God"), Paul validates the principle of justification by faith (alone) and the universal scope of the salvation it holds out to the world.

Finally (v 31), Paul allows an obvious question—better, objection—to surface. Is not all the stress so exclusively upon faith tantamount to the annulment of the law? That's certainly what looks to be the case, but Paul will have none of it, boldly asserting: "On the contrary, we are [upholding (NAB's "supporting" is too weak)] the law." We might well feel tempted to say, "Well, you could have fooled me, Paul—because abolishing the law appears to be exactly the drift of your argument." Paul will eventually find a place for the law—albeit a negative one—in the scheme of salvation. In the meantime, exploiting the very slippery meaning of the word "law" (*nomos*) in Greek, he takes up its reference to Scripture (Pentateuch) and in this sense "upholds" the law by summoning up its witness to righteousness by faith.

Scripture's Witness to Faith Shown in Abraham: 4:1-25

Introduction to Romans 4

Romans 4 is one of the more approachable chapters in the letter since it is unified around an attractive presentation of the figure of Abraham. In the face of a Jewish tradition that saw this all-important patriarch primarily in terms of obedience to divine commands, Paul's task is to bring him forward as Scripture's star witness for faith. The availability of God's righteousness to all believers has swept away the possibility of righteousness on the basis of the law understood as a legal code. But the law in the shape of Scripture (the Pentateuch), along with the Prophets, bears "witness" (NAB: "testimony") to righteousness by faith (3:21b). As in the case of the long scriptural chain in 3:10-18 (though far more attractively!), the importance of Scripture is that it gives God's view of what counts in the final, messianic age—a divine view that is, of course, decisive.

To get purchase on Paul's argument in this chapter it is important to be aware of three more general matters before entering into the details of the text. The first thing to appreciate is the place of Abraham within the Jewish tradition that is the background to the argument here. Abraham is not simply one biblical figure among many others that Paul could have chosen to illustrate his point. Abraham is the "father" of the Jewish nation, not simply in the sense of being the ancestor from whom all are descended but in a representative way that lingers on. The stances he took before God, the choices he made, and the promises he received remain definitive for his descendants. He is crucial to Israel's identity. One cannot define Israel, especially the Israel of the messianic age, without defining Abraham and what it means to be his descendants (in biblical terms, his "seed"). Hence the necessity for Paul to claim Abraham as figure first and foremost of faith rather than of obedience to law, the prevailing view in the Jewish tradition. Only if he succeeds in claiming Abraham for faith can Paul claim that it is persons and communities of faith who, as his "seed," stand in line to inherit the promises he received.

The second matter to note is the sequence of exchanges between God and Abraham (still "Abram" at this point in the original) in the biblical text, Genesis 15, that was a goldmine for Paul in his task of claiming the patriarch for faith. We can set out the sequence as follows:

- God gives Abraham an assurance concerning his future (v 1)
- Abraham points out that he is childless and has no heir (vv 2-4)
- God takes Abraham outside, points to the stars, and *promises* him, "so . . . shall your descendants be" (v 5: *the Son/Seed Promise*)
- "Abram put his *faith* in the LORD, who credited it to him as an act of *righteousness*" (v 6; emphasis added)
- A covenant-making ritual between God and Abraham (vv 7-17)
- God *promises* to give the land from the river of Egypt to the Euphrates to Abraham's descendants (vv 18-21: *the Land Promise*).

This passage clearly links faith and being found righteous in a single statement, without any mention of observance of law. It does so, moreover, in the context of two key promises that Abraham received. Despite his advanced age and the barrenness of his wife Sarah, Abraham put his faith in the first promise of God (what I call the Son/Seed Promise): that he would have a vast number of descendants. Then, on the basis of the righteous status that attended his faith in that promise, he received a second promise (what I call "the Land Promise"): that God would give the land (from the River Nile to the Euphrates) to his descendants. He received this second promise for his descendants simply on the basis of the righteous status in God's eyes that he attained through faith. The key point for Paul is that his descendants come under the scope of that promise on the same basis: through faith.

In this connection the third important matter to note is that the Land Promise had undergone considerable transformation in the Jewish tradition that Paul is presupposing. It has been "expanded" so as to include, as v 13 clearly states, "the world." This expression probably refers to "the inheritance of the world" originally bestowed on human beings by God according to the first creation account in Genesis 1:28-30. The promise in this sense would be realized in the messianic age when God's original design for human beings, long since frustrated by sin, would come true for the first time.

Within the framework of this tradition and with close attention to Genesis 15, Paul's argument proceeds basically in two stages. First (vv 1-12) he shows from Scripture that Abraham was a person found righteous in God's eyes on the basis of his faith (in the Son/Seed Promise). Second (vv 13-25) that he received the Land Promise on this basis alone— so that it might come true for the vast number of descendants he had been promised, that is, not only the Jews but also a great multitude of Gentiles who would imitate his faith.

Abraham, Person of Faith and Father of All Believers: 4:1-12

⁴:¹What then can we say that Abraham found, our ancestor according to the flesh? ²Indeed, if Abraham was justified on the basis of his works, he has reason to boast; but this was not so in the sight of God. ³For what does the scripture say? "Abraham believed God, and it was credited to him as righteousness." ⁴A worker's wage is credited not as a gift, but as something due. ⁵But when one does not work, yet believes in the one who justifies the ungodly, his faith is credited as righteousness. So also David declares the blessedness of the person to whom God credits righteousness apart from works:
⁷"Blessed are they whose iniquities are forgiven
    and whose sins are covered.
⁸Blessed is the man whose sin the Lord does not record."

⁹Does this blessedness apply only to the circumcised, or to the uncircumcised as well? Now we assert that "faith was credited to Abraham as righteousness." ¹⁰Under what circumstances was it credited? Was he circumcised or not? He was not circumcised, but uncircumcised. ¹¹And he received the sign of circumcision as a seal on the righteousness received through faith while he was uncircumcised. Thus he was to be the father of all the uncircumcised who believe, so that to them [also] righteousness might be credited, ¹²as well as the father of the circumcised who not only are circumcised, but also follow the path of faith that our father Abraham walked while still uncircumcised.

After some introductory remarks (vv 1-2) Paul moves into his scriptural proof that Abraham was a person found righteous in God's eyes by faith. The proof comes in three stages. Paul employs a rabbinic technique of biblical interpretation whereby a text from one passage receives confirmation by a text from another on the basis of a word or phrase they have in common. In this case Paul first (vv 4-5) adduces a text from the Law (Pentateuch), that is, the sentence from Genesis 15:6 that we have already discussed, and then cites (vv 6-8) a second text, Psalm 32:1-2, with which it has in common the word "credited" (the NAB unfortunately obscures this by translating "does not record"; it would be better to translate "reckoned" in both cases). Since David was held to be the author of the Psalms and was also reckoned to have been a prophet, a quotation from the Psalms provides a text from the Prophets. Thus the combination of these two texts gives Paul the dual scriptural witness to righteousness by faith from "the law and the prophets" as he had promised in 3:21.

Having cited (v 3) the first text, Genesis 15:6, linking Abraham's being found righteous in God's sight with his faith in the divine promise, Paul teases out its implications (vv 4-5). He takes an example from everyday life—from the acknowledged right of an employee to receive recompense for work done, and, on the other hand, from the corresponding lack of right to such recompense on the part of one who has not done any work at all. Employees who have worked can rest their hopes for payment on what they themselves have done. But any benefit accruing to an employee who has done nothing has to stem from the pure goodwill and favor of the employer. Since Abraham has at this point done nothing he is in the second situation. If he is to receive a "reward" (Gen 15:1) from God—the promised line of descendants—it must be on the basis of trust in God's grace and generosity only. Paul's somewhat odd expression stating faith in "the one who justifies the ungodly" probably reflects his sense that Abraham at this point is technically a Gentile and so part of that sinful world to which God is reaching out in grace. In other respects the image is close to Jesus' parable of the laborers in the vineyard (Matt 20:1-16). Because the employer there chooses to be generous, even those who have arrived at the last hour and barely worked at all receive the same payment as those who have worked all day. Like Paul, the parable projects an image of God as a God of grace above all.

Paul's second text (vv 6-8), from the Prophets in the shape of Psalm 32:1-2, recounts the experience of a person who has been led through misfortune to recognize and admit sinfulness, and so arrive at a wonderful experience of acceptance and forgiveness by God. The psalm movingly portrays the greater "blessedness" of finding a God of grace over attempts to deny one's sinfulness and claim right standing in God's eyes on the basis of one's "works." (We are close here to another parable of Jesus: that of the Pharisee and the tax collector [Luke 18:9-14].) On the basis of the link between the two texts, Genesis 15:6 and Psalm 32:1-2, Paul can assign the experience of grace-based justification recorded in this psalm to Abraham.

It is at the third stage of his scriptural argument, however, that Paul throws down his trump card. He asks at what stage Abraham received this "blessing" (= justification). Did it follow or precede his reception of circumcision? The answer is clear in the sequence of Genesis 15–17. Justification came first (Gen 15:6); circumcision followed (17:10-14, 26-27)— and did so, as Paul would have it (v 11a), simply as a "sign" or "seal" set upon a righteousness/justification already received through faith.

The consequences of this are momentous for the identity of the renewed People of God. Abraham is the "father" not only of those who are his lineal descendants (Jews) but also, and in a sense primarily, of those who follow the path (literally "walk in the steps") of the faith by which he was justified when uncircumcised (vv 11b-12). Paul has not only reclaimed Abraham as first and foremost a person of faith. He has redefined his "fatherhood" in an inclusive rather than an exclusive direction: he is "father" of a great line of Gentile believers and "father" of Jews primarily in terms of faith.

Abraham: Receiver of the Promise for All Believers: 4:13-25

[13]It was not through the law that the promise was made to Abraham and his descendants that he would inherit the world, but

through the righteousness that comes from faith. [14]For if those who adhere to the law are the heirs, faith is null and the promise is void. [15]For the law produces wrath; but where there is no law, neither is there violation. [16]For this reason, it depends on faith, so that it may be a gift, and the promise may be guaranteed to all his descendants, not to those who only adhere to the law but to those who follow the faith of Abraham, who is the father of all of us, [17]as it is written, "I have made you father of many nations." He is our father in the sight of God, in whom he believed, who gives life to the dead and calls into being what does not exist. [18]He believed, hoping against hope, that he would become "the father of many nations," according to what was said, "Thus shall your descendants be." [19]He did not weaken in faith when he considered his own body as [already] dead (for he was almost a hundred years old) and the dead womb of Sarah. [20]He did not doubt God's promise in unbelief; rather, he was empowered by faith and gave glory to God [21]and was fully convinced that what he had promised he was also able to do. [22]That is why "it was credited to him as righteousness." [23]But it was not for him alone that it was written that "it was credited to him"; [24]it was also for us, to whom it will be credited, who believe in the one who raised Jesus our Lord from the dead, [25]who was handed over for our transgressions and was raised for our justification.

Paul has shown from Scripture that Abraham found acceptance and right relationship (justification) with God through faith. His second major point is that it was to him *precisely as believer* in this first promise (the Son/Seed Promise) that the second divine promise (the Land Promise) was made. As I have indicated above, in the developed Jewish tradition this promise took in no longer just a stretch of land across what we now call the Middle East but embraced "the world" (v 13). It contained all the blessings of salvation, catching up the original "bequest" of the world to humankind in Adam. In the rather constricted argument of vv 14-16 Paul excludes any possibility that the law and the relationship with God that it would bring had anything at all to do with the operation of this promise. Because of human sinfulness, going the way of the law can only run into the brick wall of human relations with God that Paul terms "wrath" (v 15). Faith, on the other hand, brings human sinfulness before the grace of God, the true relationship that God wants to have with human beings. As in the case of Abraham, faith prepares the way for human beings to receive the promise (the Land Promise) as pure gift, thereby safeguarding its universal and inclusive scope. The promise is for *all* for whom Abraham is "father": those from the "many nations" (literally "Gentiles"), as well as those (the Jews) who proceed from the law (vv 16-17a).

At this point (v 17b), Paul makes one of the most attractive moves in the letter, theologically speaking. Abraham's role as father of all believers rests on a parity in faith. On the biblical principle, "like parent, like child," believers are descendants of Abraham and in line to receive the promise made to him and his descendants (Gen 15:18) because they believe in exactly the same way as he did. To show this, Paul explores (vv 17b-22) what was involved in Abraham's believing in the original promise (the Son/Seed Promise: Gen 15:4-5) and then relates this to Christian faith (vv 23-25). If he was to have a child—and indeed a vast line of descendants—Abraham had to believe in God in a very specific sense: in a God "who gives life to the dead and calls into being what does not exist" (v 17b). Why was this so? Because of his personal circumstances and those of his wife Sarah at the time. As far as reproductive capacity goes, there was "deadness" on both sides of the parental equation: his own advanced years and the long-standing barrenness of Sarah's womb (v 19). If in these circumstances the couple were to have a child, it could only be through the capacity of God, as Creator, to "raise the dead." Moreover (vv 20-21), Abraham's faith was not a once-off affair. It involved a perseverance in believing, a hoping against hope, until the birth of Isaac gave evidence that the promise, "so [i.e., as many as the stars] . . . shall your descendants be" (Gen 15:5), was on the way to being fulfilled. Faith shades off into hope at this stage in a way that Paul will exploit later on.

The concluding sentences (vv 23-25) draw the parallel with believers' faith. If the faith of Abraham that was credited to him for justification (v 22) involved believing in a Creator God who raises the dead, that is also true of Abraham's "descendants." We too believe in such a God, One who raised Jesus from the dead, the core tenet of the Gospel (vv 23-24; cf. 1 Cor 15:3-5; Rom 10:9; etc.). Paul can thus maintain that the key text Genesis 15:6 linking justification with faith, applies (literally "was written") just as much to us as to Abraham. If Christ was "handed over for our transgressions" (v 25a), he "was raised for our justification" (v 25b).

As in the case of Abraham, our believing too involves an element of hope. Faith looks back to the past event of God's raising of Jesus, but, as Paul will bring out in the next major section of the letter (chaps. 5–8), the resurrection of Jesus is also a pledge that God will raise our "mortal bodies" through the power of the Spirit (Rom 8:11). In this comprehensive way Paul has reclaimed Abraham for grace and faith, and presented him as the paradigm of Christian faith and hope.

With the closing sentences of this chapter Paul has well and truly emerged from his dialogue with the Jewish teacher. The first-person plural references ("we"; "our") have Christian faith and Christian hope in view. Paul would now be confident that he has clinched from his scriptural presentation of Abraham the truth that God wants to deal with human beings as a God of grace as well as a God of creative power. The way is now open to treat of the hope that emerges from faith as believers live out the renewed relationship with God (justification) they have graciously received.

2. The *Hope* of Salvation: A (Believers) 5:1–8:39

The Hope that Springs from God's Love: 5:1-11

> 5:1Therefore, since we have been justified by faith, we have peace with God through our Lord Jesus Christ, 2through whom we have gained access [by faith] to this grace in which we stand, and we boast in hope of the glory of God. 3Not only that, but we even boast of our afflictions, knowing that affliction produces endurance, 4and endurance, proven character, and proven character, hope, 5and hope does not disappoint, because the love of God has been poured out into our hearts through the holy Spirit that has been given to us. 6For Christ, while we were still helpless, yet died at the appointed time for the ungodly. 7Indeed, only with difficulty does one die for a just person, though perhaps for a good person one might even find courage to die. 8But God proves his love for us in that while we were still sinners Christ died for us. 9How much more then, since we are now justified by his blood, will we be saved through him from the wrath. 10Indeed, if, while we were enemies, we were reconciled to God through the death of his Son, how much more, once reconciled, will we be saved by his life. 11Not only that, but we also boast of God through our Lord Jesus Christ, through whom we have now received reconciliation.

We enter now upon the section of Romans (chaps. 5–8) that almost all readers find most appealing. Picking up the overall theme of the letter—that the Gospel is the "power of God [leading to] salvation" for all believers (1:16)—Paul's task is now to convey the hope for salvation that lies open for believers on the basis of the righteous status brought about through faith (5:1-2). So faith now yields to hope as the major theme. Likewise, the theme of God's righteousness (faithfulness) gives way to that of God's love. The whole section in fact begins (5:1-11) and ends

(8:31-39) with the hope that springs from God's love. Functioning like bookends holding together a series of volumes on a shelf, these two passages communicate the sense of the divine love binding together everything in between.

Paul's case for hope has to confront the present reality of life for believers. We are on the way to full salvation but not yet arrived. As far as relationship with God goes, we *are* fully "arrived." "Justified by faith" we have been brought into right relationship with God and enjoy a familial intimacy with God, attested by the Spirit (5:5; cf. 8:14-16). We have to live out this relationship, however, while bodily anchored in a world that is still far from completely redeemed. Three negative realities in particular confront believers while they are still on the way to salvation: suffering, physical mortality, and the lingering proneness to sin that, in biblical terminology, Paul refers to as "flesh" (*sarx*). Each of these realities, in its own distinctive way, can threaten the hope of salvation and Paul confronts each in due course.

The section begins (vv 1-2) with a wonderful expression of our new relationship with God on the basis of faith. From being "enemies" (cf. v 10) Christ's costly act upon the cross and our faith in that event has brought us into an aura of "peace." Like citizens of a previously hostile but now reconciled power, we have "access" to the divine presence, to live henceforth in an atmosphere of grace. It is from this sense of divine favor that hope for full salvation springs. Earlier in the letter "boasting" had been excluded because it involved putting one's reliance for salvation on human achievement inevitably doomed to fail. Now, however, we really can "boast in hope of the glory of God" because that hope rests entirely on grace. The biblical concept of "glory" runs like a golden thread throughout the letter. It refers to the attainment in full measure of that likeness to God or true humanity intended by God from the start (Gen 1:26-27). Lost through sin (Rom 3:23), the glory is now being realized through God's act in Christ.

Defiantly, Paul carries over the motif of "boasting" to the theme of suffering (vv 3-4). We may not be prepared to follow him all the way in the chain-like sequence that he formulates in these verses. Does not suffering often induce despair rather than hope? What Paul is challenging, however, is the thought of suffering as an index of the disfavor or anger of God—a conviction to which religious people are particularly inclined when suffering comes their way. Many believers in the early days of the church were undoubtedly perplexed that, despite Christ's saving work on the cross and his resurrection and ascension to God's right hand, the times remained so unmessianic. With suffering, especially persecution, and even death still around, were we truly "justified" and "at peace" with God? Are we perhaps in some sense still "in our sins" and being punished on that account? Does suffering mean that "wrath" rather than salvation awaits us at the end?

Beginning with the fine thematic statement in v 5, Paul tackles this error head on. Hope will *not* "disappoint" us on this account. We do not stand under God's wrath. How do we know? Because "the love of God has been poured out into our hearts through the holy Spirit that has been given to us" (v 5b). By "love of God" Paul does not mean our love for God but the felt experience of God's love conveyed by the Spirit. As the creative power of the "new creation" (as of the old: Gen 1:2; 2:7), the Spirit plays a number of roles in Christian life and Paul will have a lot more to say about it later on. For the present, using the biblical imaging of the Spirit as water ("poured out"), he points to the gift of the Spirit as that which assures believers, no matter what they suffer, that they stand within the favor of God; they can look to the future with hope rather than fear (cf. Rom 8:15-16).

The remaining half of the passage undergirds this hope with two "waves" of argument based on the extremity of God's love (vv 6-9; v 10). Both feature a kind of a fortiori logic as follows: if when we were sinners (God's "enemies" [v 10]) God gave up his Son to die for us and reconcile us, how "much more" (*pollōi mallon*) now that we are "friends" (through justification) can we be certain that God will complete the process and see us through to full salvation? The force of the argument (one that Paul will use again and again in this section of the letter) lies in the consideration that what God has done in the harder case (giving up the Son to die for the "ungodly"), God will certainly not fail to complete in the easier case (seeing the already reconciled through to salvation). To make the point about the extremity of God's love shown in the self-sacrificing death of Jesus, Paul asks (v 7) for what sort of person it might be thinkable to give up one's own life. Perhaps for a really good person—someone who brings great gifts to the service of humanity—we might be prepared to die. But who would be prepared to die, let alone give up the life of an only child, for a bad person or an enemy? Yet that is what God has done (vv 8-10). God has sent the Son to an alienated and hostile world, to bear the burden of that world's sinfulness and alienation through his death on a cross, in order to reconcile the world and set it back on the path to life. How, reasons Paul, when we contemplate the divine love involved in what God has *already* done in this way, can we doubt God's determination to carry through the process in what lies ahead?

That is the essential pattern of Paul's argument. A couple of further points may be made. In v 9 Paul concludes, "How much more . . . will we be saved . . . from the wrath." Many translations (but, fortunately, not the NAB) attempt to clarify the sense of "wrath" here by adding "of God." But this addition has no foundation in the Greek. Within the Jewish apocalyptic framework of Paul's argument, "wrath" does not so much denote an emotion in God but the end-time fate awaiting those who persevere in evil. In a context where all the stress is on God's love, the distancing of wrath from God at this point is likely to be deliberate. Translations that add "of God" do no service to Paul's argument.

Second and more generally, the passage is remarkable for the absolute continuity it displays between the action and love of Christ and the intention and love of God (the Father). As in 3:24-26, the initiative for Christ's loving act flows entirely from God and embodies the divine love and grace reaching out to a sinful and hostile world. There is no suggestion (as has sometimes been derived from that earlier passage) of Christ's costly act "changing" God's attitude from anger to love. The unity between Father and Son in the still-to-be-completed work of salvation allows Paul to conclude, "we . . . boast of God through our Lord Jesus Christ, through whom we have now received reconciliation" (v 11).

Christ's Gift of Righteousness and Life Outweighs Adam's Legacy of Sin and Death: 5:12-21

> [12]Therefore, just as through one person sin entered the world, and through sin, death, and thus death came to all, inasmuch as all sinned— [13]for up to the time of the law, sin was in the world, though sin is not accounted when there is no law. [14]But death reigned from Adam to Moses, even over those who did not sin after the pattern of the trespass of Adam, who is the type of the one who was to come.
>
> [15]But the gift is not like the transgression. For if by that one person's transgression the many died, how much more did the grace of God and the gracious gift of the one person Jesus Christ overflow for the many. [16]And the gift is not like the result of the one person's sinning. For after one sin there was the judgment that brought condemnation; but the gift, after many transgressions, brought acquittal. [17]For if, by the transgression of one person, death came to reign through that one, how much more will those who receive the abundance of grace and of the gift of justification come to reign in life

through the one person Jesus Christ. [18]In conclusion, just as through one transgression condemnation came upon all, so through one righteous act acquittal and life came to all. [19]For just as through the disobedience of one person the many were made sinners, so through the obedience of one the many will be made righteous. [20]The law entered in so that transgression might increase but, where sin increased, grace overflowed all the more, [21]so that, as sin reigned in death, grace also might reign through justification for eternal life through Jesus Christ our Lord.

This very famous passage in the letter is notable for the sustained comparison and contrast that it sets up between Christ and the ancestor of the human race, Adam. It has been the focus of intense theological interest, especially in connection with the doctrine of original sin. The origins of sin and its spread throughout the human race are not, however, the main thing Paul wants to affirm in this text. In somewhat parallel fashion to the passage immediately before (5:1-11), it continues Paul's case for hope. The difference is that, whereas in that previous passage Paul argued for hope in the face of human suffering, now it is death that is principally in view. There is hope for eternal life because Christ has initiated a legacy of righteousness leading to life that is far more powerful than the legacy of sin and death bequeathed to the human race by Adam.

We may be surprised to find Paul speaking enigmatically in v 12 of "one person" through whom sin and death passed on to all. Perhaps Paul's audience in Rome also scratched their heads and muttered, "Who is this 'one person' he's started to talk about?" Paul seems to presume that they will know he's talking about Adam, the "father" of the human race as a whole. He is presupposing their awareness of a Jewish tradition, found in other literature of the time, that saw Adam as initiating a legacy of death for all his descendants. In a way that has caused a lot of difficulty ever since, Paul saw Adam as passing on not only a legacy of death but doing so because he passed on a legacy of sin, which was the primary problem because it was Adam's sin and all subsequent human sinning that attracted the penalty of sin.

This view of death as a penalty for sin is not something that we necessarily want to share. For human beings, as for all other forms of animated existence, physical death is not a penalty for sin but the natural term of life. Paul, however, does not always distinguish between physical mortality and death in the more profound sense of eternal separation from God. At times he seems to be understanding the former as a kind of symbol of the latter, or at least as something that in the original design of God "ought not be"—and would not be had sin not come upon the human scene. In any case, while physical death remains the lot of every human person, Paul sees the saving work of Christ as directed to reclaiming the original design of God for human beings: that through the gift of righteousness they should regain the hope of eternal life.

There is, of course, a tension, felt already in the Jewish tradition, between sin and death coming as a legacy from Adam and the responsibility of individual human beings for their own sin. Paul, at least as he formulates matters in v 12, seems to want to have it both ways. His use of the Adam schema is, then, problematic in more than one sense and we may wonder why he introduced it at all. What it does do is illustrate the sense of a single human figure having significance for the race as a whole. In this sense and in this sense only, Adam and Christ are alike: both are figures of universal significance. In all other respects they differ: both in the contrasting legacies they brought (sin and death in the one case, righteousness and life in the other) and in the measure of their effects; where Adam represented simply a human being sinning on neutral terrain, so to speak, Christ represented a divine invasion of grace into an already alienated human situation with the capacity to turn it around and set it back on the path to life. In this way Paul makes his case for hope on the basis of the vastly superior instrumentality of Christ.

The other advantage of setting Christ over against Adam in this way, picturing him in effect as a "New Adam" (in 1 Cor 15:45 he calls him "last Adam"), is that it makes the salvation he brings not a kind of supernatural icing on the cake of human existence but the full flowering of that existence itself. If in Adam Paul tells the sin story of the human race and the destructive effects that follow when it prevails, in Christ as "New Adam" he tells the grace story of the human race and the fullness of humanity, both on an individual and a communal scale, that it brings. The difficulties attending the Adam schema are perhaps a small price to pay for such theological riches. God is in a sense "refounding" the human race in Christ, bringing to realization for the first time the original design for human beings, frustrated by human sin.

What gets the whole schema off to a difficult and possibly misleading start is that fact that in the opening statement (v 12) Paul states the negative ("Adam") side and then breaks off without formulating the corresponding positive statement about Christ. He does so to deal with a problem on the Adam side (death being presented as a punishment for sin in the absence of law) that a modern document would relegate to a footnote. The postponement of a corresponding statement on the Christ side had the unfortunate effect of focusing the attention of the theological tradition on the work of Adam and the transmission of sin to the neglect of the true focus of the passage, which, as we have seen, is Christ and his legacy of grace.

Eventually the passage settles down (at v 15) to wave upon wave of statements comparing and contrasting the effect of Adam and that of Christ. It is all designed to highlight the "much more" on the Christ side, from which flows the case for hope. A particularly attractive formulation comes in v 17, where we should not fail to note the way Paul stresses the "abundance" on the grace side. Where death "reigned" as a tyrant power, grace does not itself reign (contrast v 21) but causes others—those who receive the gift of justification—to reign themselves. In v 19 Paul expressly sets the "disobedience" of Adam, a clear allusion to Genesis 3, over against the "obedience" of Christ. Christ was "obedient to death" (Phil 2:8) in the sense that his faithful embodying of divine love in an alienated world brought him to the supremely costly death of the cross. The law in this situation was no help at all (v 20). In fact, as Paul will explain at length later on (chap. 7), it exacerbated the situation of sin (cf. 3:20; 4:15). But the increase (literally "abounding") of sin only served to highlight the greater increase (literally "superabounding") of divine grace. All comes to a triumphant climax with the "reign" of grace through justification for eternal life through Christ our Lord (v 21).

Human life is not lived on neutral terrain, in no-man's-land, as far as right living is concerned. Two forces tug on each and every human being: a force drawing toward sin and death, and a force (divine grace) for right relationship with God (righteousness) leading to life. The point of this passage is to argue for hope on the grounds that the weighting, the more powerful tug, is on the latter rather than the former side. There is a "solidarity in sin and death" (as expressed in the traditional doctrine of original sin) but God is creating a (more powerful) solidarity in righteousness and life ("original grace") in Christ.

One thing to note before we leave this passage is that Paul has introduced a literary device that will run through his discussion right up to the first part of chapter 8. He takes abstract theological terms such as sin, grace, righteousness, death, and life, and personifies them, making them actors in a drama of salvation not unlike characters in a medieval mystery play (Sin, Grace, Righteousness, Death, Life). He portrays Sin (*hamartia*) and Death (*thanatos*) as tyrant powers under whose enslaving grip Adam has brought the human race (cf. already 3:9). Correspondingly, believers are rescued by Christ from this enslavement to come under the sway of liberating powers similarly personified, namely Righteousness and Life.

The personification lends a somewhat mythological tone to the entire discussion. But, in the case of Sin in particular, Paul in no way wishes to suggest that human beings have become the helpless tools of powers somehow "outside" or separate from themselves. Sin for Paul represents the grip of radical selfishness, a deadly virus in human life that ruins relationships in all directions: relationships with God, with one's fellow human beings, with one's body, and with the wider environment. Without denying individual responsibility, Paul's view of sin is collective in that it sees the sins of individuals to be manifestations of this radical selfishness that holds all lives within its tyrannical grip. Paul undoubtedly believed that Adam truly existed as ancestor of the race, a belief that we, with a different understanding of the nature of the Genesis stories and in the light of scientific theory concerning human origins, can hardly endorse. But Adam is more important for Paul as a symbol of this collective solidarity in sin than as an individual with a personal history. Adam "models" humans relating selfishly and destructively in all directions—as Christ both models and facilitates human relating in a totally unselfish (Rom 15:3; Phil 2:5-8) and constructive way. We can endorse this symbolic view of Adam without commitment to a literalist understanding of the Fall narrative in Genesis 3, a story designed to state in story form a timeless truth about humanity in relation to God. No one sins entirely alone, and no one sins without in some sense adding to the collective sin burden of the race. Appealing to the figure of Adam, Paul presents a human solidarity in sin and death, but only as a foil or background to a (much more powerful) solidarity in grace and life.

Living Out the Righteous Status We Have Received through Christ: 6:1–8:13

Free from Sin to Live for God: 6:1-14

> [6:1]What then shall we say? Shall we persist in sin that grace may abound? Of course not! [2]How can we who died to sin yet live in it? [3]Or are you unaware that we who were baptized into Christ Jesus were baptized into his death? [4]We were indeed buried with him through baptism into death, so that, just as Christ was raised from the dead by the glory of the Father, we too might live in newness of life.

⁵For if we have grown into union with him through a death like his, we shall also be united with him in the resurrection. ⁶We know that our old self was crucified with him, so that our sinful body might be done away with, that we might no longer be in slavery to sin. ⁷For a dead person has been absolved from sin. ⁸If, then, we have died with Christ, we believe that we shall also live with him. ⁹We know that Christ, raised from the dead, dies no more; death no longer has power over him. ¹⁰As to his death, he died to sin once and for all; as to his life, he lives for God. ¹¹Consequently, you too must think of yourselves as [being] dead to sin and living for God in Christ Jesus.

¹²Therefore, sin must not reign over your mortal bodies so that you obey their desires. ¹³And do not present the parts of your bodies to sin as weapons for wickedness, but present yourselves to God as raised from the dead to life and the parts of your bodies to God as weapons for righteousness. ¹⁴For sin is not to have any power over you, since you are not under the law but under grace.

At this point in the letter Paul embarks on a long sequence devoted to Christian behavior: 6:1–8:13. Though the tone is at times exhortatory, this is not actually the section of the letter formally devoted to exhortation. That will come in the last major section (the "parenesis": 12:1–15:13). Paul's case for hope, however, takes an ethical "tack" for a very necessary reason. Throughout the letter up to this point and especially in the preceding passage (5:12-25) he has placed a very strong emphasis on God's grace in the face of human sin. In the eyes of the more morally zealous such stress on divine grace might be dangerous. It could lead some—especially recent converts from the immoral Gentile world—to conclude that continued wrongdoing might find similar divine indulgence. With such emphasis on grace and without the moral straitjacket of the Jewish law, how can they be sufficiently motivated to preserve and live out the righteousness they have acquired through faith and baptism? Will they not fall back into sin and so forfeit the salvation that their new life in Christ is holding out? If Paul's case for hope and his understanding of the law-free Gospel that underpins it is to stand up, he has to address this issue. He has to provide a new basis for Christian ethical life: to show both the necessity and possibility of living out the righteousness acquired through faith without a return to living under the constraints of the law. This is the essential role of the entire section down to 8:13.

Paul's major thesis, set out in 7:1–8:13, will be that this righteous life is possible because the Spirit has replaced the law as the energizing principle of Christian life. He prefaces this with two sequences (6:1-14; 6:15-23), both of which sound as though they may have originated as homilies given in the setting of Christian worship. In parallel fashion but appealing to slightly different images, these set out the "impossibility" of continuing to live under the dominion of Sin. Of course, Paul as an experienced pastor, knows that sin remains a continuing possibility, indeed an actuality in the life of believers. When he portrays continuing sinfulness as an "impossibility"—since believers are "dead to sin" or "free from Sin"—it is really the total *inappropriateness* of sin that he is trying to convey.

Paul begins by formulating the false suggestion (v 1) and then vigorously rebutting it (v 2)—a device he often uses to spur his argument forward. His sense of believers being "dead to sin" continues the personification begun in the previous passage, so that we should really write "Sin" rather than "sin." The argument rests on the imaging of Sin as the enslaving power of radical selfishness that has got all human beings in its grip. This for Paul is the root or cause of all actual sinning.

The most effective—if drastic—way to escape a tyrant or slave master is by dying. So, in the sequence that follows (vv 3-10), Paul reminds his audience that they have undergone such a "death" through their baptism. While this is Paul's most extended presentation of Christian baptism, his intention is not to give an instruction on this sacrament for its own sake. Presuming that the believers in Rome have already undergone such a catechesis, Paul appeals to the implications of baptism for ongoing Christian life. In a series of waves once again (vv 3-4; vv 5-7; vv 8-10) he reminds his audience over and over of the consequences of their baptismal union with Christ: their freedom from the grasp of Sin, on the one hand, and their living a new life of righteousness, on the other.

We meet here for the first time in the letter Paul's distinctive sense of postbaptismal Christian existence as life "in Christ." The risen Lord personally constitutes a sphere of influence or milieu of salvation into which believers are drawn through faith and baptism (Gal 3:27-28; 1 Cor 12:12-13). Henceforth they live "*in* Christ" (cf. v 11). Christ does not lose his individual personal identity but, nonetheless, as risen Lord and "life-giving Spirit" (1 Cor 15:45), he somehow "contains" within his person, in a communal sense, the messianic community on the way to salvation.

This life "in Christ," as Paul conceives it, is not simply like being plunged into Christ as into a tub or tank in a static sense. Rather, it involves a dynamic insertion into what might be called Christ's total "career": his death, burial, and (in due course) resurrection. Paul's repeated statements of this baptismal union with Christ are carefully precise about where believers ("we") currently are on the timeline of salvation. As "baptized into [Christ's] death" (v 3), we *have* died with Christ and indeed have been "buried" with him. "Our old self" (that is, our old Adamic existence in which we were enslaved to Sin) has been "con-crucified" with Christ. This has done away with "our sinful body" (v 6)—though not in the sense that our physical body was the cause of all the problem. (The NAB translation is not helpful here: "body" here [literally "body of sin"] simply expresses our previous connection with Adam under the dominion of Sin.) All this belongs to a past to which we are now "dead." But our union with Christ's risen life is incomplete; unlike him, we have not yet *bodily* emerged from the "tomb." If we have been united with him in death, "we *shall* also be united with him in the resurrection" (v 5).

While not yet fully sharing Christ's resurrection, our union with him already imposes on us both the necessity and the possibility to "live [literally "walk"] in newness of life" (v 4). That is, our present life in the world must display the qualities that belong to the new creation. We have to live in the present time as people who belong to the future, awaiting its fulfillment in hope.

Paul expresses this positive direction of present Christian life as "living for God," as Christ "lives for God" (vv 10-11). This attractive phrase expresses the reality of the relationship with God that we now have: our entire existence lovingly directed to the service of the Father. Put another way: since our life "in Christ" is interchangeable with the sense of Christ "in us," the risen Lord continues in the bodily lives of believers the "living for God" that characterized all stages of his existence (cf. Phil 2:6-11).

A little exhortation (vv 12-14) draws all this together. Death to Sin through baptismal union with Christ should mean that Sin, in the sense explained, should no longer have any "rule" in believers' life in the body, a "rule" that would make one obey its "desires." While "desire" often has a sexual overtone in Paul, he probably has a more extensive pattern of sinful behavior in mind: a selfish lust for domination and control, destructive of relationships in all directions.

Life in the body can go in that direction. The concrete actions of one's life (NAB "parts of your bodies") can be made available to Sin as "weapons" or instruments for "wickedness" (v 13a). But, equally, life in the body can be and ought to be enlisted for "righteousness." As "people brought back to life from the dead" (through baptism) believers can offer their bodies to God as "weapons" or instruments of righteousness (v 13b). As

Christ embodied "the righteousness of God" in the world offering it reconciliation and life (3:21-22; 2 Cor 5:18-21), so the bodily life of believers
can be an extension of that saving faithfulness as they live out in the world
the righteousness they have received as gift through faith. While Paul
can speak negatively of the body at times (8:13), from passages such as
this, and from his theology overall, a very positive and engaging spirituality of Christian life in the body should emerge.

Something of a throwaway line concludes the passage (v 14). Paul
assures his audience that Sin will not have power over them on the surprising grounds that they "are not under the law but under grace." Those
whose objections he is countering in this section (cf. 6:1) surely saw the
removal from the law, or at least its nonimposition upon Gentile converts,
as the problem—as something that would lead to the reign of Sin. For
Paul it is the solution! He will deal with the law's connection with sin in
due course (7:7-25). In the meantime, he simply throws out that challenge
and offers what would appear to be a parallel homily on the possibility
and necessity of living righteously, apart from the law, in the present era.

The New Obedience: 6:15-23

15What then? Shall we sin because we are not under the law but
under grace? Of course not! 16Do you not know that if you present
yourselves to someone as obedient slaves, you are slaves of the one
you obey, either of sin, which leads to death, or of obedience, which
leads to righteousness? 17But thanks be to God that, although you
were once slaves of sin, you have become obedient from the heart
to the pattern of teaching to which you were entrusted. 18Freed from
sin, you have become slaves of righteousness. 19I am speaking in
human terms because of the weakness of your nature. For just as
you presented the parts of your bodies as slaves to impurity and to
lawlessness for lawlessness, so now present them as slaves to righteousness for sanctification. 20For when you were slaves of sin, you
were free from righteousness. 21But what profit did you get then
from the things of which you are now ashamed? For the end of those
things is death. 22But now that you have been freed from sin and
have become slaves of God, the benefit that you have leads to sanctification, and its end is eternal life. 23For the wages of sin is death,
but the gift of God is eternal life in Christ Jesus our Lord.

Once again, this sounds very like the kind of homily Paul would
have given to his converts from the Gentile world. It rests upon a sus-

tained image from that world with which those converts would have been all too familiar: slavery. Slavery is not an attractive image and Paul apologizes at one point (v 19a) for using it. Elsewhere (especially in Galatians) he portrays Christian life as a life of freedom in contrast to a former slavery. Here, however, the image of slavery runs across the transition from the former life to the new.

The sentence in which Paul formulates the image (v 16) is one of the most convoluted that he ever wrote, and no translation can really make it clear without explanation. The precise image is that of a slave transferring from one master (a bad one) to another (a good one). The slave's situation is greatly improved following the transfer, but as a slave he is still under obedience to a master. Neither during the transfer nor following it is there a period when obedience is not required. Applied to the present life of believers, the image makes the point that believers have passed from one servitude and obedience to another. They have not passed out of obedience into a moral vacuum. Having left the service of Sin, they have entered a new obedience to Righteousness (personified within the image).

In terms of the image, slaves under the former (bad) master had to obey whether or not they wanted to and whether or not they approved of what they were required to do. Under the new (good) master, however, whom they love and trust, slaves may well obey willingly, "from the heart." This is what Paul seems to have in mind when he speaks of believers having "become obedient from the heart to the pattern of teaching to which you were entrusted" (v 17). The "pattern of teaching" may refer to some kind of catechetical code of moral instruction given to converts from the Gentile world. But Paul says that believers have been entrusted to the "pattern" rather than the pattern to them. It is more likely that Jesus Christ is the pattern to whom believers have been "delivered" through faith and baptism. His whole "career" offers a model of unselfish love to which believers should conform. (Paul puts forward Christ as precisely such a pattern of behavior in the Christ hymn he cites in Phil 2:5-11.)

After a word of apology for the image (v 19a), Paul pursues (vv 19b-23) the contrast between the old obedience and the new with particular focus on the very different outcomes in either situation. Whereas in their previous life, his audience presented their bodies as slaves to impurity (literally "uncleanness") and lawlessness, with ever more lawlessness the result, so now they should present their bodies as slaves to their new master, Righteousness, where "sanctification" will be the result (v 19b). Set over against "lawlessness" and "things of which you are now ashamed," sanctification refers to the transformation of life in a moral sense to which God's gift of righteousness should lead. The final outcomes in either case are "death," that is, "eternal death," on the one hand, "eternal life," on the other.

So we can set up two contrasting sequences in regard to the servitude or "slavery" involved in either case:

- slavery to Sin ("lawlessness"), leading to "uncleanness," leading to eternal death
- slavery to Righteousness, leading to "sanctification," leading to eternal life

Operative in both cases is a key axiom of the biblical tradition to the effect that righteousness leads to life—along with its negative contrary: that sin leads to death. It is interesting that while Paul can speak on the negative side of Sin having death as its "wages" (slaves received "pocket money" in the ancient world), he avoids any suggestion of payment in the new situation. Eternal life is the "gracious gift" (*charisma*) of God. Grace remains the beginning and end of all.

Taken together, both passages—originally homilies, as I like to suppose—set Christian moral life on a firmly christological base. Living in the milieu of grace should in no sense lead to a moral free-for-all. On the contrary, the intimate and living union with Christ forged by baptism sets believers free from the deep-seated selfishness that is the origin of all sin and allows the unselfish love of Christ to well up within them, making their continuing life in the body, in all its aspects, a willing service to God. There is a fine spirituality here as well as a Pauline basis for Christian ethics.

Free from the Law: 7:1-6

> ⁷:¹Are you unaware, brothers (for I am speaking to people who know the law), that the law has jurisdiction over one as long as one lives? ²Thus a married woman is bound by law to her living husband; but if her husband dies, she is released from the law in respect to her husband. ³Consequently, while her husband is alive she will be called an adulteress if she consorts with another man. But if her husband dies she is free from that law, and she is not an adulteress if she consorts with another man.
>
> ⁴In the same way, my brothers, you also were put to death to the law through the body of Christ, so that you might belong to another, to the one who was raised from the dead in order that we might bear fruit for God. ⁵For when we were in the flesh, our sinful passions,

awakened by the law, worked in our members to bear fruit for death. [6]But now we are released from the law, dead to what held us captive, so that we may serve in the newness of the spirit and not under the obsolete letter.

Romans 7 is devoted entirely to the topic of the law of Moses. Since freedom from that particular law has long since ceased to be an issue for Christians, this chapter of the letter may appear to have little relevance for us today. Paul's views on the law are also the area where his writings give greatest offense to Jews, for whom the law—or the Torah as they prefer to call it—is a treasured way of life rather than a demanding moral straitjacket. As we have remarked already, Paul is an antithetical thinker. He loves to present material in pairs of opposites, affirming the positive by setting it over against the corresponding negative. In this respect it is not quite true to say that Romans 7 is devoted to the law and nothing else, as though it were a kind of separable treatise on the topic. On the contrary, Paul's depiction of the law in this chapter is a negative foil to what he wants to affirm later about the Spirit. This means that Romans 7 cannot be considered in isolation from Romans 8:1-13, where the hope flowing from Christian life in the Spirit is the principal concern. So, on behalf of Paul, I have to ask the reader to bear with his negative portrayal of the law because what he says about the law is essential to understanding his very positive depiction of life in the Spirit. In fact, as we shall see, that positive motif itself briefly breaks through the surface in a preliminary way early in chapter 7 (v 6).

Having made clear to his audience that they are—or very much ought be—free from the clutches of Sin (6:1-23), Paul now assures them that they should consider themselves similarly free from the law (7:1-6). He says at this point that he's speaking to brothers and sisters "who know the law" (v 1). We naturally think here in first instance of believers of Jewish background. But the community in Rome may contain many believers of Gentile origin, who, perhaps at the time of their initial conversion, have taken on the practice of the Jewish law. Whether willingly or not, they may have been persuaded that unless they adhered to it, they could not be saved. Paul's law-free exposition of the Gospel will not get a sympathetic hearing in Rome unless he can persuade such Gentile believers that the law is not for them. Any person baptized in Christ, whether Jew or Gentile, is free from the claims of the law.

Once again Paul reaches for an image, one taken from marriage law (vv 2-3). Spouses are bound to each other by law as long as both remain alive. The death of one spouse leaves the surviving partner free to marry someone else. Rather unattractively, Paul slants everything toward the female partner and maintains that the law would hold her an adulteress were she to consort with another man while her husband was still alive. If he dies, however, she is free to marry another. His death has set her free from the law that bound her.

This single truth—that her freedom from law has come about through death—is the key point when the image is applied to the situation of the believer (v 4). Within the image, the woman obviously represents the believer; the first husband the law (of Moses); and the new husband whom she is free to marry, Christ, the risen Lord. Strictly speaking, the image limps, because the law does not die; it is the believer who dies, through his or her baptismal union with Christ (cf. 6:3-5). The simple point Paul is making, however, is that freedom has come about through a death and that required "death" is something believers have already undergone through having been "put to death . . . through the body of Christ."

While the reference may be to the physical body of Christ that died upon the cross, it is more likely that "body" here carries the wider sense it has for Paul of instrument of communication or belonging. "Body of Christ," then, would have its characteristic Pauline sense where it refers to believers' union with Christ as a personal corporate sphere of salvation, a union brought about through baptism and elsewhere expressed as living "in Christ" (6:11). As I noted earlier, Paul's sense of this union with Christ is dynamic. Believers are joined to him in his total "career": death, burial, and resurrection. In this way they have been put to death with him as far as the law is concerned.

This sense of union with Christ allows Paul to pursue the marital image in a more attractive direction (v 4b). The "marriage" of believers to the risen Lord can "bear fruit for God" in the way that marriages are normally "fruitful": that is, through the begetting of offspring. The "offspring" in the present case are the good works that flow from believers' union with the risen Lord. In this way Paul sees the "new obedience," the capacity for believers to "live out" the gift of righteousness they have received, as entirely the product of their ("marital") union with the risen Lord. This understanding of Christian ethical life preserves the "grace" and "gift" aspect of the new righteousness. It gathers up the human contribution into the divine creativity without denying the reality of that contribution or belittling its genuine role. Once again Paul provides here a basis for a Christian spirituality of responsible action in the world stemming from deep personal intimacy with Christ as risen Lord.

To highlight and celebrate the new ethical possibility Paul character-istically plays it off against the negative situation when "we" were "in the flesh" and under the regime of the law (v 5). "Flesh" here has its typical biblical sense where, beyond a reference to human existence as such, there are overtones of that existence as weak, prone to mortality and sin, hostile to God. Simply as human we are always in some sense "in the flesh." God's action in Christ, however, has liberated believers from being "in the flesh" in the sense of being totally determined by these negative factors. The problem with the law, as Paul will shortly explain (vv 7-25), is that it exacerbates rather than quells these impulses of the flesh. Within the lingering marital image, union with it could only make us "fruitful for death" (v 5). Now, however (v 6), free from the law, dead to that old "partner," we can render service in "newness of the spirit" in contrast to the oldness of letter (NAB: "under the obsolete letter")—an echo, it would seem, of prophetic texts such as Jeremiah 31:31-33 and Ezekiel 36:26-27 that Paul read as indicating divine intention to replace the regime of the law with that of the Spirit (cf. 2 Cor 3:5-9; Rom 2:29).

The two cryptic statements in vv 5-6, in which Paul sets the contrast between the past and present situation of believers, in fact anticipate, respectively, the extended descriptions of life "under the law" and "life in the Spirit" that are now to follow. The negative statement in v 5 out-lines the sin-provoking encounter with the law that leads to death (vv 7-13; vv 14-25), while v 6 anticipates the righteousness-producing effect of the Spirit that leads to (eternal) life (8:1-13). If we think that both state-ments need considerable unpacking, that is precisely what Paul, in his characteristic mode of negative (law) before positive (Spirit), now sets out to do.

The Fatal Encounter with the Law: 7:7-13

⁷What then can we say? That the law is sin? Of course not! Yet I did not know sin except through the law, and I did not know what it is to covet except that the law said, "You shall not covet." ⁸But sin, finding an opportunity in the commandment, produced in me every kind of covetousness. Apart from the law sin is dead. ⁹I once lived outside the law, but when the commandment came, sin became alive; ¹⁰then I died, and the commandment that was for life turned out to be death for me. ¹¹For sin, seizing an opportunity in the command-ment, deceived me and through it put me to death. ¹²So then the law is holy, and the commandment is holy and righteous and good.

> [13]Did the good, then, become death for me? Of course not! Sin, in order that it might be shown to be sin, worked death in me through the good, so that sin might become sinful beyond measure through the commandment.

Several times in our journey through Romans we have found Paul tossing off very negative statements about the law. Through the law comes "consciousness [= experience] of sin" (3:20); "the law produces wrath" (4:15); it enters in that "transgression might increase" (5:20a); its absence (rather than its presence) removes believers from the power of sin (6:14-15). The assault on the law reached a climax with the negative statement we have just been discussing, to the effect that the law awakens sinful passions "to bear fruit for death" (7:5). Granted that the law was given by God, granted also Paul's claim to be "supporting" it (3:31), Paul cannot postpone any longer an explanation of what he has been saying about the negative effects of life under the law. The explanation follows in two stages: vv 7-13 describe an encounter with the law in the form of a quasi-historical narrative told in the past tense; vv 14-25 explore the same encounter from the inside, as it were, describing in the present tense what it feels like to be held captive under the law.

Throughout, of course, Paul is speaking of the Mosaic law, reflecting a particular controversy of his own day: how far, if at all, observance of the law should be required of Christian believers, especially those coming from the Gentile (non-Jewish) world. That controversy is remote from our concerns today. Paul's treatment of the law does, however, have a more general and abiding relevance. What he says about the uselessness, or indeed the destructiveness, of addressing a particular legal code to a human situation where the root problem of sin has not been addressed, is valid for all attempts to impose a system of values or legal code where the same situation prevails. And we should keep in mind that his lively depiction of the uselessness of purely external law in this situation is all designed to pave the way for his subsequent (8:1-13) indication of the Spirit as the only effective source of freedom and moral capacity. We have, then, to see the present passage as one side, the negative side, of a diptych that will remain to be matched by the positive description of life in the Spirit.

Both the encounter with the law (vv 7-13) and the description of life under its rule (vv 14-25) are set in the first-person singular. This has naturally led to the conclusion that Paul is describing his own experience of life under the law. For a variety of reasons this traditional view has largely lost currency. It is difficult to relate the struggle he describes to the religious formation of a Jew under the law. Nor does it agree with the report he gives about his past life in Philippians 3:4-6, where he describes himself as "blameless" in regard to the righteousness required by the law. It is much more likely that Paul is employing at this point a well-known rhetorical technique of his time called "speech in character." Within this literary convention, the "I" who speaks here voices in a generalizing sense the experience of "Everyman" (or "Everywoman") confronted by the law.

With respect to the identity of the "I" in the first section (vv 7-13), however, we need to be a bit more precise. Unmistakable allusions to the Fall story in Genesis 2–3 (especially the reference to Sin's deception in v 11) lend the "I" an Adamic aura. While Adam did not live under the law of Moses, which, of course, came much later, Paul sees the fact that he received an explicit commandment from God (not to eat the fruit of a particular tree [Gen 2:17; 3:3]) as placing him in a situation similar to that of those (the Israelites) who were later to be "under the law" (cf. already 5:14) promulgated by Moses. Moreover, as the "I" tells the story, the encounter with the law comes in the shape of a commandment from the Decalogue (the Ten Commandments) given to Israel at Sinai (Exod 20:17; Deut 5:21). It seems that Paul wants his audience to hear the "I" speaking in tones evocative both of Adam *and* Israel. Israel's experience of the law is told in terms of the effect God's command had on Adam. Paul wants us to understand that the law, far from exempting Israel from the fate and failure of Adam, actually put those who came under it (the Jews) into the same Adamic plight as the rest of humankind.

Paul begins (v 7) in his characteristic way of making a false suggestion and then vigorously rebutting it. The suggestion is that the law is to be identified with sin—a conclusion that might well be drawn from the nasty things he has been saying about the law up till now. Paul sets about disentangling any intrinsic connection between the law and sin, while describing how its onset, in the shape of "the commandment," led to its becoming the tool or instrument of sin. This came about, not through any fault in the law itself—later described as "holy and righteous and good" (v 12)—but because of a latent tendency in human beings that it provoked into life. The law came in the shape of the specific commandment "You shall not covet" (v 7: literally "You shall not desire"). Paul is thinking of the prohibition Adam received not to eat of the (desirable [cf. Gen 3:6]) fruit of the tree but expressing it in terms of a truncated form of the final commandments of the Decalogue (the ones prohibiting coveting of the neighbor's wife or possessions). "The commandment" thus becomes a prohibition of "desire" as such.

"Desire" here (Greek *epithymia*) does not have primarily a sensual, let alone sexual, sense. Paul uses it to express the tendency of unredeemed human beings to chafe at the limits of the human, to yearn for and seek to grasp the power and moral autonomy that belongs to the Creator alone. Since, in Paul's view, all sinful acts proceed from this basic tendency to rebel, it is the provocation of "desire" in this sense that leads to the domination of Sin as enslaving tyrant power—literally, to Sin's "becoming alive" (v 9). Without (or before the coming of) the commandment this tendency lay dormant. The imposition of the command provoked and brought to life the very thing it sought to suppress.

Since the commandment evoked "desire" and desire led to the domination of Sin, the ultimate consequence, as Sin's "wages" (6:23), was death. The statement "I died" (v 10) cannot be literally true, since the "I" lives on. Paul is referring to the onset of (physical) mortality as a consequence of sin and as a harbinger or symbol of death in the more profound sense of eternal alienation from God. Paul is, in fact, reading the Genesis 2–3 narrative in a way very close to its original meaning: that is, as a story in mythological form attributing the limitations imposed on human life (specifically the loss of immortality) to human desire to grasp beyond the limits of the human, to desire the freedom and autonomy that belongs to the Creator alone. Paul is simply extending the range of that story to include Israel's experience under the law of Moses as well.

While Paul's evocation of the Genesis story may have that law specifically in view, there is a more general reference that we can perhaps all recognize. We are all familiar with situations where the external imposition of rules and regulations provokes the tendency to rebel and carry out the behavior they are specifically designed to suppress. Wise parents and teachers are particularly careful around adolescents in this regard. Paul seems to see the law of Moses as addressed to human beings in a quasi-adolescent stage of growth, where the tendency to regard God as an oppressive rival rather than a loving sharer of life remains unaddressed. Paul attributes to Sin the falsehood about God that the serpent used to deceive Eve in the original Fall story (v 11). Sin portrays the commandment as the unreasonable imposition of a God who wants to cut human beings down to size, rather than what it truly is: a divine protection against a tendency in human nature ("desire") that would lead to death rather than life.

The law for all its intrinsic goodness (v 12), as hijacked by Sin had—and continues to have (vv 14-25)—this totally counterproductive effect in human life. It cannot eradicate but in fact exacerbates the very rebelliousness in human nature that it seeks to suppress. What then was/is its role? Why was it given by God? To lead to death? Paul again (v 13) rejects this understandable but false inference, and goes on to hint at a role for the law in the scheme of salvation. Within a wider divine purpose God gave the law (to Israel) precisely to make sin reveal its true colors, to unmask the latent rebellion in the human heart in all its destructiveness, to bring it to the surface, so to speak, where it could be recognized ("in order that it might be shown to be sin" [v 13c]) and dealt with (in the Christ event) once and for all (8:3-4).

In short, God used the law much as a counselor, suspecting that a client's life is being controlled by a hidden, subconscious anger of which the person is unaware, might seek to provoke that anger and bring it to the surface, where it can be recognized for what it is and dealt with effectively. Such a tactic will doubtless involve some ugly scenes. But bringing the anger to consciousness is an essential part of the healing process. In similar fashion, Paul can somehow see God allowing an "increase" of sin (5:20a) on the way to a wider triumph of grace (5:20b).

If this is indeed his thinking, it is easy to see how this view of the divine action could lead to the charge—which Paul dismisses as false and blasphemous—that he teaches "we should do evil that good may come of it" (3:8). What we have to keep in mind is that his understanding of the law's negative working arises, not out of intrinsic hostility to the law, but out of extreme pessimism in regard to human nature aside from and unredeemed by the grace of Christ. We can only rightly assess Paul's negative statements about the law in the light of his contrary sense of the surpassing force of God's grace ("Where sin abounded, grace 'hyperabounded'" [see 5:20]).

Life under the Law: The Fatal Tension: 7:14-25

14We know that the law is spiritual; but I am carnal, sold into slavery to sin. 15What I do, I do not understand. For I do not do what I want, but I do what I hate. 16Now if I do what I do not want, I concur that the law is good. 17So now it is no longer I who do it, but sin that dwells in me. 18For I know that good does not dwell in me, that is, in my flesh. The willing is ready at hand, but doing the good is not. 19For I do not do the good I want, but I do the evil I do not want. 20Now if [I] do what I do not want, it is no longer I who do it, but sin that dwells in me. 21So, then, I discover the principle that when I want to do right, evil is at hand. 22For I take delight in the law of God, in my inner self, ²³but I see in my members another principle at war with the law of my mind, taking me captive to the law of sin that dwells in my members. ²⁴Miserable one that I am! Who will deliver me from this mortal body? ²⁵Thanks be to God through Jesus Christ our Lord. Therefore, I myself, with my mind, serve the law of God but, with my flesh, the law of sin.

This is one of the best known passages of Paul's letter to Rome. It had great appeal for central figures in the Christian tradition such as Augustine and Luther, and the influence of their interpretations has been great. Almost every reader or hearer of the passage can identify with the struggle so vividly described here: the tension arising out of knowing what one ought to do, while sensing the lack of capacity to carry it into effect. It is the age-old human dilemma memorably summed up by the Roman poet Ovid: "I see the better and approve it; But I follow the worse" (*Metamorphoses* 7.19-21).

It is unlikely, however, that Paul intends the struggle so powerfully described here to be something characteristic of present Christian life. Some aspects of the passage, it is true, do convey that impression. Most notable is the fact that the account is told in the present tense. The use of the present, however, can be explained as part of the literary form being used (the "speech in character" mode), lending vividness and drama to arrest the reader. Above all, there is one key factor of present Christian experience notably absent: the experience of the Spirit. The absence of the Spirit from the passage contrasts sharply with its presence in the one to follow (8:1-13). The contrast, as I have already noted, is central to Paul's running argument as a whole in that, where 7:14-25 presents the moral struggle without the aid of the Spirit, 8:1-13 presents the same struggle where the Spirit, rather than Sin, is the dominant force. To refer both passages indiscriminately to present Christian life blunts the contrast and renders ineffectual Paul's dramatic portrayal (in 8:3-4) of God's intervention in Christ to release the Spirit.

Looking at the passage in more detail, we see that it is very repetitive. After a thematic introduction in v 14, it describes the same basic moral dilemma over and over in a series of three waves (vv 15-17; vv 18-20; vv 21-23). All then builds up to a climax, culminating in the desperate cry voiced in v 24: "Miserable one that I am! Who will deliver me from this mortal body? [literally "from the body of this death"]." We seem to break through to a "Christian" perspective with the indication of Christ in the first half of v 25a, though curiously the latter half of that verse, in rather an anticlimax, states the dilemma once more. (The "premature" aspect of v 25a has led many interpreters, rightly in my view, to regard it as an addition that a pious early copyist could not refrain from making.)

In each of the waves the "I" voices fundamental agreement with the law and a genuine willingness to obey its commands. Continually frustrating this purpose, as indicated at the close of each wave, is the presence of Sin as enslaving, indwelling power. Sin compels the "I" to obey its commands rather than those of the law. The overall rhetorical effect of the three waves is a powerful depiction of the futility, in ethical terms, of simply imposing the law (of Moses) or any external legal obligation on persons where the fundamental internal problem remains unresolved. The problem with the law, good and holy though it be in itself (v 12), is that it does not get "inside" human beings and deal with the real issue: the radical selfishness and desire for absolute autonomy that Paul, in biblical speak, dubs "flesh." Far from countering this, as Paul has just shown in 7:7-13, the imposition of law simply stirs it up, leading to the dominance of Sin in all manner of wrongdoing. What is required is a solution that will involve entry right into the sinful human situation to address the problem at its noxious core. This is what Paul will describe in the corresponding, positive wing of the diptych in the passage to follow (8:1-13). The present description of the plight of the "I" confronted by the law is simply the preparatory foil to the divine rescue operation and its lasting effects to be described there.

It is best, then, to read the passage, not as a description of present Christian life, but as a "looking back" from the vantage point of the present life of believers to the moral dilemma, the ethical "impossibility," of the situation apart from the grace of Christ and the assistance of the Spirit. Alongside the time contrast ("before" and "after"), and perhaps more fundamental, is a contrast between human beings struggling to fulfill moral demand unaided by God and human beings turning to God and ultimately helped by God through the assistance of the Spirit. Seeing the contrast in this "timeless" way restores its relevance for believers here and now. There will doubtless be many times when we will resonate the struggle voiced by the "I" here and find it descriptive of where we feel ourselves to be. Rather than concluding, however, that this is the "normal" situation for believers—a conclusion that leads to an overly pessimistic spirituality—we should perhaps ask whether we are not at this point looking too much to ourselves and our own resources rather than to God and the assistance of grace. In this way the passage can become for us, as it has been for many, a genuine aid in the discernment of spirits.

Life in the Spirit: Freedom to Live as God Wants: 8:1-13

8:1Hence, now there is no condemnation for those who are in Christ Jesus. 2For the law of the spirit of life in Christ Jesus has freed you from the law of sin and death. 3For what the law, weakened by the flesh, was powerless to do, this God has done: by sending his own Son in the likeness of sinful flesh and for the sake of sin, he condemned sin in the flesh, 4so that the righteous decree of the law might be fulfilled in us, who live not according to the flesh but according to the spirit. 5For those who live according to the flesh are concerned with the things of the flesh, but those who live according to the spirit with the things of the spirit. 6The concern of the flesh is death, but the concern of the spirit is life and peace. 7For the concern of the flesh is hostility toward God; it does not submit to the law of God, nor can it; 8and those who are in the flesh cannot please God. 9But you are not in the flesh; on the contrary, you are in the spirit, if only the Spirit of God dwells in you. Whoever does not have the Spirit of Christ does not belong to him. 10But if Christ is in you, although the body is dead because of sin, the spirit is alive because of righteousness. 11If the Spirit of the one who raised Jesus from the dead dwells in you, the one who raised Christ from the dead will give life to your mortal bodies also, through his Spirit that dwells in you. 12Consequently, brothers, we are not debtors to the flesh, to live according to the flesh. 13For if you live according to the flesh, you will die, but if by the spirit you put to death the deeds of the body, you will live.

We now enter into what is everyone's favorite chapter of Paul's letter to Rome. As I have been arguing, however, this opening section of Romans 8 really concludes the long sequence in ethical tone that Paul began at 6:1. If there is to be hope for eternal life—the chief topic of Romans 5–8 as a whole—that hope rests on believers having the capacity to live out the gift of righteousness they have received through faith. Within that wider section, the sequence making up 6:1–8:13 asserts both the necessity and possibility of living righteously. Paul has dramatically showed the "impossibility" of so living under the law. Now, in strong contrast, he shows the possibility of so living created by God through the gift of the Spirit. This leads back to a more explicit assertion of hope (in the face the sufferings of the present time) that is the subject of the remainder of Romans 8 (vv 14-39).

We immediately detect the palpable change of tone and air of relief with the opening, "There is no condemnation for those in Christ Jesus" (v 1). Within the apocalyptic framework of Paul's thought the "condemnation" would be that which would fall on sinful human beings at the last judgment. For those "in Christ Jesus," that is, those who through faith and baptism have been incorporated into the risen Lord as corporate "sphere of salvation," the prospect of such condemnation falls away. Paul will in fact evoke the last judgment scene at the close of the chapter (vv 31-39) and, as a final assurance of hope, dramatically defy any spiritual power to attempt to bring accusation against the faithful or separate them from the love of God made visible in Christ Jesus (v 39). "No condemnation!" then, is a kind of thematic slogan for chapter 8 as a whole.

In the sentences that follow Paul gives the grounds for this confident assertion, tracing it all back to the action of God, sending the Son to defeat Sin and release the life-giving, empowering Spirit (vv 2-4). The reason that there is "no condemnation" for those in Christ Jesus is that the regime of Sin leading to death (literally "the law of sin and death") has been replaced by the "law of the Spirit [leading to] life" (v 2). (Paul addresses the assurance in the second person singular ["has freed *you*"] to make it a response to the anguished cry of the "I" in the passage preceding.) It is important to note that the "law" (of sin and death) on the negative side does not refer to the Mosaic law as such, but to the regime, the enslaving control that Sin set up in human beings as described so vividly in the preceding chapter; the law of Moses may have exacerbated this regime of Sin but, as Paul has been at pains to stress, it is not identical to it. Correspondingly, on the positive side, Paul speaks of the Spirit metaphorically as "law" in implicit allusion, I believe, to the prophetic texts Jeremiah 31:33 and Ezekiel 36:26-27. Taken together, these state the divine intent in the messianic age to place the Spirit "within" the hearts of the people as a new "law" communicating the capacity to obey. Paul sees what God has done in Christ to be the fulfillment of that divine pledge.

In a long, theologically rich sentence (vv 3-4) Paul traces the liberation right back to God's action in Christ. Faced with the impotence of the law to remedy the situation (the dominance of Sin in human life), God sent the Son to deal with the problem at its radical core. Where the law remained external and for that reason impotent, the Son came "in the likeness of sinful flesh." As in 2 Corinthians 5:21 ("[God] made him to be sin who did not know sin"), Paul does not hesitate to stress the radicality of the Son's entrance into the sinful human situation. There, personally bearing (on the cross; cf. 3:24-25) the cost of that entry, Christ dealt with sin (literally "and for the sake of sin"), so that the "condemnation" that would have fallen on human beings (cf. v 1) falls instead on the real villain: "Sin in the flesh."

The upshot is that the righteousness that the law required but could not bring about ("the righteous decree of the law") "might be fulfilled in us," who live now (literally "walk now"), not according to the flesh, but according to the Spirit (v 4). Notice that Paul does not say, "that we might fulfill," but "might be fulfilled in us." The passive indicates the action of God and the sense that the new righteousness ("the walking"), while it is "ours" because expressed in our bodily life (cf. 6:12-13), is fundamentally the achievement of God's Spirit within us. This significant detail wards off any suggestion of a return to a "works-righteousness" ethic, safeguarding the new era of grace. The ecumenical implications of the passive are significant. It respects the Protestant insistence upon grace, while preserving the Catholic sense that the "works" of believers, while entirely the product of the Spirit, really do contribute to God's future for humanity and the world.

Before we leave this theologically rich sentence, we should note its trinitarian shape. God (the Father) sends the Son to release in human affairs the empowering Spirit. While Paul, of course, does not have the developed doctrine of the Trinity that emerged centuries later in the church, his thought does fall into a trinitarian pattern. The present text enables us to claim that the ethical life of believers, our capacity to live out the gift of righteousness, is entirely the product of the triune God within us. It is the "extension," the embodiment in human living, of that "righteousness of God" that, in the person of the Son, represents the faithfulness of the Creator to the world. As Paul says in the bold text to which I have often appealed: "[God] made him to be sin who did not know sin, so that we [who *were* sinners] might become the righteousness of God in him" (2 Cor 5:21).

The following sentences (vv 5-11) spell out this new capacity. Typically, Paul casts a glance back for a while (vv 5-8) at the negative. He contrasts living "according to the flesh" with the new capacity to live "according to the spirit." There remains a degree of tension within present Christian life. It is still *possible* to live according to the flesh, with the "hostility" to God and destiny to (eternal) death that that way of life will bring. It is still possible to live in that way, but crucially and in stark contrast to the preceding situation under the law (7:14-25), it is not *necessary* to do so. What had been a fatal tension, tearing the "I" apart (7:24), has become a constructive tension, impelling believers constantly to grow within the new freedom created in them by the Spirit, in life and "peace" with God. Here we must keep in mind Paul's biblical sense of "flesh" (*sarx*) as referring not simply to human sensuality ("sins of the flesh") but to a whole pattern of life that is self-absorbed, selfish, and hostile to God. Clearly contrary to the flesh in this sense is the impact of the Spirit, because the Spirit is really nothing other than the ongoing impact of the utterly unselfish love of Christ. When believers live "according to the spirit" they are allowing Christ to live out in their bodily life the divine love that led him to give himself up for us all (Rom 5:6-10; cf. Gal 2:20).

Paul expresses this in a variety of ways in vv 9-11. Notice how interchangeably he speaks now of the Spirit, now of Christ as risen Lord. Where in the former situation under the law, it had been Sin that called the shots as indwelling power (7:17, 20, 23) with a destiny to death, now believers have Christ or the Spirit of God dwelling within them—not calling the shots but setting them free to respond to the promptings of grace. While the body may be mortal (NAB "dead" does not catch the sense) because of sin (that is, destined to physical death as a legacy of sin), the Spirit means "life because of righteousness" (v 10). (The NAB translates Paul's noun "life" as an adjective, "alive," seriously weakening the sense.) This last phrase recalls the axiom stemming from the biblical tradition to the effect that righteousness leads to life. Despite the prospect of physical death, believers are destined to eternal life because of the righteousness that the Spirit is working within them. The One (God the Father) who was faithful to the sole truly righteous one (Jesus), vindicating his obedience (5:19) by raising him from the dead, will also be faithful in raising those who have received as gift (3:21-26) and live out in the Spirit the righteousness required for eternal life. The wheel has come full circle; the long "ethical journey" that began in 6:1 is reaching its end. Paul has underpinned his case for hope by showing the necessity and the possibility for believers to live out the righteousness required for life.

As a pastor, as in 6:12-13, Paul cannot resist a word of warning and exhortation (vv 12-13). Believers owe no "debts" to the flesh. To go that way—which is still possible!—is to turn back to death. If, on the contrary, through the power of the Spirit dwelling within, believers "put to death the deeds of the body," that will be their path to life. I have always wondered why Paul wrote here "deeds of the body" rather than "deeds of the flesh"—as if physical existence (body) were in itself a negative factor. Perhaps it was a slip on his part, because elsewhere the body is a neutral factor that can be placed either at the service of sin or of righteousness (6:11-12). Christian spirituality has a long history of taking it out on the body, as though that were the problem, rather than curbing selfishness in all its manifestations. Paul's remark here may have played its part in fostering that ultra-ascetical tendency. Whatever he may have meant, the overall direction is clear: allowing the utter unselfishness of Christ to well up within sets believers on the path to life. That hope now emerges once more (v 14; cf. 5:1-11) as explicit theme.

The Hope of Salvation in the Sufferings of the Present Time: 8:14-39

Children and Heirs of God: 8:14-17

> ¹⁴For those who are led by the Spirit of God are children of God. ¹⁵For you did not receive a spirit of slavery to fall back into fear, but you received a spirit of adoption, through which we cry, "*Abba*, Father!" ¹⁶The Spirit itself bears witness with our spirit that we are children of God, ¹⁷and if children, then heirs, heirs of God and joint heirs with Christ, if only we suffer with him so that we may also be glorified with him.

Central to hope is the experience of the Spirit. Paul had briefly alluded to the gift of the Spirit as communicator of a sense of God's love early in this section of the letter: "and hope does not disappoint, because the love of God has been poured out into our hearts through the holy Spirit that has been given to us" (5:5). In an attractive little passage he now invites his audience to explore the experience of closeness to God at greater depth.

To this end Paul invokes the motif of believers as "children [sons and daughters] of God." In using this language of believers he is not coining a new metaphor for Christian life but applying to them a standard designation that had a long prehistory with respect to Israel in the Old Testament (see Exod 4:22-23; Deut 14:1; Isa 1:2-4; Hos 1:10; 11:1; Wis 18:13; etc.). The privilege of being God's "sons" (or "daughters") flows from Israel's election as a people enjoying a status of closeness to God shared by no other nation. It marks Israel off from other nations and is more or less interchangeable with the sense of being "the people of God." In the centuries leading up to the rise of Christianity the description acquired a distinctly eschatological tone and came to refer to the righteous Israel of the messianic age destined to "inherit" (as God's "sons and daughters") all the blessings of salvation. It is in this eschatological sense that Paul introduces the language of "sonship" (more inclusively, "divine filiation") here. Those who "are led by the Spirit" are those who, through the power of the indwelling Spirit (8:9-10), preserve and live out the righteousness communicated to them through Christ. As such, they are here and now God's "children" destined to "inherit" eternal life (v 14).

But in the present "overlap of the ages" situation, where suffering and the prospect of death remain, believers need assurance that they enjoy this status. It is the Spirit that supplies the guarantee. Characteristically ruling out the negative before asserting the positive, Paul insists that the Spirit we have received is not one of slavery communicating fear. On the contrary, we have received (a) Spirit that makes us cry out, "*Abba*, Father" (vv 15), clear testimony that we enjoy here and now a filial status (v 16). In the NAB translation Paul refers to this "Spirit" as one of "adoption." While in secular Greek "adoption" is the standard translation of the term *huiothesia*, "adoption" was not a social practice in the Jewish milieu that is the more immediate context of the argument. Rather than adoption, much more likely present is the sense of Israel's filial status in relation to God. This suggests that "Spirit of sonship" is a more accurate (albeit less gender-inclusive) translation here. Paul is applying to believers—of both Jewish and Gentile background—the privilege of divine filiation that hitherto belonged to Israel alone.

Paul is making that application on a wholly christological basis quite lacking in the Jewish tradition. In pointing to the "*Abba*" cry he seems to be alluding to a phenomenon so well-known and characteristic of Christian life as to require no further explanation. It is generally agreed that in this address to God—one of the rare instances where the New Testament records the original Aramaic—we have a reminiscence of Jesus' own distinctive address to the Father. The New Testament tradition preserved the Aramaic (in Mark 14:36 and Gal 4:6 as well as here) because, as the informal address within the family to the male parent ("Dad"), it had a nuance of familiarity and intimacy that the Greek *patēr* ("Father") could not quite convey. In the two Pauline instances the "*Abba*" cry is placed on the lips of believers. But the impulse to address God in this intimate way comes from the Spirit, which as we have seen is for Paul hardly separable from the impact of the risen Lord, welling up within believers because of their existence "in Christ." In the persons of the baptized the Son continues to express, through the Spirit, the intimacy of his relationship with the Father. Once again (cf. 8:3-4) we encounter Paul's sense of believers being drawn here and now into the communion of love that is the Trinity.

From the status of being God's "children" it is a short step to that of being "heirs" (v 17)—terminology that, in turn, evokes the promise to Abraham spelled out in chapter 4. In calling believers "heirs of God" Paul is designating them as the intended beneficiaries of that promise of "inheriting the world" that God gave to Abraham "and to his descendants" (4:13, 16), an "inheritance" that catches up all the blessings of salvation.

But, as Paul made more explicitly clear in Galatians (3:16, 26), believers are descendants (literally "seed") of Abraham, and hence heirs, in virtue of their baptismal union with Christ. They are "heirs of God" as "coheirs of Christ," and as such they have to follow the pattern of his entrance into the inheritance: they have to share his sufferings in order to share also his glory (v 17b). The motif of suffering reenters the argument as the context in which hope must be exercised in the present time.

Creation Groans for Freedom: 8:18-22

[18]I consider that the sufferings of this present time are as nothing compared with the glory to be revealed for us. [19]For creation awaits with eager expectation the revelation of the children of God; [20]for creation was made subject to futility, not of its own accord but because of the one who subjected it, in hope [21]that creation itself would be set free from slavery to corruption and share in the glorious freedom of the children of God. [22]We know that all creation is groaning in labor pains even until now.

Contemporary ecological concern has led to renewed focus on this passage. Does Paul's indication of the "groaning" of creation make him an environmental theologian? Concern for the environment was hardly a burning issue in his day and he would doubtless be amazed by the attention recently devoted to this passage in that cause. Nonetheless, by reading the passage in a way that goes beyond his thought but remains faithful to its overall direction I think it is possible to find some meaning here for our contemporary concern.

As already noted, at this point in the letter the motif of suffering has returned as the context in which believers must exercise hope (v 17b). The opening sentence (v 18) picks this up as a major statement of theme: "the sufferings of this present time are as nothing compared with the glory to be revealed for us." The NAB translation in the last phrase ("for us") could suggest something external to human beings. Paul's expression is rather ambiguous and is certainly open to the sense of a glory to be revealed not only to us but in us as well. In this latter sense "glory" (*doxa*) is Pauline shorthand for humanity arrived at its final state in the scheme of salvation. It connotes the "likeness to God" ("image") intended by the Creator from the beginning (Gen 1:26-27) and already displayed in the risen Lord as "last Adam" (1 Cor 15:45).

The development of the thesis that glory to be revealed outweighs present suffering follows in four clearly defined stages. Quaint though it sounds, the first three all feature a "groaning" motif. They can be distinguished according to the subject of the groaning: in vv 19-22 "creation" groans; in vv 23-25 "we" groan; in vv 26-27 there is reference to groans uttered by the Spirit. A fourth and final stage in vv 28-30 rounds off the sequence setting the whole process within the inexorable unfolding of God's eternal plan.

Crucial to the understanding of the first passage (vv 19-22) is recognizing that Paul is drawing here on a biblical and postbiblical Jewish tradition that saw the nonhuman created world as intimately bound up with the fate of human beings. "Creation" (*ktisis*) progresses when the human race progresses; it suffers a fall when human beings fall. Both share, in brief, a "common fate." The tradition goes back ultimately to the biblical creation story where human beings, bearing the image of God, are given dominion over the earth (Gen 1:26-28; also Ps 8:5-8). A more immediate background to the present text is Genesis 3:17-19 where the earth is cursed because of Adam's sin and, as a result, yields its fruits only grudgingly, requiring human toil and sweat. Correspondingly, on the same "common fate" principle but in a reverse direction, there is the sense that a coming salvation of human beings (usually Israel) will redound positively upon creation as well. Creation will both share in and testify to the final restoration, encompassing a renewal that is cosmic in scale (Isa 11:6-9; 43:19-21; 55:12-13; Ezek 34:25-31; Hos 2:18; Zech 8:12).

In line with this tradition, to bolster his argument for hope, Paul points to an "eager expectation" on the part of creation (v 19) that is manifested as a "groaning in labor pains even until now" (v 22). The intervening sentences (vv 19-21) explain why creation has this expectation. The reason is that, when human beings, in the person of Adam, fell from favor with God, creation also took a "fall": the earth was cursed because of Adam's sin and transformed from being a garden to being an object of hard, unremitting labor. It was subjected in this way to "futility" in the sense of being rendered unable to fulfill its true purpose in right relationship and harmony with human life. In a mythic way that may appeal to the imagination rather than hard logic, Paul personifies "creation" and pictures it as submitting to this subjection "unwillingly," not of its own accord but because of "the one who subjected it" (v 20). It is not immediately clear who he means by this "subduer." Most interpreters prefer to see a reference to God, since God is the one who curses the earth in Genesis 3:17-19. Grammatically, however, it is equally possible to see here an indication of the one whose fault actually brought about the divine subjection: namely, Adam. A reference to Adam, standing in for the entire human race, fits well with the wider context of Romans and opens up significant interpretive possibilities, as I hope to show.

Whatever the precise reference of the "subduer," Paul's point, spelled out in the following verse (v 21) is that, when creation was subjected against its will in this way, it continued to cherish a hope that, if and when the human situation of disobedience was reversed, it too, on the "common fate" principle, might also benefit. More literally, it too might be set free from its bondage to decay and have some share in the "freedom" (from mortality) regained by human beings as a consequence of their restored right relationship with God (righteousness). It is the sense that this hope is about to be realized that accounts for creation's current "eager expectation," expressed in the "groaning [together] in labor pains even until now" (v 22).

As I have said, the passage is highly mythological, appealing to the imagination rather than strict theological reasoning. Nonetheless, I do believe that it has some contribution to make to an ecological theology. It evokes the creation texts of Genesis 1–3 that set human relationship with the nonhuman remainder of creation as a key element in human relationship with God, texts where human beings are given responsibility for the rest of creation and where, as a consequence, the "fates" of both are inevitably intertwined—for good and for ill. In v 20 we seem to have an allusion to the sin story of the human race told in Adam—a story that redounds ruinously upon the nonhuman world as well. It is not fanciful to see exploitative and destructive human pollution of the environment as part of that sin story, along with other evils. But also present (v 21), and closer to what Paul wants directly to affirm in the passage, is the hint of the grace story told in the "last Adam," Christ. It is the "much more" powerful nature of that grace story over the sin story that forms the true basis for hope (5:15-17, 20). If creation has suffered and continues to suffer from the ravages of human sin, there is hope that it may also benefit when and where the grace story prevails—because a new "subduer," Christ, has faithfully and successfully played the role that Adam muffed. If and when human beings align themselves with that grace story, and take a contemplative rather than an exploitative attitude toward the wider nonhuman world that is the essential context for human life, then hope on a cosmic as well as a human scale may prevail.

The Groaning of "Ourselves" and the Spirit: 8:23-30

> [23]and not only that, but we ourselves, who have the firstfruits of the Spirit, we also groan within ourselves as we wait for adoption, the redemption of our bodies. [24]For in hope we were saved. Now hope that sees for itself is not hope. For who hopes for what one sees? [25]But if we hope for what we do not see, we wait with endurance.
>
> [26]In the same way, the Spirit too comes to the aid of our weakness; for we do not know how to pray as we ought, but the Spirit itself intercedes with inexpressible groanings. [27]And the one who searches hearts knows what is the intention of the Spirit, because it intercedes for the holy ones according to God's will.
>
> [28]We know that all things work for good for those who love God, who are called according to his purpose. [29]For those he foreknew he also predestined to be conformed to the image of his Son, so that he might be the firstborn among many brothers. [30]And those he predestined he also called; and those he called he also justified; and those he justified he also glorified.

Creation groans with respect to what it discerns happening to human beings (vv 19-22). Now Paul indicates, as a further cause for hope, a "groaning" of human beings with respect to themselves. What prompts this groaning is the presence of the Spirit, which Paul refers to as "firstfruits." This phrase stems from the harvest ritual of Israel. Israelites took the firstfruits of the harvest to the temple as an acknowledgment that the entire yield of the land is God's gift and in anticipation of the full harvest to follow. Here the direction of the divine-human transaction is reversed in the sense that God gives the Spirit to believers as a pledge or "down payment" (2 Cor 1:22; 5:5) of the full "harvest" (eternal life) to follow. As firstfruits in this sense the Spirit stirs up within believers a kind of "holy restlessness" with their present situation. Displayed in their groaning, this restlessness becomes a further index of hope.

The groaning involves a waiting for "adoption" (so the NAB translation, v 23b). As believers are already God's "children" (vv 15-16), "adoption" is hardly an appropriate translation for something they still await. The Greek word *huiothesia*, which Paul goes on to define here as "the redemption of our bodies," is best taken to refer to the outward disclosure of our status as God's sons and daughters that will occur when our bodily existence is conformed to that of the risen Lord—just as resurrection disclosed his status as divine Son (1:4). Currently, our bodily existence is "enslaved" to suffering and decay (cf. v 21). Salvation will not consist in redemption *from* the body, as though attachment to the body were the whole problem. What we await is the liberation of our bodily existence from all that imprisons it here and now, so that it may share the glorious state of the risen Lord (vv 29-30).

Paul regularly refers salvation to the future. Here (v 24a) he speaks of it in the past tense ("we were saved") but immediately adds (though NAB reverses the order) "in hope." The past tense conveys the sense that the hope we have is so secure that through hope we really are already in a situation of salvation.

"But," the audience might well respond, "where is the evidence that salvation is all but present in this way?" Paul forestalls such a response with a little "excursus" on hope (vv 24b-25). Hope is operative, not when what is hoped for is in view, but precisely when it is not. When we wait for a bus that we can just make out in the distance, we confidently expect it to arrive in due course. It is when it is nowhere in view that we have to hope that it will come at all. So, for believers hope is not an optimism based on encouraging aspects of the present situation. The final situation is not in sight, nor is it easily imagined. Christian hope, like that of Abraham (4:18-21), involves an unseeing patience (literally "endurance"). It places its trust entirely in the faithfulness of God to make good the final installment of salvation already pledged through the gift of the Spirit.

Paul is, then, remarkably certain about the final outcome in connection with salvation while completely "agnostic" about the details. But he does concede that such "visionless" hoping is difficult for human beings. Hence his indication of an assistance rendered to believers in this situation of weakness by the Spirit (vv 26-27). As the NAB translation has it, when we do not know how to pray as we ought, the Spirit intercedes for us with sighs (literally "groans") too deep for words. The translation suggests that the "problem" is *how* to pray—a rendering that has brought comfort to many down the ages. The actual Greek wording suggests rather that the problem is not how to pray but *what* to pray for. Because we cannot "see" the end God has in store for us, we do not know how to pray for it properly. But, says Paul (v 27), the Spirit does know the will of God in this respect, and comes to our aid with groans so deep within us as to be below the level of consciousness.

This is an elusive passage. It may well be one place where we touch upon a mystical awareness in Paul's thought. Mystical experience, which of course is not so rare as often supposed, involves an inward awareness of and communication with the divine that transcends everyday human consciousness, thought, and speech. It bears on a union where the barrier between time and eternity slips away, where there seems to be some glimpse or foretaste even of what the perfected union with God might contain. The journey inward is a journey to the future or, to put it in more strictly Pauline terms, a journey to that hidden glory that the Spirit is nurturing here and now, and of which the risen existence when it comes will be the full revelation.

A final comment (v 28) draws together the various phases of the argument for hope that have been stated. Paul appeals to an axiom of the Jewish tradition expressing the sense that, under God's providence for the elect (literally "those who love God"), "all things" conspire together to bring about "good." "All things" could refer to and include the nonhuman creation (vv 19-22). It more likely refers to the sufferings of the present time that form the context for hope. Other things being equal, these would normally be considered "evil." But for those whose lives are enveloped by God's love even these things work for "good"— that is, the full realization of God's purpose in their regard.

The ultimate basis for hope is the inclusion of believers in the inexorable unfolding of this divine plan, already well under way. Paul spells out the particular divine acts of the process in a step-like sequence of clauses (vv 29-30) reminiscent of a similar pattern in 5:3-4. All five verbs ("foreknew"; "predestined"; "called"; "justified"; "glorified") belong to the language used in the Jewish tradition to describe God's favors to Israel. Paul is now applying this terminology and the privileges it evokes to the renewed people of God made up of Jewish and Gentile believers. The awkward expression "foreknew" is biblical speak for election (e.g., Jer 1:5). "Predestined" here should not be given the notorious and troubling meaning that it has often carried in the Christian tradition: that is, in reference to an eternal decree of God freely assigning some human beings to salvation, some to eternal damnation, prior to any act or deserts on their part. The "predestination" in view here is entirely positive and not at odds with human freedom. The reference is simply to the design God has had in mind for human beings from creation onward. It is no more "predestining" of human existence in a controlling sense than the plans and hopes good parents might cherish for their children who must grow up and assume adult freedom and independence.

Just once Paul breaks into the sequence to spell out this "predestination" in christological terms (v 29b). The language is carefully chosen and must be given full weight. "Conformed to the image of his Son" does not mean simply becoming like Christ in a general kind of way. The sense is more that of participating in the image (of God) that Son *is*. As Son of God and "last Adam" (1 Cor 15:45) the risen Lord displays and recaptures for humanity the dignity of being in the divine image and likeness according to the original design of God (Gen 1:26-27; cf. 2 Cor 3:18; 4:4, 6). His resurrection has revealed him to be God's Son in a unique sense (Rom 1:3-4). When other human beings (believers) attain the same risen state, then he will be "firstborn" within a large family. He will be surrounded in his risen glory with a large company of "brothers and sisters" who share his filial status in relation to God.

That is God's ultimate design for human beings, and it is well under way. "Calling" refers to the summons of the Gospel that is already, through the ministry of apostles such as Paul, spreading across the world. "Justified" refers, as we have seen at length, to the divine declaration of being right with God that follows the hearing of the Gospel with faith.

All these divine acts belong to the past for believers. Yet Paul places the final divine act—"glorification"—in the past as well. Elsewhere (e.g., 5:2) "glory" refers to the final destiny of the justified, their arrival at the state of "likeness to God" intended by the Creator from the start (reversing the "lack" indicated in Rom 3:23). Paul may be using the past tense ("he also glorified") as an expression of certainty: what God has set in motion will so certainly be brought to term that we can speak of the entire process as already achieved. It may be, however, that he writes "glorified" on the basis of a hidden glorification already under way. In vv 19 and 21 he spoke of a glory that is to be "revealed" (vv 19-21). Moreover, a splendid sentence in 2 Corinthians 3:18 describes glorification as a process already under way:

> All of us, gazing with unveiled face on the glory of the Lord, are being transformed into the same image from glory to glory, as from the Lord who is the Spirit.

These parallels suggest that Paul thinks of a glorification already in process. Like the status of being "children of God," it is still a hidden thing, consisting above all in the new relationship with God flowing from justification. The glory will be publicly revealed when believers, through resurrection, share in the glory of their risen Lord.

The resurrection of Christ is not, then, an "exception" or an "irruption" into the normal course of human affairs. It is the paradigm and pledge of humanity reaching its proper goal when the sin story of human life told in Adam is overtaken and consumed by the grace story told in Christ. What the present sequence (8:18-30) contributes in particular is inclusion of the nonhuman created world within the scope of that divine design.

The Coming Victory of God's Love: 8:31-39

[31]What then shall we say to this? If God is for us, who can be against us? [32]He who did not spare his own Son but handed him over for us all, how will he not also give us everything else along with him? [33]Who will bring a charge against God's chosen ones? It is God who acquits us. [34]Who will condemn? It is Christ [Jesus] who died, rather, was raised, who also is at the right hand of God, who indeed intercedes for us. [35]What will separate us from the love of Christ? Will anguish, or distress, or persecution, or famine, or nakedness, or peril, or the sword? [36]As it is written:

"For your sake we are being slain all the day;
     we are looked upon as sheep to be slaughtered."

[37]No, in all these things we conquer overwhelmingly through him who loved us. [38]For I am convinced that neither death, nor life, nor angels, nor principalities, nor present things, nor future things, nor powers, [39]nor height, nor depth, nor any other creature will be able to separate us from the love of God in Christ Jesus our Lord.

If Romans 8 is everyone's favorite chapter of the letter, this concluding passage must rival the hymn to love in 1 Corinthians 13 as the all-time favorite text of Paul. The apostle, at his rhetorical best, rounds off his argument for hope with a defiant challenge to any power or circumstance that might seem to separate believers from the triumphant power of God's love.

We recall that chapter 8 began with the bold assertion: "there is no condemnation for those who are in Christ Jesus" (v 1). The excluded condemnation would be a verdict that, within the apocalyptic framework of Paul's thought, might be given at the coming great judgment. In the present passage Paul evokes imaginatively that great assize, puts believers on trial, so to speak, and dares any power to challenge the verdict of acquittal already given by God (justification). Above all, the continuance of suffering in present Christian life cannot be interpreted as a sign of divine disfavor or an indication that believers are in for a rough time at the judgment. Nothing and no one can separate believers from the love of God already so powerfully displayed in the Christ event.

The phrase, "If God is for us" (v 31b) could almost stand as the theme of the entire letter. Catching up the earlier theme of God's "righteousness" (1:17; 3:21-26), Paul thinks of God the Creator as eternally faithful, eternally "on the side of" human beings, even when they are unfaithful, indeed "hostile" to God. Returning to the "logic" of the passage with which the entire section began (5:1-11), he evokes the sense of what God has already done at extraordinary cost in order to assert absolute confidence that God will see the process through to completion (v 32). The phrase "[God] did not spare his own Son" consciously echoes the language of Genesis 22:16 (LXX). The angel who stays Abraham's hand from slaying his son Isaac praises him for being prepared "not to spare" his beloved Son. The suggestion is that what God did not in the end require of Abraham, God did require of God's self: the "giving up" to death of his own Son, Jesus. Nowhere else does Paul express the divine "vulnerability" displayed in the Christ event so poignantly as here. The extremity of divine love already shown in that event, when in fact we were "sinners" and "hostile" (5:6-10), guarantees that God will continue to be "for us" to the end—that God will in fact give us "all things" with him, namely the full residue of salvation. Evoking more explicitly the final court scene, Paul defies any being to get up and bring a charge against the elect, when God has already delivered (in justification) a verdict of acquittal and when the defense attorney is none other than the risen Lord himself (vv 33-34).

The perspective then moves from the heavenly court to the suffering situation that is the lot of the believers' lives in the present (vv 35-39). As earlier (in 5:1-11), the abiding issue is how that suffering is to be interpreted. Are the sufferings listed at length in v 35 to be regarded as punishments that God allows angelic powers to inflict on believers? Are they signs, therefore, of a distance, indeed a separation, from divine love? The key phrase comes at the beginning of the quotation of Psalm 44[45]:22 in v 36: "*For your sake* we are being slain all the day." The sufferings come about not because believers are separated from God but precisely because of their union with Christ, whose suffering they are sharing in order in due course to share his glorification (v 17b).

The closing sentences (vv 37-39) evoke the scene of a victorious general's triumphant procession through the streets of Rome. In all these trials we conquer overwhelmingly (literally "we are hyper-conquerors") through the One (Christ) who has loved us (cf. Gal 2:20). Neither the trials themselves ("death, . . . life"), nor the powers that may be thought to stand behind them (angels, principalities, etc.) can be thought as coming between us and the love of God made manifest in Christ Jesus, our Lord. The list reflects the worldview of Paul's day, where various spiritual or demonic powers were seen as manipulating social and political forces prevailing in the present world, including, above all, the empire of Rome. While victory is not yet complete, these are the forces that will be compelled in the end to walk captive in the triumphant procession of Christ (cf. Col 2:15). We may not share the worldview behind Paul's list but we can surely add items that we see as threatening us here and now. In this way we can bring our own lives under the scope of his overwhelming confidence that all trials that believers endure are encompassed within the faithful love of God and built into the eventual realization of the divine saving purpose on our behalf.

3. The *Hope* of Salvation: B (Israel): 9:1–11:36

We arrive now at the third major section of Paul's letter to Rome. The three chapters are held together by a single theme: God's faithfulness to that great bulk of Israel (the Jewish people) that has not come to faith in the crucified Messiah. For many years this section of the letter was regarded as a treatise on this topic, more or less separable from the rest of the letter. This judgment no longer stands. It is now recognized that Paul's attitude to his ancestral people was a matter that he had to clear up if he was to receive a welcome from the believing community in Rome, many of whose members remained closely attached to the Jewish heritage. If his treatment of Israel in Galatians had become more widely known, he had a lot of work to do to counter the impression that he had written off Israel. This "hard work" is very evident in the strong assertions of anguish over the fate of his people with which each of the three chapters begins (9:1-3; 10:1; 11:1-2).

Beyond the issue that Israel constituted for Paul in light of his impending visit to Rome, this section of the letter has acquired new relevance today as the relationship of Christianity to Judaism has moved from the periphery to the center of theological interest. What Paul will ultimately say about God's abiding faithfulness to Israel at the close of this section (11:11-32) is actually the New Testament's most positive statement concerning the future of the Jewish people. With tragic results, it has historically been neglected while texts from the gospels, especially those of Matthew and John, have largely shaped Christian attitudes to Jews and Judaism. In this respect and in a post-Holocaust context, no area of Romans is of greater importance for Christian reflection and study than these three chapters.

That said, this is far from the easiest area of Romans to work through. For the most part Paul deploys long scriptural arguments, many of which will seem arbitrary and unconvincing to readers today. Apart from the very significant theological issue in regard to Judaism, there is not all that much to arrest contemporary theological interest and, on the contrary, several areas where Paul's reasoning and conclusions are distinctly problematic and off-putting. Above all, we have to interpret the section as a whole and look particularly to the terminus arrived at (in the latter half of chap. 11). It is seriously misleading to rest at stations along the way and derive from them theologies of independent and lasting validity. In reality they are simply intermediate stages in a long rhetorical journey.

Paul in fact addresses the issue of God's faithfulness to Israel in a roundabout way, coming at it from several angles. An opening strong avowal of concern for his people, Israel, sets up the issue (9:1-5), which is then addressed in three stages: (1) a long scriptural survey (9:6-29) establishes God's sovereign freedom to bring into existence an end-time people solely on the basis of grace without regard to ethnic identity or human deserts; (2) from the aspect of human response, Paul explores (9:30–10:21) the reasons for Israel's failure to respond to the Gospel; (3) since the divine calling and gifts are irrevocable, Gentile believers must not discount Israel's eventual salvation within the unfathomable wisdom of God (11:1-36).

Paul's Personal Anguish and the Privileges of Israel: 9:1-5

> [9:1]I speak the truth in Christ, I do not lie; my conscience joins with the holy Spirit in bearing me witness [2]that I have great sorrow and constant anguish in my heart. [3]For I could wish that I myself were accursed and separated from Christ for the sake of my brothers, my kin according to the flesh. [4]They are Israelites; theirs the adoption, the glory, the covenants, the giving of the law, the worship, and the promises; [5]theirs the patriarchs, and from them, according to the flesh, is the Messiah. God who is over all be blessed forever. Amen.

Paul gives no formal introduction to the question of Israel but simply states his anguish as though answering a charge already put to him (9:1-3). As if to sharpen the intensity still further, he catalogues the privileges of Israel in what would appear to be a traditional list (vv 4-5). Most of the items ("election"; "calling"; "divine filiation" [NAB: "adoption"]; "glory"; "promise[s]") are familiar to us from the preceding sections of the letter. In a way that greatly raises the stakes, they have in fact been attributed to the renewed People of God made up of Jewish and Gentile believers. The culminating privilege is that from Israel stems the Messiah according to his natural descent (literally "according to the flesh"). This is the deep irony coloring the entire section. Precisely with respect to this supreme privilege Israel has failed: she has not recognized the Messiah who came from her according to his natural origins, whereas a great number of Gentiles have believed in him and so have come into the privileges and the inheritance that once seemed focused upon Israel alone. (Whether the final sentence of v 5 refers to Christ as "God" or whether it should be regarded as an independent expression of praise ["doxology"] is disputed. The latter seems more likely.)

The Elective Pattern of God's Working: 9:6-29

The Elective Pattern Shown in Scripture: 9:6-21

⁶But it is not that the word of God has failed. For not all who are of Israel are Israel, ⁷nor are they all children of Abraham because they are his descendants; but "It is through Isaac that descendants shall bear your name." ⁸This means that it is not the children of the flesh who are the children of God, but the children of the promise are counted as descendants. ⁹For this is the wording of the promise, "About this time I shall return and Sarah will have a son." ¹⁰And not only that, but also when Rebecca had conceived children by one husband, our father Isaac—¹¹before they had yet been born or had done anything, good or bad, in order that God's elective plan might continue, ¹²not by works but by his call—she was told, "The older shall serve the younger." ¹³As it is written:

"I loved Jacob
but hated Esau."

¹⁴What then are we to say? Is there injustice on the part of God? Of course not! ¹⁵For he says to Moses:

"I will show mercy to whom I will,
I will take pity on whom I will."

¹⁶So it depends not upon a person's will or exertion, but upon God, who shows mercy. ¹⁷For the scripture says to Pharaoh, "This is why I have raised you up, to show my power through you that my name may be proclaimed throughout the earth." ¹⁸Consequently, he has mercy upon whom he wills, and he hardens whom he wills.

¹⁹You will say to me then, "Why [then] does he still find fault? For who can oppose his will?" ²⁰But who indeed are you, a human being, to talk back to God? Will what is made say to its maker, "Why have you created me so?" ²¹Or does not the potter have a right over the clay, to make out of the same lump one vessel for a noble purpose and another for an ignoble one?

The thought that Israel's failure to believe the Gospel has jeopardized her hold on the privileges is not just a problem in regard to Israel. It puts in question the validity of God's own word. Has God been unfaithful to the scriptural promises in which these privileges were guaranteed? It is with this question, an intensely *theo*logical question in the strict sense, that Paul begins (v 6a) his long discussion. He will first reassess the scriptural evidence down the patriarchal generations to show that God's way of dealing with Israel has always proceeded with sovereign freedom independent of human deserts (vv 6b-21). He then (vv 22-29) shows that the present composition of the renewed people of God—a Gentile majority and a Jewish minority—is in accordance with a pattern announced long beforehand in the prophetic Scriptures of Israel.

As we have seen when considering Paul's earlier survey of Scripture in chapter 4, the whole destiny of Israel is tied to God's promise to Abraham "and to his descendants" (literally "seed"). The issue Paul now raises, beginning with this first patriarchal generation (v 6b), concerns just who constitutes this "seed of Abraham." If all physical descendants of Abraham, simply by dint of natural ("fleshly") descent, are "seed" in this sense, then the promise would have to apply equally to Ishmael and the nation he fathered (the Arabs). But Scripture makes it quite clear that the promise is only to run in the line of Isaac, who, in the circumstances of his birth (cf. Gen 18:1-15), is clearly marked out as a child of promise. Here is a first indication that the promise will follow an elective pattern, dependent not on physical descent or race but only on God's free choice.

Paul pursues the scriptural evidence into the next patriarchal generation (vv 10-13). The promise did not run equally in Isaac's twin sons, Esau and Jacob. On the contrary, even before they were born and therefore before either had the chance to earn or forfeit the grace in any way, God once again showed a clear preference for the younger (Jacob) over the elder (Esau). (The reference in v 13 to God's "hating" Esau, quoting Malachi 1:2-3, reflects a Semitic way of expressing a choice of one party over another; God does not "hate" Esau in our sense.)

Paul allows for a moment (vv 14-18) that this reading of the divine action could imply that God is unjust: his treatment of persons is so unequal. The objection is barely stated before it is swept aside in a further scriptural justification of God's freedom. Two key figures of the Exodus generation, Moses and Pharaoh, were dealt with in contrasting ways. To Moses (Exod 33:19) God proclaims his right to show mercy to whomever he will. Pharaoh, on the other hand, had his heart "hardened" (Exod 4:21; 7:3; 9:12; 14:4, 8, 17); in seeking to hold Israel back he became willy-nilly an instrument for the display of God's power and glory throughout the world (Exod 9:16).

Paul may be paving the way here for his later claim that Israel's current resistance to the Gospel represents a similar "hardening" that will serve its wider proclamation (11:7, 25). But his main point is to insist that God, in order to be truly God, must retain, as the scriptural record shows, sovereign freedom. The operation of the promise cannot be held in check or conditioned by human response or human deserts, whether good or bad.

All very well but such action on God's part ("hardening" Pharaoh's heart) appears to eliminate human freedom and responsibility to such an extent as to render God's finding fault with human beings quite unreasonable. Does it not make us simply puppets in the divine hand? To counter this final form of the objection Paul introduces (vv 19-21) a stock biblical image designed to exclude the very thought of human protest against the sovereign freedom of the Creator. The image derives from the potter's freedom to shape clay into vessels of any kind he chooses: some for noble, others for humble usage. Like the clay, the human creature has no right to complain, "Why have you created me so?" (v 20c).

This is hardly Paul at his best. Human beings are not lifeless clay. Paul adduces the image to illustrate and evoke a basic biblical dogma—one emerging above all from the book of Job—that, in the end, the Creator, as Creator, has the right to proceed in a way totally unaccountable to human beings. This is the sole point being made. It is seriously misguided to press out of the homely image more wide-ranging theological conclusions (as in the long-standing debate over "predestination"). We have here neither Paul's first nor his last word on the nature and working of God.

The Present ("Mixed") Composition of the Believing Community Foretold in Scripture: 9:22-29

²²What if God, wishing to show his wrath and make known his power, has endured with much patience the vessels of wrath made for destruction? ²³This was to make known the riches of his glory to the vessels of mercy, which he has prepared previously for glory, ²⁴namely, us whom he has called, not only from the Jews but also from the Gentiles.

²⁵As indeed he says in Hosea:
"Those who were not my people I will call 'my people,'
    and her who was not beloved I will call 'beloved.'
²⁶And in the very place where it was said to them, 'You are not
    my people,'
    there they shall be called children of the living God."

> [27]And Isaiah cries out concerning Israel, "Though the number of the Israelites were like the sand of the sea, only a remnant will be saved; [28]for decisively and quickly will the Lord execute sentence upon the earth." [29]And as Isaiah predicted:
>
> "Unless the Lord of hosts had left us descendants,
>   we would have become like Sodom
>   and have been made like Gomorrah."

Up to this point Paul has shown (at least to his own satisfaction!) that God gave sufficient indication in Scripture that the divine way of proceeding would be unconditioned by human response or deserts. It is now time to show how the present situation in regard to the end-time people of God—Gentiles included; Jews, save for a "remnant," excluded—has equally been foretold and foreshadowed in Scripture. If such is the case, then God's word cannot be said to have "failed" (v 6a).

It must be said at the outset that Paul could have gone about this demonstration far more clearly than he does. It begins (v 22) with a question, "What if," that in the end receives only an implied answer, "Well, isn't that God's right!" Ironically, God has placed Israel in the role of Pharaoh, whereas the believing community, now so largely made up of Gentiles, has become the beneficiary of the mercy God appeared to promise to Israel through Moses. God has let Israel become, in its unbelief, "vessels of wrath made for destruction" (better: "ripe for destruction"; Paul does not say "consigned to destruction"). God has endured this situation with much "patience" for two reasons: to display wrath (what happens to human beings when they fall out of living relationship with their Creator; cf. 1:18-31) and make known his power—presumably in the sense that, as was the case with Pharaoh, the current "hardening" of Israel serves the wider proclamation of the Gospel.

On the positive side, the "vessels of mercy" (v 23) must refer to the present community of believers, "called" into being out of the Gentiles and a small Jewish remnant. That such was to be the constitution (at least for the time being) of God's end-time people Paul again (vv 25-29) finds verified in Scripture. Hosea (2:23; 1:10) foretold the calling of a "not-my-people" (that is, the Gentiles) to be God's people, and Isaiah (10:22; 1:19) foresaw the whittling down of Israel's numbers to a small, faithful remnant (NAB's "decisively and quickly" in v 28 is better translated "completing and curtailing"). These prophetic texts show that the present paradoxical constitution of the community, along with the current unbelief of Israel, is fully in accord with what God had foreseen and declared long before.

Taken in isolation, this passage has given rise to what is possibly the most terrifying doctrine ever to be drawn from Scripture: "double predestination" (Augustine; Calvin). This theory holds that God has from all eternity elected some for salvation and some for damnation, a fate determined quite prior to and independent of human response and behavior. To this it must be said that Paul does not have the fate of individual human beings in view here. He is taking a collective view of Jewish and Gentile response to God, thinking of communities rather than individuals. Moreover, what he says here is only one element of a total theological solution he is working toward in an attempt to square the apparent failure of Israel with the biblical doctrine of election and the faithfulness of God. It is all simply one block in whole theological edifice that he is building in these chapters. To isolate this passage from its wider context and derive a complete theology from it is totally—and dangerously—misleading. It is not a Pauline "station" on which to linger long.

Israel's Failure to Respond to the Gospel: 9:30–10:21

Israel's "Stumble" before the Righteousness of God: 9:30–10:4

[30]What then shall we say? That Gentiles, who did not pursue righteousness, have achieved it, that is, righteousness that comes from faith; [31]but that Israel, who pursued the law of righteousness, did not attain to that law? [32]Why not? Because they did it not by faith, but as if it could be done by works. They stumbled over the stone that causes stumbling, [33]as it is written:
   "Behold, I am laying a stone in Zion
      that will make people stumble
      and a rock that will make them fall,
      and whoever believes in him shall not be put to shame."
[10:1]Brothers, my heart's desire and prayer to God on their behalf is for salvation. [2]I testify with regard to them that they have zeal for God, but it is not discerning. [3]For, in their unawareness of the righteousness that comes from God and their attempt to establish their own [righteousness], they did not submit to the righteousness of God. [4]For Christ is the end of the law for the justification of everyone who has faith.

Paul has considered the present paradoxical makeup of the renewed people of God (Jews largely excluded; Gentile believers included) from the aspect of God's characteristic way of acting and declared intention (in Scripture). He now takes up the same issue from the point of view of human response: why has Israel failed in regard to the Gospel, where so many Gentiles have responded in faith?

Behind Paul's opening summing up of the situation is one of his favorite images: that of athletes running in a race (cf. also Phil 3:12-16; 1 Cor 9:24-27). If the prize is "righteousness," that is, the right relationship with God on which salvation depends, the Gentiles were originally not entered into the race at all. The righteous status they received through faith came as a pure gift of God's grace bestowed on them as "ungodly" sinners (Rom 4:5). Israel, on the other hand, was really entered in the race to gain righteousness, "pursuing" that goal through practice of the Jewish law ("as if it could be done by works" [v 32]). Pursuing righteousness in this way, Israel misread the purpose of the law. It was never intended to communicate the righteousness required for salvation. As earlier sections of the letter have made clear (3:20; 5:20; 7:13), the law's role was the negative one of preparing the way for faith by convicting Israel of sin. What ultimately caused Israel to "stumble" in the race was the "stone" that God laid down on the track in fulfillment of an announcement made in Isaiah 22:16 (combined with 8:14). The "stone of stumbling" and the "rock of falling" is the crucified Messiah Jesus (cf. the parallel reference in 1 Cor 1:23). Israel "stumbled" at this Messiah because accepting such a Messiah meant accepting that, along with the sinful remainder of the world, this was the kind of redemption that Israel needed. It meant accepting the verdict (elaborated in Paul's prophetic accusation in Rom 2:1–3:20) that Israel would never be a righteous nation on the basis of the law but would have to throw itself in faith upon the mercy of a gracious God.

Paul once again (10:1; cf. 9:1-3) expresses his deep personal concern for Israel and acknowledges the "zeal for God" that lies behind her pursuit of righteousness through the law (v 2a). But it is a zeal that is "not discerning" (literally "not according to knowledge") in the sense that it fails to recognize what God has done in Christ and clings to its own perception of what is required (v 2b). It does not "submit" to the "righteousness of God" that is being graciously offered through the Gospel's proclamation of the crucified Messiah (3:21-26) but misguidedly, in the face of this divine offer, seeks to establish a righteousness of "their own" (v 3). It fails to see that Christ is "the end of the law" (v 4). His appearance and his redemptive work have simply brought to a close its (negative) role in the scheme of salvation, leaving the way open for justification to be available for "everyone" (that is, Gentiles as well as Jews) simply on the basis of faith.

Once again, as contemporary readers, we have to realize how offensive Paul's strictures against the law of Moses and those who adhere to it as a means of righteousness sound in Jewish ears. Jews can point to so many texts in Scripture that clearly and unequivocally present the Torah as a path of righteousness (e.g., Lev 18:1-5, a text cited but then relegated to inferior status by Paul: Gal 3:12; Rom 10:5). Paul's use of Scripture is indeed highly selective. Even if we read the final statement (v 4) in the sense preferred by many scholars, "Christ is the goal [*telos*] of the law," the situation is not greatly ameliorated, since the Torah is then simply subsumed into the role of pointing to Christ. What we have to recognize is that Paul is reading everything "back" from his faith in the crucified Messiah, which has totally turned upside down his former worldview as a devout Jew. He is perhaps projecting onto his fellow Jews something of the preconversion attitude that led him for some time to be so zealous a persecutor of the followings of the crucified Christ. We can be sympathetic to what he is doing here. But we need not— perhaps should not—follow him all the way. While nothing masks human need for the *gift* of salvation so successfully as misguided religious zeal, that failure is not tied to any particular religion nor is the faith that overcomes it tied to any particular religious system. Both attitudes are possible within theistic systems and both are equally possible within Judaism and Christianity.

The "Nearness" of Righteousness by Faith: 10:5-13

[5]Moses writes about the righteousness that comes from [the] law, "The one who does these things will live by them." [6]But the righteousness that comes from faith says, "Do not say in your heart, 'Who will go up into heaven?' (that is, to bring Christ down) [7]or 'Who will go down into the abyss?' (that is, to bring Christ up from the dead)." [8]But what does it say?
"The word is near you,
in your mouth and in your heart"
(that is, the word of faith that we preach), [9]for, if you confess with your mouth that Jesus is Lord and believe in your heart that God raised him from the dead, you will be saved. [10]For one believes with the heart and so is justified, and one confesses with the mouth and so is saved. [11]For the scripture says, "No one who believes in him will be put to shame." [12]For there is no distinction between Jew and Greek; the same Lord is Lord of all, enriching all who call upon him. [13]For "everyone who calls on the name of the Lord will be saved."

Paul has shown, at least to his own satisfaction, the fundamental cause of Israel's failure in respect to the Gospel. In the remainder of chapter 10 (vv 5-21) we are shown why responsibility for that failure rests entirely with Israel and not with God. As a first stage of this demonstration (vv 5-13) Paul sets up in rather quaint terms a contrast between the difficulty of the quest for righteousness through the law and the ease or "nearness" of finding it through faith. He first quotes (v 5) the words of Leviticus 18:5 to show how righteousness through the law, if it is to result in the gaining of (eternal) life, requires an arduous and complete fulfillment. He then (vv 6-8) takes a text from Deuteronomy (30:12-14), which in its original context proclaims that the "commandment" is neither "hard" nor "far off." In a very arbitrary way Paul strips this text of its clear reference to performance of the Mosaic law and makes it speak instead of the "ease" and "nearness" of finding righteousness by faith (with "going down into the abyss" being substituted for "crossing the sea" in the original Deuteronomic text).

The essential point Paul takes from Deuteronomy is the ease of what God requires. In contrast to the effort involved in keeping the law, righteousness by faith simply requires submission to and an acknowledgment of what God has already done—in the Christ event. To ask (v 6), "'Who will go up into heaven?' (. . . to bring Christ down)" is tantamount to denying that God has already sent (from heaven) the only Son (8:3-4). To ask, "'Who will go down into the abyss?' (. . . to bring Christ up from the dead)" is to deny that he died for our sins and was raised by God "for our justification" (4:25). Righteousness by faith excludes such questions ("Do not say . . ." [v 6]). It simply insists that people have access to Christ and the justification he brings in the preached word of faith. In the words of an earlier text of Deuteronomy (9:4) the required word is "near" in the sense of being simply a matter of making with one's lips the basic Christian confession that Jesus is "Lord" (v 8: cf. Phil 2:11) and believing in one's heart that God has raised him from the dead. Such confession proceeding from faith brings right relationship with God and sets the believer on the way to salvation (vv 9-11).

Earlier in the letter (3:29-30) Paul had established a common basis for justification by appealing to the oneness of God. In similar fashion he now (vv 12-13) rules out separate paths to salvation on the grounds that all simply call upon one and the same "Lord," Jesus Christ. Just as there was "no distinction" in regard to sin (3:23), so there is "no distinction" in regard to access to the "riches" made available in Christ to all who call upon his name. This common access to the riches of Christ (2 Cor

8:9) fulfills the prophecy of Joel (2:32 [LXX 3:5]) that *"everyone* who calls on the name of the Lord will be saved" (v 13).

Israel Has Heard but Not Responded to the Gospel: 10:14-21

[14]But how can they call on him in whom they have not believed? And how can they believe in him of whom they have not heard? And how can they hear without someone to preach? [15]And how can people preach unless they are sent? As it is written, "How beautiful are the feet of those who bring [the] good news!" [16]But not everyone has heeded the good news; for Isaiah says, "Lord, who has believed what was heard from us?" [17]Thus faith comes from what is heard, and what is heard comes through the word of Christ. [18]But I ask, did they not hear? Certainly they did; for

"Their voice has gone forth to all the earth,
and their words to the ends of the world."

[19]But I ask, did not Israel understand? First Moses says:

"I will make you jealous of those who are not a nation;
with a senseless nation I will make you angry."

[20]Then Isaiah speaks boldly and says:

"I was found [by] those who were not seeking me;
I revealed myself to those who were not asking for me."

[21]But regarding Israel he says, "All day long I stretched out my hands to a disobedient and contentious people."

Paul now explores more deeply the failure of Israel to join those who call on the name of the Lord (v 13). Where has the breakdown occurred and which of the parties involved—God, the preachers of the Gospel, or Israel—is responsible for it? Paul outlines the total process leading up to the "calling" that brings salvation (vv 14-15). God has set the process in motion. Preachers have gone out and preached the Gospel throughout the world. No deficiency can be pointed to on that side of the communication. The breakdown has occurred in the area of response. Here too Israel cannot be excused on the basis of not having "heard" the message, since, as the psalmist foretold, it has already gone to the "ends of the world" (v 18; Ps 19:4). Nor, continues Paul, can Israel claim not to have "understood" (v 19a). What precisely it was that Paul thinks Israel did not understand is difficult to discern. The answer must lie in the further scriptural texts (Deut 32:21; Isa 65:1; Isa 65:2) that Paul adduces to rule out this final excuse (vv 19b-21). But his appeal to Scripture here is more than ordinarily elusive. He seems to be proposing that, had Israel really "listened" to these texts, she would have understood that God always intended to include the Gentiles in the community of salvation and made her "jealous" on that account—namely, that she would have to share the riches of salvation with the nations of the world. Had she really "heard" and "understood" those divine declarations, she would not now be so resistant to the summons of an inclusive Gospel.

Once again, we can only observe Paul's attempting to find a way through the bitter issue of Israel's unbelief with a use of Scripture that remains to us arbitrary and forced. He is attempting to show believers that if one reads Scripture in light of what God has actually done, that is, in the light of Christ, then one can "hear" it speaking the language of righteousness by faith, hear it explaining that the present situation of Gentile faith and Jewish unbelief was not an unforeseen catastrophe where the whole divine scheme of salvation went awry. On the contrary, it was something foreseen in Scripture, hence planned by God all along, and so capable of being taken up into a wider scheme that is yet to fully unfold.

Biblical thinkers, Paul included, did not keep rigidly separate divine action and human freedom to the extent that we do today. Acts of human freedom, whether positive or negative, can also be the expressions of the will and influence of God. Things that have happened can be seen as the will of God simply because they have taken place, and also because they are able to be incorporated into a wider divine plan. Reasoning along these lines allows Paul to wrestle with Israel's unbelief in the puzzling way he does at this point in Romans.

Israel's Final Inclusion in the Community of Salvation: 11:1-36

God Has Not Rejected Israel—The "Remnant": 11:1-10

> [11:1]I ask, then, has God rejected his people? Of course not! For I too am an Israelite, a descendant of Abraham, of the tribe of Benjamin. [2]God has not rejected his people whom he foreknew. Do you not know what the scripture says about Elijah, how he pleads with God against Israel? [3]"Lord, they have killed your prophets, they have torn down your altars, and I alone am left, and they are seeking my life." [4]But what is God's response to him? "I have left for myself seven thousand men who have not knelt to Baal." [5]So also at the present time there is a remnant, chosen by grace. [6]But if by grace, it is no longer because of works; otherwise grace would no longer be grace. [7]What then? What Israel was seeking it did not attain, but the elect attained it; the rest were hardened, [8]as it is written:

"God gave them a spirit of deep sleep,
  eyes that should not see
  and ears that should not hear,
down to this very day."
⁹And David says:
  "Let their table become a snare and a trap,
    a stumbling block and a retribution for them;
    ¹⁰let their eyes grow dim so that they may not see,
    and keep their backs bent forever."

By the close of chapter 10 Paul has vindicated the faithfulness of God and the efficacy of the Gospel. But he appears to have done so at the price of cutting out from salvation that large bulk of Israel that has not responded to the message of the Gospel in faith. Has the divine attempt to be inclusive of the Gentiles proved "exclusive" with respect to Israel? What is the remaining status of this people? They appear to have rejected God's offer of salvation in Christ. Does this mean that God has rejected them?

Paul's response to this shocking suggestion falls into three parts. For a while (vv 1-6) he defends God's faithfulness to Israel by pointing out that not all Jews have in fact at the present time been rejected. He himself, "an Israelite, a descendant of Abraham, of the tribe of Benjamin" (v 1b), is a living refutation of this. So too is the Jewish-Christian block within the community of believers. This is no mere relic of Israel absorbed with loss of identity into the greater number. It represents a faithful "remnant," chosen by God's grace and foreshadowed in the divine response to the prophet Elijah (vv 2b-4; cf. 1 Kgs 19:10, 14), with whom Paul identifies himself. God pointed out to Elijah that, contrary to his lament, he was not the one faithful Israelite left standing: there were seven thousand others who had not "knelt to Baal." So Paul can point to the still sizeable number of believers of Jewish origin (v 5). This "remnant," chosen by grace, not on the basis of "works" (keeping the law), is (v 6) a first indication that God has not rejected the chosen people (literally "his people whom he foreknew" [v 2a]).

But where does this leave the remainder of Israel? They, says Paul, were "hardened" (v 7c). They have been placed—Paul clearly means through the action of God—in the same situation as Pharaoh, whose heart, as Paul has already indicated (9:17-18), God hardened in the interests of a wider divine purpose (the proclaiming of God's name throughout the earth). Soon (vv 11-24) Paul will point to a similar divine purpose in regard to Israel's present hardening. For a while, though, he lingers (vv 8-10) on the hardening process. He cites texts from the Law (Pentateuch; Deut 29:4 [LXX 29:3]) and the Prophets (Psalms; Ps 69:22-23 [LXX 68:23-24]) at some length to provide reliable scriptural testimony to the fact that this hardening was something foreseen and announced beforehand by God. The quotations are unattractively negative and raise again the whole issue of how such divine action can coexist with human freedom and responsibility. Paul has already adverted to this issue (9:19)—and dealt with it dismissively (9:20-21). He does not open it up again. While not surrendering human responsibility, in line with a biblical frame of thought that did not distinguish between God's permissive and God's intended will, he simply attributes everything that happens—including human failure and sin—as somehow willed by God and held within a wider divine purpose. He is now ready to lift his audience's eyes to that wider salvific vision.

Israel's "Stumble" Salvific for the Gentiles: 11:11-24

¹¹Hence I ask, did they stumble so as to fall? Of course not! But through their transgression salvation has come to the Gentiles, so as to make them jealous. ¹²Now if their transgression is enrichment for the world, and if their diminished number is enrichment for the Gentiles, how much more their full number.

¹³Now I am speaking to you Gentiles. Inasmuch then as I am the apostle to the Gentiles, I glory in my ministry ¹⁴in order to make my race jealous and thus save some of them. ¹⁵For if their rejection is the reconciliation of the world, what will their acceptance be but life from the dead? ¹⁶If the firstfruits are holy, so is the whole batch of dough; and if the root is holy, so are the branches.

¹⁷But if some of the branches were broken off, and you, a wild olive shoot, were grafted in their place and have come to share in the rich root of the olive tree, ¹⁸do not boast against the branches. If you do boast, consider that you do not support the root; the root supports you. ¹⁹Indeed you will say, "Branches were broken off so that I might be grafted in." ²⁰That is so. They were broken off because of unbelief, but you are there because of faith. So do not become haughty, but stand in awe. ²¹For if God did not spare the natural branches, [perhaps] he will not spare you either. ²²See, then, the kindness and severity of God: severity toward those who fell, but God's kindness to you, provided you remain in his kindness; otherwise you too will be cut off. ²³And they also, if they do not remain in unbelief, will be grafted in, for God is able to graft them in again. ²⁴For if you were cut from what is by nature a wild olive tree, and grafted, contrary to nature,

into a cultivated one, how much more will they who belong to it by nature be grafted back into their own olive tree.

With this passage Paul's consideration of Israel's current situation finally turns in a positive direction. In the wider design of God, Israel's present "hardening" is neither meaningless nor final. In the opening question, "did they stumble so as to fall?" (v 11a), the "race" image surfaces once more. Israel may have "stumbled" in the race (and been "overtaken" by the Gentiles) but this does not mean that she has "fallen" so badly as to be out of it altogether (v 11b). On the contrary (v 11c) Israel's "stumble" with respect to the Gospel has provided both the scope and the impetus for the same Gospel to bring "enrichment" (cf. 10:12) on a wider scale. And that is not the end of the matter. Paul hopes that the sight of the Gentiles being enriched by the Gospel will provoke a "jealousy" in Israel that will ultimate lead to her own salvation.

It is by no means clear how Paul saw this "jealousy" motif operating in practice—and whether in fact it "worked"! At any rate, he says that he "magnifies" his ministry to the Gentiles (v 13; NAB's "I glory in my ministry" misses the point entirely). That is, he makes its success well known. The aim, presumably, is that, struck by the gifts of love, joy, and peace prevailing in the Gentile communities through the gift of the Spirit, Jews who have previously resisted the Gospel may be led to think again. Thus Paul can claim that his apostolate to the Gentiles is also to some degree inclusive of his own people as well (v 14).

Using the "much more" (a fortiori) argument familiar from chapter 5, Paul strikes a note of great confidence in respect to this hope for Israel. If (the negative case) their (temporary) "rejection" has meant "the reconciliation of the world," that is, the saving extension of the Gospel to the Gentiles, how much more effective will (the positive case) their "acceptance" be! Will it not be the prelude to the resurrection of the dead (literally "life from the dead"), the final consummation of all things in the reign of God (cf. 1 Cor 15:22-28)?

Paul adduces three images—two brief, one developed at length—to underpin this hope. The first (v 16a) picks up the "firstfruits" idea familiar from Paul's statement about the Spirit in 8:23. The offering of the firstfruits of the harvest—or, as here, the dough (Num 15:17-21)—consecrates the rest as well. Likewise—the second image (v 16b)—the holiness of a "root" extends to the branches as well. In both cases, "firstfruits" and "root," Paul seems to have in mind the "fathers" (patriarchs; cf. 9:5), especially Abraham. Because of them, a "holiness" remains in Israel.

The third image, the "Wild Olive," builds on the second and develops it in an extended allegory (vv 17-24). With respect to this image Paul has been severely criticized on the grounds that, as a townsman, he got agricultural practice quite wrong. Normally, orchardists will graft a cultivated olive onto uncultivated ("wild olive") stock in order to promote hardiness and resistance to disease. In Paul's allegory, the natural branches ("the Jews") have been removed and "wild" stock (the Gentiles) grafted in. As a matter of fact, evidence has come to hand showing that the practice as Paul describes it was not unknown. Regardless of the practice, the allegory's chief role is to serve as a strict warning to Gentile believers, whom Paul is directly addressing now (v 13a). They are not to write off Israel. If God has been able to graft them (the wild olive) in "against nature," as it were, how much easier it will be for God to graft in the natural branches (Israel). And how easy, too, it would be for God to cut *them* out if they prove unworthy of the "kindness" they have received. Again, we can only say, how different relations between Christians and Jews down the ages would have been had Paul's warning to Gentile believers here not been so largely ignored.

The "Mystery" of the Final Salvation of "All Israel": 11:25-32

[25]I do not want you to be unaware of this mystery, brothers, so that you will not become wise [in] your own estimation: a hardening has come upon Israel in part, until the full number of the Gentiles comes in, [26]and thus all Israel will be saved, as it is written:

"The deliverer will come out of Zion,
   he will turn away godlessness from Jacob;
   [27]and this is my covenant with them
   when I take away their sins."

[28]In respect to the gospel, they are enemies on your account; but in respect to election, they are beloved because of the patriarchs. [29]For the gifts and the call of God are irrevocable.

[30]Just as you once disobeyed God but have now received mercy because of their disobedience, [31]so they have now disobeyed in order that, by virtue of the mercy shown to you, they too may [now] receive mercy. [32]For God delivered all to disobedience, that he might have mercy upon all.

Paul now brings his reflection on the fate of Israel to a climax. What he announces here (v 25) he describes as a "mystery": that is, an aspect of God's plan for the events of the end time, hidden from ordinary human knowledge but disclosed to those with prophetic gifts, such as himself. The "mystery" here concerns not so much the fact that Israel will find inclusion—Paul has made that clear already—but the circumstances that have to run their course before the climactic event occurs. A substantial portion of Israel will undergo the period of "hardening" already mentioned and this will endure until the full number of the Gentiles has "entered in" to the community of salvation. Then and only then, in a reversal of conventional expectation, will "all Israel" be saved (v 26a): that is, when the majority that is presently hardened joins the "remnant" (Jewish-Christian believers) that has already come to faith.

A composite quotation from Isaiah (59:20-21a and 27:9) puts a scriptural seal on this forecast. The "deliverer who will come from Zion" (v 27) is best referred to Christ. Isaiah foresaw that God, in covenant faithfulness, would send a Messiah to Israel, whose role as "deliverer" would not be a political one but rather the removal of sin. That this was the kind of "deliverance" that Israel, along with the Gentile world, needed, Paul has made abundantly clear in the early part of his letter (2:1–3:20, 23). He takes Isaiah's text as a firm divine declaration that Christ's deliverance of Israel in this respect will ultimately win through.

In conclusion (vv 28-32) Paul offers a series of antithetical couplets reflecting on the paradoxical operation of God's mercy. Former expectations of the priority of Israel vis-à-vis the Gentiles in regard to salvation have been drastically reversed. Israel may now be where the Gentiles once were: in a state of "hostility" to God (v 28). But this hostility is temporary: for the benefit of the Gentiles ("on your account"), as Paul has explained (11:11-12). It is temporary because Israel, as God's chosen people ("in respect to election"), remains "beloved because of the patriarchs." The ultimate basis for hope, as Paul insists in a memorable sentence, is that "the gifts and the call of God are irrevocable" (v 29). Here we see the fundamental principle of the letter—God's abiding faithfulness ("righteousness") to human beings—driven home to its conclusion. Human failure cannot have the last word over against God. If Israel was the first beneficiary of God's favor, Israel will be included in the end.

A hope, then, attaches uniquely to Israel. But its coming into operation will follow the "grace and mercy" pattern already operative in the case of the Gentiles (vv 30-32). Like them, Israel is going through a time of "disobedience" in order to experience at depth the mercy of God. God has "delivered all" (that is, Jews as well as Gentiles) to "disobedience" in order that all may experience God as God truly wishes to be: a God of grace and mercy. The common bind in sin and alienation from God that Paul labored to establish early in the letter (3:23; 5:12) is well on the way to being encompassed and finally overcome by a common solidarity in grace (5:21).

Hymn to God's Inscrutable Wisdom: 11:33-36

> ³³Oh, the depth of the riches and wisdom and knowledge of God!
> How inscrutable are his judgments and how unsearchable his ways!
> > ³⁴"For who has known the mind of the Lord
> > or who has been his counselor?"
> > ³⁵"Or who has given him anything
> > that he may be repaid?"
> ³⁶For from him and through him and for him are all things. To him be glory forever. Amen.

This short hymnic passage concludes not merely the discussion of Israel in chapters 9–11 but the entire presentation of the Gospel up to this point. Paul began by carefully according a "priority" as regards salvation to the Jews ("for the Jew first" [1:16]). But in the course of the exposition that priority has been radically reversed, at least as far as the "program" of salvation goes. God is including "all" (Jews and Gentiles) within the community of salvation but doing so in a way that reverses and confounds conventional (especially conventional Jewish) expectation. Hence this concluding hymn to divine wisdom. To absorb and dispel any lingering doubts concerning the validity of his inclusive Gospel Paul catches up his audience in an overwhelming sentiment of awe and praise. Evoking the book of Job, the hymn weaves together a remarkable pattern of motifs and echoes from the Wisdom tradition of Israel.

4. Living Out the Gospel in Love: 12:1–15:13

Christian Life as "Rational Worship": 12:1-2

> ¹²:¹I urge you therefore, brothers, by the mercies of God, to offer your bodies as a living sacrifice, holy and pleasing to God, your spiritual worship. ²Do not conform yourselves to this age but be transformed by the renewal of your mind, that you may discern what is the will of God, what is good and pleasing and perfect.

Paul has now concluded the presentation of the Gospel as he understands and proclaims it. Following a pattern set in earlier letters (Gal

5:13–6:19; 1 Thess 4:1–5:22; later Col 3:1–4:6; Eph 4:1–6:20) he devotes the last major section of the letter (12:1–15:13) to an instruction (Greek *parenesis*) on the implications of the Gospel for Christian living, especially life in community. After a brief introductory summons (12:1-2), he gives a fairly generalized series of instructions (12:3–13:14), before concluding with a more specific plea for tolerance in the matter of food (14:1–15:13). Rather than responding closely to circumstances in the Roman community, the exhortation addresses the kind of issues that Paul, as missionary and pastor, knew to be significant for communities trying to live the Gospel in the Mediterranean world. Despite the distance between that world and ours, much of what he says here remains highly relevant today.

The introductory summons (vv 1-2) consists of two long sentences laden with riches for Christian theology and life. Continuing the note of God's inclusive mercy from the preceding passage (11:30-32), he entreats his audience to make their life in the body a continual act of worship to God (v 1). "Worship" (Greek *latreia*), we may recall, was listed as one of the privileges of Israel (Rom 9:4). Christian believers no longer worshiped at the Jerusalem temple. Christ's sacrificial death on the cross had rendered otiose the kind of sacrifices offered there. A new kind of worship has come into being. In contrast to the offering of (dead) animals in the temple, this is a "living sacrifice," consisting of everyday life, lived out in a way that is "holy and acceptable to God."

The NAB translates the final phrase of v 1 as "your spiritual worship." The Greek word translated "spiritual"—*logikos*—is equally translatable as "rational." In light of what Paul says in the sentence to follow, I think this is preferable, and so would render the whole phrase as "the worship you owe as rational beings."

In the second sentence (v 2) Paul warns his audience not to conform themselves to the present age but to "be transformed" by a "renewal of mind" that will allow right discernment of the will of God. At the beginning of the letter, as part of his prophetic accusation, Paul had pointed out how the Gentile world's lapse into idolatry involved a misuse of the human mind. It had been "darkened" and rendered futile in its thinking because of its refusal to know God (1:19-21). The present appeal, with its stress upon "renewal" of the mind, seems to respond to and reverse that failure. Renewed by grace the human mind is now capable of discerning the will of God and what is "good and pleasing and perfect." There is no thought of returning to the Jewish law for ethical guidance. With striking confidence in the capacity of the renewed mind, Paul insists that moral life is now to proceed from this renewed faculty of discernment. The

Greek word translated "discern"—*dokimazein*—has the sense of "test," of weighing a situation's pros and cons before arriving at a decision. The stress on the role of the mind in the new ethical life leads me to prefer the translation "rational worship" at the end of v 1.

Taken in this way, these two sentences contain a spirituality and a theory of ethical discernment that is both suggestive and open-ended for our time. Because of the vast cultural and historical gap, Scripture provides believers today with little concrete guidance for the ethical dilemmas of modern life. Science and technology, in particular, throw up ethical challenges unimaginable in the biblical world of the Gospel. In this context Paul's stress on the capacity of the "renewed mind" to discern, his sense of the need to test (allowing for some measure of trial and error), his use of the language of the surrounding secular world ("good and pleasing and perfect") offer an important biblical charter to contemporary spirituality and moral theology.

The Exercise of Different Gifts within the Community: 12:3-8

> [3]For by the grace given to me I tell everyone among you not to think of himself more highly than one ought to think, but to think soberly, each according to the measure of faith that God has apportioned. [4]For as in one body we have many parts, and all the parts do not have the same function, [5]so we, though many, are one body in Christ and individually parts of one another. [6]Since we have gifts that differ according to the grace given to us, let us exercise them: if prophecy, in proportion to the faith; [7]if ministry, in ministering; if one is a teacher, in teaching; [8]if one exhorts, in exhortation; if one contributes, in generosity; if one is over others, with diligence; if one does acts of mercy, with cheerfulness.

Within this general sense of Christian living as "rational worship" (vv 1-2), Paul begins to fill out the picture with a more detailed account of how relationships within the community ought to proceed. The basic rule is that each should have a "sober" appreciation of the gift (of the Spirit) that has been given to him or her at the moment of coming to faith (v 3). Presupposed here is a conviction on Paul's part that every believer on coming to faith receives from the Spirit a distinct gift that he or she is to contribute to the building up of the community of faith. By "sober appreciation" Paul means a due perception of one's own gift—not hankering after or pretending to have the gifts of others, not vaunting one's own gift over that of others. Community life flourishes in good relationships when each one rightly discerns his or her own gift and exercises it effectively for the common good. Paul illustrates (vv 4-5) this vision of community life by appealing to the image of a "body." The image was employed widely in the ancient world—as also today. For Paul, of course, the community of believers is not only *like* a body, it *is* a body in the sense of constituting the "body of Christ" (cf. especially 1 Cor 12:12-27).

The rest of the passage (vv 6-8) consists of an illustrative list of the various gifts and the appropriate exercise that belongs to each. The distinction in each case between the gift (e.g., being a teacher) and its exercise (teaching) seems designed to urge each person to see to the exercise of their own particular gift as effectively as possible and not to "stray" beyond it in an attempt to exercise gifts apportioned by the Spirit to others. The list of gifts reflect the early "charismatic" stage of Christian community life before various functions were assigned to set offices and ministries. It is not surprising, then, that prophecy—the gift of discerning God's working in various events and God's will for the community—should head the list. Other gifts (teaching, exhortation) have to do with the initiation of new converts into the essentials of Christian faith and behavior, while others (ministry, contributing, doing acts of mercy) bear on seeing to the administration and fair distribution of community resources. The final three gifts (v 8bcd) all seem to be concerned in some way with the exercise of charity. Paul explicitly calls attention to the quality with which the benefit is to be communicated. Those on the receiving end should gain the sense that to serve them is a privilege not a burden.

Love in Action within and beyond the Community: 12:9-21

⁹Let love be sincere; hate what is evil, hold on to what is good; ¹⁰love one another with mutual affection; anticipate one another in showing honor. ¹¹Do not grow slack in zeal, be fervent in spirit, serve the Lord. ¹²Rejoice in hope, endure in affliction, persevere in prayer. ¹³Contribute to the needs of the holy ones, exercise hospitality. ¹⁴Bless those who persecute [you], bless and do not curse them. ¹⁵Rejoice with those who rejoice, weep with those who weep. ¹⁶Have the same regard for one another; do not be haughty but associate with the lowly; do not be wise in your own estimation. ¹⁷Do not repay anyone evil for evil; be concerned for what is noble in the sight of all. ¹⁸If possible, on your part, live at peace with all. ¹⁹Beloved, do not look for revenge but leave room for the wrath; for it is written, "Vengeance is mine, I will repay, says the Lord." ²⁰Rather, "if your enemy is hungry, feed him; if he is thirsty, give him something to drink; for

> by so doing you will heap burning coals upon his head." ²¹Do not
> be conquered by evil but conquer evil with good.

Having set out the various gifts that should flourish in a Christian community, Paul now lists a series of qualities that ought attend the interplay of gifts. The qualities will function as "oil" ensuring a fruitful interaction of gifts and the services that flow from them to others. Significantly, love—"sincere" love—heads the list. Up to this point in the letter "love" (Greek *agapē*) has referred to God's love (5:5-8; 8:31-39). The "love" now asked of believers represents an outflow into community life—and even to outsiders beyond the community—of that divine love that reached out to the world in Christ. In continuity with this divine love, the love characteristic of believers is not simply a passive waiting for occasion to arise; it actively seeks opportunity to go into operation (vv 10-11).

The succinct injunctions that follow (vv 12-16) tumble one after the other in no particular order. Some concern attitudes to be maintained in the present time, when believers are still on the way to salvation: hope, endurance, perseverance in prayer (v 12). Some refer to actions toward fellow believers: contribution to the needy; hospitality (v 13); fellow-feeling both in joy and in sorrow (v 15); a sober and humble appreciation of one's own standing (v 16). The advice to bless, rather than curse, persecutors (v 14)— an echo of the teaching of Jesus (Matt 5:44; Luke 6:27-28)—more likely has aggravating nonbelievers in view. It anticipates the sustained instruction on nonretaliation with which the instruction as a whole ends (vv 17-21).

In the command to refrain from retaliation (v 17) and to live peaceably with all (v 18), we meet Paul's sense of Christian life as a drama played out on a world stage before a hostile, noncomprehending audience (cf. 1 Cor 4:9; 2 Cor 2:14-15), which is nonetheless a field ripe for conversion (cf. Phil 2:15-16). The world may not understand but it may be impressed when believers express in the outward pattern of their lives the vulnerable love they have already experienced from God. Nonretaliation means leaving "vengeance" to God (v 19a), as commanded by Deuteronomy 32:35, quoted in v 19b. The meaning is not the hope that refraining from retaliation will lead to one's enemies receiving all the more severe punishment at the judgment ("wrath") from God. Rather, it is a surrender of one's cause to God in the confidence that God in comprehensive wisdom will see to an outcome that is just.

Beyond passive nonretaliation, Christian love should go over to the offensive, so to speak, reviving with food and drink the hungry and thirsty enemy (v 20a; Prov 25:21). The meaning of the subsequent comment—that this will "heap burning coals upon [the enemy's] head"—is obscure. Taking it to mean that such generosity will only serve to increase the severity of the punishment to be meted out (eschatologically) by God adheres more closely to the original meaning of the phrase in Proverbs 25:22. But a "punitive" understanding along these lines runs counter to the thrust of the present passage as a whole, which is devoted to love in action. It is far more likely, in line with the final injunction to "conquer evil with good" (v 21), that conversion rather than punishment of the enemy is in view. The "love" required of Christians then becomes a true reflection and extension of the divine love that offered reconciliation to an evil and hostile world in Christ (2 Cor 5:18-21) and, in resurrection, triumphed over that evil to inaugurate the new creation.

Duties toward Civil Authorities: 13:1-7

> ¹³:¹Let every person be subordinate to the higher authorities, for there is no authority except from God, and those that exist have been established by God. ²Therefore, whoever resists authority opposes what God has appointed, and those who oppose it will bring judgment upon themselves. ³For rulers are not a cause of fear to good conduct, but to evil. Do you wish to have no fear of authority? Then do what is good and you will receive approval from it, ⁴for it is a servant of God for your good. But if you do evil, be afraid, for it does not bear the sword without purpose; it is the servant of God to inflict wrath on the evildoer. ⁵Therefore, it is necessary to be subject not only because of the wrath but also because of conscience. ⁶This is why you also pay taxes, for the authorities are ministers of God, devoting themselves to this very thing. ⁷Pay to all their dues, taxes to whom taxes are due, toll to whom toll is due, respect to whom respect is due, honor to whom honor is due.

A very odd passage confronts us here. Abruptly, Paul enjoins his audience to "be subordinate to the higher authorities," that is, the civic authorities in Rome. In support of this command he embarks on a line of reasoning that has no parallel elsewhere in his letters. There is no mention of Christ and his saving work—indeed nothing distinctly Christian about the theological argument deployed, with its very conventional stress on rewards and punishments. The command to be subject to the presently ruling authorities displays not a trace of the Pauline sense that the whole framework of the present era is passing away and that believers' true "citizenship" is in heaven (Phil 3:20). It is tempting to regard the passage as an interpolation into the original Pauline text of the letter, but there no basis in the manuscript tradition for regarding the passage as non-Pauline. Since it has always been part of the canon, we have to deal with it as best we can.

There is in fact a plausible historical setting for the inclusion of the passage in Paul's letter to Rome. Just before Paul wrote there was civil unrest and rioting in the imperial capital protesting against abuses in the collection of taxes and tariffs (vv 6-7). Aware of such a climate of civic disturbance and suspecting or knowing that the Christian community was divided on the matter, Paul may have been anxious lest the highly vulnerable churches adopt an attitude that would bring them into conflict with the authorities. An exalted sense of Christian freedom and detachment from the world may have led some members to consider themselves exempt from paying taxes and tariffs (cf. Jesus' response to Peter in the matter of the temple tax in Matt 17:26-27). More particularly, some may even have been citing Paul's sense of Christian freedom to justify such an attitude. This would provide an added reason for fearing that a visit from Paul might serve to inflame the situation further. It is understandable, then, that Paul, forewarned of the disturbances by friends in the community, should signal in advance a conventional attitude to civic authority and specifically endorse the payment of taxes and tariffs. The prospect of his arrival, then, when he announces it shortly, will arouse no fear that he is going to the stir the pot.

Awareness of such a context should largely determine the interpretation of the passage. It has been made to bear a far heavier weight of theological construction than it warrants. Theologies of church-state relations have been erected on it. Supporters of autocratic governments and totalitarian regimes (e.g., Nazi Germany; Apartheid South Africa) have demanded civil obedience in its name. To modern sensibility the divine guarantee accorded here to earthly rulers—above all the appeal to obey for conscience' sake (v 5)—seems naïve and simplistic in the extreme. No allowance is made for the abuse of power on the part of human authority; nor is there any thought that on occasion it is the good rather than the bad who feel the brunt of penal sanction (cf. vv 3-4), whether through mistake or through miscarriage of justice. In situations where the conditions of just government that it presupposes do not exist, the text loses all credibility. Moreover, in the modern democratic state where authority derives immediately from the people, regularly exercising their democratic right to choose their government, the theological assertion that all authority derives from God needs a great deal of nuance.

We have to recognize, then, that for his own particular reasons at the time, Paul is expressing here the conventional view that human rulers wielded divine authority, a view widespread in the ancient world as a whole, as well as in the Jewish biblical and postbiblical tradition (e.g., Isa 10:5-6; 41:2-4; etc.). The text ought not be uncritically isolated from its time and context to bear a more universal and timeless validity.

On a more positive note, it does offer a valid reminder that no government is a law entirely unto itself. In the Christian perspective, all exercise of authority is accountable to the supreme authority, God. For Christians too the text can signal that believers cannot simply withdraw from civic responsibility and participation on the plea that their true "citizenship" is in heaven (Phil 3:20). Acceptance and exercise of that responsibility forms part of the "rational worship" owed to God in the present time (12:1-2).

Fulfilling the "Debt" of Love: 13:8-10

> [8]Owe nothing to anyone, except to love one another; for the one who loves another has fulfilled the law. [9]The commandments, "You shall not commit adultery; you shall not kill; you shall not steal; you shall not covet," and whatever other commandment there may be, are summed up in this saying, [namely] "You shall love your neighbor as yourself." [10]Love does no evil to the neighbor; hence, love is the fulfillment of the law.

This very attractive little passage with its focus on "love" resumes and completes the exhortation begun in 12:9, "Let love be sincere." "Love," then, brackets the whole sequence in between. No obligation, from the most sublime to the most mundane (payment of tariffs and taxes!), stands apart from this core requirement of the Christian life.

Paul skillfully ties the passage to the one before by picking up the note of payment of debt (vv 6-7). Christians are not exempt from the requirement to pay what they owe (v 8). But in one area they will never be able completely to discharge a debt. Love (*agapē*) is an inexhaustible debt they have contracted through the divine love received from God in Christ. This costly love (8:32), which grasped them even as "enemies" (5:10), has created in them a corresponding (inexhaustible) "debt" of love owed to fellow human beings, deserving or undeserving as the case may be.

Somewhat surprisingly Paul supports the commendation of love by speaking of its as the "fulfillment" of the law (v 8a; v 10b). To readers who have been led to see the ethical requirements of the Jewish law as the sole and irreplaceable guide to righteous living Paul insists that it is love that provides a sufficient and more fundamental basis. He cites four commandments (prohibitions) of the law relating to conduct toward the neighbor and throws in—not without a hint of disdain perhaps—"and whatever other commandment there may be" (v 9a). These are all summed up in a single precept from Leviticus, "You shall love your neighbor as yourself" (19:18; cf. Gal 5:14).

The added comment "Love does no evil to the neighbor" (v 10a) sounds rather negative and inadequate at first. Surely love is about a lot more than refraining from harm. But the commandments cited are all prohibitions, the implication being that this is the law's way: negatively to restrain rather than positively to empower. Love, on the other hand, picking up the commandment of Leviticus 19:18, invites one to place oneself precisely in the position of the neighbor and allow one's action to flow from the question, "What would I desire in this situation?" rather than, "What ought I do or refrain from doing in this situation?" Love is the "fulfillment" (*plērōma*) of the law (v 10b) in the sense that it fulfills all that the law requires, yet actively goes beyond it. For Paul, of course, it is the indwelling power of the Spirit, that enables the "righteous decree of the law" to be fulfilled in believers through love (8:4).

Living as People of the Day: 13:11-14

> [11]And do this because you know the time; it is the hour now for you to awake from sleep. For our salvation is nearer now than when we first believed; [12]the night is advanced, the day is at hand. Let us then throw off the works of darkness [and] put on the armor of light; [13]let us conduct ourselves properly as in the day, not in orgies and drunkenness, not in promiscuity and licentiousness, not in rivalry and jealousy. [14]But put on the Lord Jesus Christ, and make no provision for the desires of the flesh.

Paul concludes the more general part of his exhortation on an eschatological note. Discharging the debt of love, especially in difficult circumstances, becomes easier when believers recognize "the time" in which they now stand. The further they proceed in their Christian life, the closer they are to the day of "salvation"—the day when the returning Lord will rescue them from the present age and draw them into the fullness of his risen life.

Paul in fact seems to be drawing on a baptismal instruction or hymn, which might have run as follows (cf. Eph 5:14):

> The hour has come to wake from sleep.
> The night is advanced; the day is at hand.
> Cast off, the works of darkness
> and put on the armor of light.

The image behind this hymn and the instruction Paul has built on it is that of people waking from sleep at the start of the day. Christian life is "located" in that half-hour or so of darkness immediately preceding the dawn. Though it is still dark, the diligent are already up and about. They have cast off their night attire ("the works of darkness") and are putting on their day clothes ("the armor of light") to be ready for the work of the day as soon as it is light. The behavior listed in v 13 tallies well with reports from ancient authors of what went on in the taverns of Rome at night. Such "works of darkness" belong to the past that believers have cast off in order to clothe themselves with "the Lord Jesus Christ" (v 14a; cf. Gal 3:27; Col 3:10-11). Contrary to the self-indulgence ("the flesh") that gives rise to such vices (v 14b), the "attire" in which they should now present themselves is the pattern of his unselfish love welling up within them through the Spirit. Two millennia later, with no "end" to the age in sight, Paul's exhortation obviously has less force. But, as "children of light and children of the day" (1 Thess 5:5; cf. Eph 5:8) we can still see ourselves within the attractive image that it displays.

Tolerance in Christian Community Life: 14:1–15:13

The Tolerance Incumbent on All: 14:1-12

14:1Welcome anyone who is weak in faith, but not for disputes over opinions. 2One person believes that one may eat anything, while the weak person eats only vegetables. 3The one who eats must not despise the one who abstains, and the one who abstains must not pass judgment on the one who eats; for God has welcomed him. 4Who are you to pass judgment on someone else's servant? Before his own master he stands or falls. And he will be upheld, for the Lord is able to make him stand. 5[For] one person considers one day more important than another, while another person considers all days alike. Let everyone be fully persuaded in his own mind. 6Whoever observes the day, observes it for the Lord. Also whoever eats, eats for the Lord, since he gives thanks to God; while whoever abstains, abstains for the Lord and gives thanks to God. 7None of us lives for oneself, and no one dies for oneself. 8For if we live, we live for the

Lord, and if we die, we die for the Lord; so then, whether we live or die, we are the Lord's. [9]For this is why Christ died and came to life, that he might be Lord of both the dead and the living. [10]Why then do you judge your brother? Or you, why do you look down on your brother? For we shall all stand before the judgment seat of God; [11]for it is written:

"As I live, says the Lord, every knee shall bend before me, and every tongue shall give praise to God."

[12]So [then] each of us shall give an account of himself [to God].

Save for the instruction concerning civil authorities (13:1-7), Paul's exhortation so far has been quite general. Now (14:1) he begins to address a more specific issue: what believers may eat and drink, and—to a lesser extent—whether they have to reckon and observe holy days. At our distance it is not easy to get a clear picture of what really was the issue at stake. Nor is it easy to identify the parties involved, as Paul seems to refer to them. He initially refers to the "person weak in faith" (14:1-2). Toward the end he summons the "strong," with whom he clearly identifies himself, to "put up with the failings of the weak" (15:1). It soon becomes clear that the "weak [in faith]" are those who have qualms about eating meat and drinking wine; they also observe particular days. The strong tend to belittle the weak (vv 3a, 10b), who in turn "pass judgment on" (= "condemn") the strong (vv 3b, 10a).

Since the law of Moses prescribed many rules concerning dietary matters, the obvious solution is to identify the "weak" with believers of Jewish background and the strong with those of Gentile origin. But this is too simplistic. The Jewish law, while it did enshrine holy days, did not forbid the consumption of meat or wine. Some believers of Jewish background, such as Paul himself, clearly numbered themselves among the strong, while some Gentile converts may have remained attached to practice imposed on them by Jewish-Christian instructors strict in observance of the law. Rather than a rigid Jew/Gentile equivalence to weak/strong, respectively, it seems best to conclude that the determining factor was heightened Jewish sensitivity in regard to dietary law in a predominantly Gentile social context where the purity of food, especially meat, could not be guaranteed.

In 1 Corinthians 8–10 Paul deals with a more or less parallel situation where the issue concerned the lawfulness of eating meat that had been used in pagan sacrifices. The sale of such high quality meat in the marketplace provided an affordable source of protein for the poor. The situation Paul addresses in Romans may not be as specific as this but what seems most likely is that some believers, strongly influenced by the Jewish law, abstained from all meat on the grounds either that the meat available might have been associated with worship of idols or that it might not have been slaughtered in such a way as to exclude all blood (*kosher* requirement); they may have abstained also from wine on the grounds that it may have been used in pagan rituals (libations) or otherwise contained impurities. Paul dubs such abstainers "weak in faith" in the sense that their faith in the one true God was not sufficiently robust to free them from scruples in regard to the taint of idolatry and so allow them to eat and drink in good conscience. While basically aligning himself with the strong and directing the main thrust of his instruction to them, Paul calls for tolerance and mutual acceptance on the part of both parties.

We do not know whether Paul has information that the issue he is addressing here was a lively one in the Roman community at the time. He may simply be giving instruction on the basis of general awareness that it is one that exercised almost all communities of believers scattered around the Mediterranean world. Perhaps too, as in the case of his instruction to submit to civil authorities (13:1-7), he may have been seeking to defuse in advance an issue that his own arrival in Rome might otherwise inflame. The strong should not presume that he intended to champion their cause, making his own arrival even less welcome to the weak. Whatever may have been Paul's motivation in addressing the issue, it is remote from anything exercising believers today. Nonetheless, Paul never addresses an issue without summoning up the depth of his theology and pastoral sensitivity, and this is no exception. There are riches here for theological and pastoral reflection.

The opening section, 14:1-12, makes an appeal for tolerance that, formally at least, addresses both groups—though it is likely that Paul is really talking to the strong all the time. It is unlikely that the weak would respond positively to being addressed as such. Paul may couch his exhortation as an appeal to both parties in order to appear evenhanded and not be requiring the strong to bear the full burden of tolerance—though in effect that is what seems to be the case in the end. Behind the appeal lies the deeper theological truth that each and every believer is in some sense a servant or slave to their Lord, Jesus Christ. Every single act of human life—including the most basic ones of eating and drinking—come under the framework of this "service" to the risen Lord. Everything is performed with "thanksgiving" to him (v 6b) whose resurrection has vindicated the essential "goodness" of all things in a new creation where old legal distinctions between "holy" and "profane," "clean" and "unclean" simply fall away (v 14).

In the service of this Lord, just as everything is holy, everything is done with accountability to him alone (vv 7-12). It is not for slaves to look sideways, so to speak, to judge their fellow slaves. Since, living or dying, "we" (believers) live for the Lord, who "purchased" us at the cost of his own death, it is to him alone that each must render an account.

The sense of Christian life as a "slavery" to the risen Lord has, as in 6:15-23, its less attractive aspects. But the unattractiveness of the image in itself is surely overcome by the thought of the One in whose "service" believers are enlisted. In terms of the scriptural quotation from Isaiah 45:23 (v 11; also Phil 2:9-11) the whole existence of believers is caught up in his subjection of the universe to God to bring in the new creation. It is not inappropriate, then, that the ringing sentences of vv 7-9 ("None of us lives for oneself, and no one dies for oneself. For if we live, we live for the Lord.") feature so frequently at Christian funerals and similar celebrations of life and death. Addressing a very particular and time-located issue, Paul has once again reached into the depths of his theology to conjure up a superb vision of Christian life, in all its aspects, as lived with thanksgiving and accountability, in the service of the Lord. As a later Pauline letter sums it up: "whatever you do, in word or in deed, do everything in the name of the Lord Jesus, giving thanks to God the Father through him" (Col 3:17).

The Tolerance Asked Particularly of the Strong in Faith: 14:13-23

[13]Then let us no longer judge one another, but rather resolve never to put a stumbling block or hindrance in the way of a brother. [14]I know and am convinced in the Lord Jesus that nothing is unclean in itself; still, it is unclean for someone who thinks it unclean. [15]If your brother is being hurt by what you eat, your conduct is no longer in accord with love. Do not because of your food destroy him for whom Christ died. [16]So do not let your good be reviled. [17]For the kingdom of God is not a matter of food and drink, but of righteousness, peace, and joy in the holy Spirit; [18]whoever serves Christ in this way is pleasing to God and approved by others. [19]Let us then pursue what leads to peace and to building up one another. [20]For the sake of food, do not destroy the work of God. Everything is indeed clean, but it is wrong for anyone to become a stumbling block by eating; [21]it is good not to eat meat or drink wine or do anything that causes your brother to stumble. [22]Keep the faith [that] you have to yourself in the presence

of God; blessed is the one who does not condemn himself for what he approves. ²³But whoever has doubts is condemned if he eats, because this is not from faith; for whatever is not from faith is sin.

Paul now addresses his plea for tolerance in community life more directly to the strong. The basic principle that will govern this somewhat rambling paragraph appears in the second clause of the opening verse (v 13b): "resolve never to put a stumbling block or hindrance in the way of a brother [or sister]." This principle reflects a more general New Testament belief that the more powerful and authoritative members in a community can have an influence for ill as well as for good upon the fate of the "little ones," and hence bear a graver responsibility (cf. Mark 9:43; Matt 18:6-7; Luke 17:1-2). Taking up this idea, Paul requires from one group (the strong) a particular form of action—or rather a refraining from action—not required of the other party (the weak). He does so on the grounds that the latter are vulnerable in a way that the former are not: pressuring them to act (eat meat and drink wine against their conscience) puts in jeopardy their very salvation.

Personally, Paul fully identifies with the view of the strong to whom he appeals. He is as fully convinced as they are in their robust faith that no taint of idolatry adheres to created things in themselves. But what determines the ethical quality of human action is not simply the objective order but the disposition of the subject as well. Hence, when a person, albeit erroneously, thinks that something is "unclean"—in the technical sense of a religious taboo—that thing really is unclean for that person. Social pressure created by the example or derision on the part of the strong may induce the weak in faith to eat in bad conscience and that really does put their eternal salvation at risk.

Hence to create a "stumbling block" in this way is to proceed "no longer in accord with love" (v 15b). The reasoning stems from Paul's conviction that a believer can never look upon a fellow believer in any other way than as a brother or sister whom Christ "loved" and for whom he "delivered himself up" (1 Cor 8:11; Gal 2:20). This truth confers upon the brother or sister a preciousness that simply overwhelms all other considerations. Paul is appealing, then, to the strong to display toward their fellow believers whose faith is weak the same kind of self-sacrificing love that they themselves when "weak" (Rom 5:6) received from Christ. While in absolute terms they are free to eat and drink as they like, in the name of a deeper sense of freedom proceeding from love, they ought refrain from so doing in the presence of the weak.

In support of this Paul makes a (for him) rare appeal to "the kingdom of God" (v 17). This phrase normally refers to the future blessings of salvation that the faithful are destined to "inherit" (1 Cor 6:9; 15:50; Gal 5:21). But believers already breathe the "atmosphere" of the kingdom in the present gifts of "righteousness, peace, and joy in the holy Spirit." In comparison with such blessings, the freedom to eat and drink what one likes pales into insignificance. It is not always for the best that freedom find outward expression. To allow it to remain inward for the sake of a higher good is perfectly honorable both before God and in the sight of human beings (v 18). The important thing is to cooperate in God's work of building up the community (v 19). It would be a terrible thing to destroy God's work through disputation over food (v 20a).

In conclusion (vv 22-23) Paul reasserts his basic sense of human moral action. The key thing is that outward action should proceed from inner conviction formed by faith. To go against that conviction is to act against conscience and so to sin (v 23). External expression is nothing without inner integrity and conviction that one is acting in right relationship with God. Thus Paul's treatment of an issue in itself remote from our concerns draws on principles of far wider and continuing application: the acceptance of outward restriction in the cause of a deeper freedom and the need to respect conscience, even when less enlightened, in the interests of love.

The Example of Christ: 15:1-6

> [15:1]We who are strong ought to put up with the failings of the weak and not to please ourselves; [2]let each of us please our neighbor for the good, for building up. [3]For Christ did not please himself; but, as it is written, "The insults of those who insult you fall upon me." [4]For whatever was written previously was written for our instruction, that by endurance and by the encouragement of the scriptures we might have hope. [5]May the God of endurance and encouragement grant you to think in harmony with one another, in keeping with Christ Jesus, [6]that with one accord you may with one voice glorify the God and Father of our Lord Jesus Christ.

Identifying himself explicitly with the strong in faith, Paul concludes his appeal for tolerance by pointing to the example of Christ. Rather than "pleasing [themselves]" the strong ought to "support" (a better translation than the NAB's "put up with") the weaknesses of the weak. Strong persons are those who, besides carrying their own burdens, have strength left over to shoulder those of others too. This will mean not "pleasing oneself" in the sense of allowing one's own self-interest to be the determining principle of action—the precise meaning of acting "according to the flesh" in the biblical language prominent earlier in the letter (7:6; 8:3-11). Pleasing one's neighbor (v 2) rather than oneself, does not mean a facile attempt to make the neighbor happy at all costs. It means placing one's life project at the service of the (common) "good" in a way that makes for the "building up" of the community as a whole.

The ultimate motivation is the example provided by Christ (vv 3-4). The statement that he "did not please himself" does not refer to some isolated act but to the whole dynamic of his saving "career" on our behalf, culminating in the "obedience unto death" of the cross (Phil 2:8). Rather than pointing explicitly to this event, Paul cites Psalm 69:10 (LXX: 68:10), one of the texts most frequently cited in the early Christian tradition in connection with the passion of Christ. The psalm foreshadows the way in which the sinless One bore the cost of human violence and sin in place of those (ourselves) who were too "weak" (Rom 5:10) to bear it themselves. It is this divine act of love, welling up within believers because of their existence "in Christ," that should inspire them, similarly, to bear the "weaknesses of the weak." Read thus in the light of Christ, this scriptural text—as all of Scripture (v 4)—functions as an "instruction." It motivates endurance and encouragement to take on the unselfish, harder way by communicating a sense of "hope" that the God who responded to the obedience of Christ by raising him from the dead will similarly vindicate those who follow the unselfish pattern of his love. Mention of "hope" leads Paul, then, to round off the exhortation to tolerance in quasi-liturgical mode with a prayer-wish for community harmony and peace (v 5). This will bring about a unified, communal "glorifying" of God (v 6), reversing the human refusal to glorify God that was the essence of idolatry and lapse into the power of sin (1:21-23).

Christ's "Acceptance" as a Model for Community Acceptance: 15:7-13.

⁷Welcome one another, then, as Christ welcomed you, for the glory of God. ⁸For I say that Christ became a minister of the circumcised to show God's truthfulness, to confirm the promises to the patriarchs, ⁹but so that the Gentiles might glorify God for his mercy. As it is written:

"Therefore, I will praise you among the Gentiles
and sing praises to your name."

¹⁰And again it says:
  "Rejoice, O Gentiles, with his people."
¹¹And again:
  "Praise the Lord, all you Gentiles,
    and let all the peoples praise him."
¹²And again Isaiah says:
  "The root of Jesse shall come,
    raised up to rule the Gentiles;
  in him shall the Gentiles hope."
¹³May the God of hope fill you with all joy and peace in believing,
so that you may abound in hope by the power of the holy Spirit.

This small section at first sight seems to provide a second, quasi-parallel conclusion to the instruction on tolerance in matter of food. But whereas previously Paul spoke in terms of the strong and the weak within the community, here the focus appears to lie more broadly on the divine action with respect to Jews (literally "the circumcised") and the Gentiles. In this broader aspect it may be intended as a conclusion to the entire body of the letter (1:16–15:13) where the Jew-Gentile duality bulks so large. Nonetheless it is addressed primarily to believers of Gentile origin and repeats—albeit on a somewhat different basis—Paul's summons to generosity in attitude and community life.

The summons rests on a familiar biblical pattern of motivation whereby what one has received from God, one is bound to extend to fellow human beings (cf. Deut 24:17-22; Matt 18:32-33). On this basis the summons to mutual "acceptance" (the NAB translation "Welcome" is weak) is the "acceptance" that the Gentile believers, precisely as Gentiles, have received from Christ (v 1), which Paul goes on to elaborate with yet another reflection on his saving work in relation to both Jews and Gentiles. With respect to the Jews, Christ's "ministry" (becoming a *diakonos*) was impelled by divine faithfulness to promises God had made to the patriarchs of Israel (v 8; cf. 3:2; 9:4). For the Gentiles a different "economy" was operative. They had not received promises as Israel had, though Israel guarded on their behalf the promise to Abraham that did concern them (4:16-17; Gal 3:8, 14, 15-22, 29). The benefit that came to them in Christ came as an act of pure "mercy" to those who were, by definition, "Gentile sinners" (v 9a). If they, as Gentiles, had experienced God's "acceptance" in such measure, how ready ought *they* be to pass that acceptance on.

The exhortation concludes with a chain of scriptural quotations that support this view of Christ's role vis-à-vis the Gentiles. By selecting texts from all three parts of Scripture—the Torah (Deut 32:43 in v 10), the Prophets (Isa 11:10 in v 12), and the Writings (Ps 18 in v 9b)—Paul can summon up a broad and unanimous scriptural witness to the divine intent, through the ministry of Messiah Jesus, to draw from the nations of the world the praise and glorification of God that is the authentic human response to God (reversing the lapse recorded in 1:21-23). The final quotation (v 12) in fact presents the Messiah of Israel (literally "the root of Jesse" [father of David]) as the one who will "rise" to "rule the Gentiles" and become the object of their hope. Another prayer-wish (v 13) rounds off the entire exhortation on this note of hope, communicated by the Spirit (cf. 8:23).

Ending the body of the letter (1:16–15:13) in this way Paul has brought the wheel full circle. All began in 1:18-32 with the message of doom and wrath lying on the Gentile world because of its failure to "glorify" God (1:21-23). Now through the faithful work of Christ, God has drawn the Gentile world back to glorification and in this given them the hope of entering into the "inheritance" intended from the start to be the destiny of humankind.

CONCLUSION: 15:14–16:27

Paul's Ministry of the Gospel to the Gentiles: 15:14-21

[14]I myself am convinced about you, my brothers, that you yourselves are full of goodness, filled with all knowledge, and able to admonish one another. [15]But I have written to you rather boldly in some respects to remind you, because of the grace given me by God [16]to be a minister of Christ Jesus to the Gentiles in performing the priestly service of the gospel of God, so that the offering up of the Gentiles may be acceptable, sanctified by the holy Spirit. [17]In Christ Jesus, then, I have reason to boast in what pertains to God. [18]For I will not dare to speak of anything except what Christ has accomplished through me to lead the Gentiles to obedience by word and deed, [19]by the power of signs and wonders, by the power of the Spirit [of God], so that from Jerusalem all the way around to Illyricum I have finished preaching the gospel of Christ. [20]Thus I aspire to proclaim the gospel not where Christ has already been named, so that I do not build on another's foundation, [21]but as it is written:

"Those who have never been told of him shall see,
and those who have never heard of him shall understand."

Paul has completed his presentation of the Gospel of which he is "not ashamed" (1:16a). He has summoned the community of believers in Rome to allow their way of life to be shaped by this vision of the Gospel—specifically to allow the generosity and mercy they, as Gentiles, have received from God to flow through to their own relationships, both within and outside the community (12:1–15:13). Now it is time to present *himself* more directly to them, not simply as minister of the Gospel to the Gentiles but as one intending to pay them a visit. To indicate travel plans, to send greetings to various individuals and offer prayers for the well-being of the recipients was standard procedure in ancient letter writing. But Paul's task goes beyond simple convention. He has to announce his visit without alienating the Roman community or putting them on the defensive. At the same time, he must preserve the sense of himself as an apostle charged with responsibility for the Gentile churches and looking to a future field of action (Spain) for which he hopes the community will play a significant supportive role.

Diplomatically he acknowledges that he has admonished them, when they were well capable of admonishing each other (v 14). If he has written "rather boldly" (v 15a) it has not been as though addressing people needing original conversion but by way of "reminder" of the Gospel they already know. He has done so in virtue of the "grace" (*charis*) given him by God (v 15b). Paul expands on this "grace," applying to himself a striking image (v 16). It is taken from the liturgical worship of the Jerusalem temple in a way that the NAB translation doesn't bring out sufficiently clearly. More literally, Paul describes himself as "a minister of Christ Jesus to the Gentiles, serving the Gospel of God as a priest, so that the offering [consisting] of the Gentiles may be acceptable [to God], sanctified by the Holy Spirit." Paul is not portraying himself as a priest in the later Christian sense. He is alluding to the temple ritual of sacrifice in which the service of the priest ensured that what was brought by the people as an offering was truly holy and acceptable to God. In the present situation, the previously "unclean" Gentiles (1:24, 26-27, 28-31), hitherto denied access to God, have through their conversion made an "offering" of themselves to God. Paul's role as "priest" is to ensure that they come before God no longer as "unclean" but as truly acceptable because sanctified through the Holy Spirit.

From consideration of his apostolic role Paul moves on to state what he has actually achieved in virtue of the role. He can "boast" about it (v 17) because it does not rest on anything he has achieved by himself but solely on what Christ as risen Lord has worked through him (v 18). What has attested the presence of the risen Lord has been not only the success of the preaching in leading the Gentiles to "obedience" (cf. "obedience of faith" 1:5) but the marvelous phenomena ("signs and wonders"), worked through the power of the Spirit, that have attended the proclamation (v 19a). The "signs and wonders" probably allude to miracles of healing and perhaps exorcisms, confirming an impression of Paul also conveyed by Acts (14:8-10; 16:16-18, 25-26; 20:9-12; 28:8-9).

The effect of this impulse of the risen Lord (v 19b) has been the completion of a mighty arc of evangelization taking in the whole of the eastern Mediterranean seaboard to the borders of what would now be the modern state of Albania ("Illyricum"). At face value, the claim is extraordinary. Paul's preaching was confined to the great cities and even in them probably reached only a small proportion of the population. His aim, it seems, was not to reach each and every individual but to proclaim Christ "to the ends of the earth," thus fulfilling a divine condition for the return (Parousia) of the Lord (cf. Mark 13:10).

In the sweep of this missionary activity, Paul's task has been essentially that of the pathfinder, the pioneer. His policy has been not to build on another's foundation but to press on outward to those regions where Christ has "not been named," that is, where other missionaries have not been active and churches not yet established (v 20; cf. 2 Cor 10:16). With a breathtaking sense of his central role in salvation history Paul can even relate (v 21) to his own career a scriptural text (Isa 52:15b) that originally referred to the Suffering Servant figure of Isaiah. All is designed, however, to explain why he has not appeared in Rome until now and to prepare the way for the bombshell he is about to launch: the information that he *is* now intending to visit—not to build there on a foundation already laid but to establish a base for further missionary activity in the West.

Paul's Travel Plans: Rome and Then Spain: 15:22-33

[22]That is why I have so often been prevented from coming to you. [23]But now, since I no longer have any opportunity in these regions and since I have desired to come to you for many years, [24]I hope to see you in passing as I go to Spain and to be sent on my way there by you, after I have enjoyed being with you for a time. [25]Now, however, I am going to Jerusalem to minister to the holy ones. [26]For Macedonia and Achaia have decided to make some contribution for the poor among the holy ones in Jerusalem; [27]they decided to do it,

and in fact they are indebted to them, for if the Gentiles have come to share in their spiritual blessings, they ought also to serve them in material blessings. [28]So when I have completed this and safely handed over this contribution to them, I shall set out by way of you to Spain; [29]and I know that in coming to you I shall come in the fullness of Christ's blessing.

[30]I urge you, [brothers,] by our Lord Jesus Christ and by the love of the Spirit, to join me in the struggle by your prayers to God on my behalf, [31]that I may be delivered from the disobedient in Judea, and that my ministry for Jerusalem may be acceptable to the holy ones, [32]so that I may come to you with joy by the will of God and be refreshed together with you. [33]The God of peace be with all of you. Amen.

Paul has explained how his apostolic activity in the East and policy of not trespassing on regions where other evangelists have been at work have prevented him from visiting the community at Rome up till now (v 22). With no further scope for his work in the East, the impulse of the Gospel is driving him to look elsewhere, namely, to Spain. This will provide the opportunity to fulfill at last his long-standing desire to visit the community in Rome (vv 22-23). Paul wants not only to see them in passing. After they have enjoyed each other's company for a time, he hopes to be "sent on [his] way there" by them—the latter phrase containing a clear hint of a hope to receive support for his new mission from a community well placed, geographically and financially, to offer it (v 24).

Between Paul and Rome—and ultimately Spain—lies a more immediate task. He has to journey back to the East, to Jerusalem, conveying to the community of believers there (NAB "the holy ones"; better "the saints") the financial contribution that he has been collecting from his Gentile communities in accordance with the agreement described in Gal 2:9-10. The collection was no mere relief measure for a community in need. For Paul it was a key symbol of the overall unity of the churches, Jewish and Gentile, bound by the one Gospel. More specifically, it was an acknowledgment on the part of the Gentile churches that, through a remarkable exercise of God's mercy, they, "the wild olive" (11:16-18), had been grafted upon Israel, currently represented by the Jewish-Christian "remnant" in Jerusalem; they continued to draw "nourishment" ("spiritual blessings") from that original "root." The privilege of having shared in these (superior) spiritual blessings has created for them an "obligation" to ensure that a similar sharing takes place on the (lesser) material level. Paul singles out the churches in Greece ("Macedonia and

Achaia") for their special willingness in this regard (vv 26-27). When he has discharged this responsibility, he will visit Rome en route to Spain (v 28), confident that he will do so both with Christ's blessing and bringing such blessing in "fullness" (v 29).

Very much on Paul's mind is the precarious nature of his mission to Jerusalem. First, he will be under threat from the Jewish majority in Jerusalem that has not come to faith in Jesus as the Christ (literally "the disobedient in Judea"); they regard him as a renegade and subverter of the ancestral faith. Second, and far more poignantly, there is the prospect that even fellow believers in Jerusalem will spurn both the collection and what its acceptance would symbolize: the acknowledgment of Gentile believers as full "citizens" in the renewed people of God. Such rejection would undermine Paul's entire missionary project and the theological vision behind it. Hence his earnest request that the prayers of the Roman community that both dangers be averted should accompany his Jerusalem mission (vv 30-31). If it be God's will that such prayers be answered, he will come to Rome "with joy" for a time of mutual "refreshment" before leaving for Spain (v 32). We do not know exactly what transpired when Paul did arrive in Jerusalem, but the later account given in Acts 21:15-40 might suggest that his fears concerning his reception were only too well founded.

Commendation of Phoebe and Greetings: 16:1-16

16:1I commend to you Phoebe our sister, who is [also] a minister of the church at Cenchreae, 2that you may receive her in the Lord in a manner worthy of the holy ones, and help her in whatever she may need from you, for she has been a benefactor to many and to me as well.

3Greet Prisca and Aquila, my co-workers in Christ Jesus, 4who risked their necks for my life, to whom not only I am grateful but also all the churches of the Gentiles; 5greet also the church at their house. Greet my beloved Epaenetus, who was the firstfruits in Asia for Christ. 6Greet Mary, who has worked hard for you. 7Greet Andronicus and Junia, my relatives and my fellow prisoners; they are prominent among the apostles and they were in Christ before me. 8Greet Ampliatus, my beloved in the Lord. 9Greet Urbanus, our co-worker in Christ, and my beloved Stachys. 10Greet Apelles, who is approved in Christ. Greet those who belong to the family of Aristobulus. 11Greet my relative Herodion. Greet those in the Lord who belong to the family of Narcissus. 12Greet those workers in the Lord,

Tryphaena and Tryphosa. Greet the beloved Persis, who has worked hard in the Lord. [13]Greet Rufus, chosen in the Lord, and his mother and mine. [14]Greet Asyncritus, Phlegon, Hermes, Patrobas, Hermas, and the brothers who are with them. [15]Greet Philologus, Julia, Nereus and his sister, and Olympas, and all the holy ones who are with them. [16] Greet one another with a holy kiss. All the churches of Christ greet you.

It is not surprising that Paul should conclude his letter to Rome, in line with letter-writing convention, with a series of greetings. What is striking is the length of the list and the number of persons greeted—especially in view of the fact that he is writing to a community that he has not himself founded. The extent of the list is perhaps strategic. It demonstrates the wide basis of support Paul already enjoys in Rome. The greetings also allow him, through compliments attached to the names, to win over those he knows only by repute.

Preceding the greetings proper is a commendation for Phoebe (vv 1-2), described as a "deacon" (NAB: "minister") of the church at Cenchreae, and clearly the bearer of Paul's letter to Rome. While we cannot read into the title "deacon" (not "deaconess"!) all the features attaching to the office in the later church, the description implies that Phoebe exercised a ministry of "service" in a continuing and recognized capacity (12:7), making her a person of stature within her own community and beyond. Phoebe deserves to be welcomed and assisted in every way because she has been a "benefactor" to many and to Paul (v 2). "Benefactor" (Greek: *prostatis*) suggests that Phoebe is a woman of some means, who has exercised a ministry of hospitality in Cenchreae in a way that had earned recognition both from her own community and from fellow believers passing through. Paul's unstinted commendation of Phoebe is an important indication of the leadership exercised by women in the early communities.

In the remainder of the list (vv 3-16) Paul greets twenty-four individuals by name, plus two others indicated simply by their relationship to persons named. For most of the list, that is, for the first sixteen individuals mentioned, Paul adds some epithet to the name, indicating either some special relationship to himself or else the recognition the persons named enjoy in the wider church. Of the twenty-four individuals named, nine are women. More significant still is the fact that these women bear more than half the epithets denoting "service" and "labor" on behalf of the community and the Gospel. Particularly noteworthy is the first named on the list, Prisca. Together with her husband Aquila, Prisca worked closely with Paul, hosting house churches in several communities (Corinth, Ephesus, Rome) after he had moved on. Andronicus and Junia (v 7) likely represent another missionary couple, both—including the woman Junia—being hailed not only as "apostles" but as "outstanding" in that category. As a whole, the list of those greeted sheds considerable light on the structure of the community of believers in Rome—groups meeting in house churches—and of the leadership and apostolic activity exercised by members without discrimination of gender.

The whole sequence concludes (v 16) with the command to greet one another with "a holy kiss": a gesture through which believers communicated to each other a sense of the love (*agapē*) distinctive of Christian life. By having himself included in this exchange of love Paul enters right into the heart of the community in Rome gathered to hear the letter.

A Warning and Further Greetings: 16:17-23

> [17]I urge you, brothers, to watch out for those who create dissensions and obstacles, in opposition to the teaching that you learned; avoid them. [18]For such people do not serve our Lord Christ but their own appetites, and by fair and flattering speech they deceive the hearts of the innocent. [19]For while your obedience is known to all, so that I rejoice over you, I want you to be wise as to what is good, and simple as to what is evil; [20]then the God of peace will quickly crush Satan under your feet. The grace of our Lord Jesus be with you.
>
> [21]Timothy, my co-worker, greets you; so do Lucius and Jason and Sosipater, my relatives. [22]I, Tertius, the writer of this letter, greet you in the Lord. [23]Gaius, who is host to me and to the whole church, greets you. Erastus, the city treasurer, and our brother Quartus greet you.

The admonition contained in vv 17-20 breaks abruptly into the sequence of greetings (which continues in vv 21-23). There is also a striking change of tone: the community is urged to avoid troublemakers, whose behavior and influence is described in the darkest tones. It is not unusual to encounter severe warnings toward the close of Pauline letters (Gal 6:12-13; Phil 3:2, 17-19; 1 Cor 16:20b). But, that said, the admonition remains an oddity in Paul's letter to Rome. Until now, when rejecting contrary positions, he has offered arguments against the substance of those positions. Here, in a way at odds with the plea for tolerance in 14:1–15:13, he simply attacks the bad faith of those who defend them. Much of the language and the general tone is redolent of the post-Pauline tradition found in the Pastoral Letters (1–2 Timothy; Titus). My inclination is to regard this passage as an interpolation into the original text by a writer in the Pauline tradition who felt authorized to issue a warning in the name of the Apostle, adding in conclusion the customary grace (v 20b).

After the intrusive warning, the greetings resume, though now they come from Paul's coworkers rather than from the Apostle himself. First is Timothy, the coworker mentioned more frequently and with greater commendation than any other in the Pauline letters. Paul signals the unique status of Timothy by making his greeting stand ahead and independently of the remaining three. Then Paul's (long-suffering?) scribe, Tertius, emerges from customary scribal anonymity to send his own greeting "in the Lord" (v 22), the last phrase signaling that in writing the letter he is performing a Christian as well as a purely professional service. Finally come greetings from important persons in the Corinthian community, the first being Gaius, whom Paul baptized (1 Cor 1:14) and who is currently Paul's host. Erastus (cf. Acts 19:22), "the city treasurer," could well be the same person mentioned in a first-century AD Latin inscription from Corinth. His title shows that the Gentile communities founded by Paul did not lack some members of reasonably high social status in the wider civic community.

Concluding Doxology: 16:25-27

> [25][Now to him who can strengthen you, according to my gospel and the proclamation of Jesus Christ, according to the revelation of the mystery kept secret for long ages [26] but now manifested through the prophetic writings and, according to the command of the eternal God, made known to all nations to bring about the obedience of faith, [27]to the only wise God, through Jesus Christ be glory forever and ever. Amen.]

The doxology making up these verses appears in this place in most manuscripts. Some omit it altogether; some locate it at the end of chapter 14 or chapter 15. Its textual credentials are therefore uncertain. Nowhere else does such a long doxology appear in a Pauline letter, and, while its content echoes some important themes and phrases of Romans, the style and phraseology are reminiscent of the post-Pauline tradition seen in Colossians, Ephesians, and the Pastoral Letters. These considerations lead most scholars to regard it as a later addition.

While such may be the case, it forms a not inappropriate conclusion to Paul's most weighty letter. The doxology develops (v 25c) the notion of the Gospel in terms of "mystery," a term that communicates the sense of the community's being given privileged access, through revelation, to God's plan for the working out of the final events of salvation. As in Colossians and Ephesians (Col 1:26-27; 2:2; Eph 3:3-6, 9) the mystery particularly concerns the Gentiles' sharing in the privileges of salvation, previously understood as pertaining to Israel alone. The present revelation (v 26) of the once-hidden mystery refers to the Christ-event, made known "through the prophetic writings" and ultimately to "all nations to bring about the obedience of faith." "Prophetic writings" in all likelihood refers not to the prophets of the Old Testament but to later writing considered "prophetic" in the sense of being filled with revelatory power. Taking into account the time when the doxology is likely to have been composed, these "writings" could include New Testament texts such as the letters of Paul, and specifically Romans itself. In this sense the doxology would subtly include Paul's letter to Rome among the instruments whereby God's design to summon the entire world to "an obedience of faith" is achieved. By not only resuming key themes of the letter but also drawing it into the very scheme of salvation it proclaims, the doxology provides a very fitting tribute and conclusion to the crowning work of Paul's own hand.

Glossary of Pauline Terms and Concepts

Apostle

In Paul's case we have to set aside the notion of the twelve apostles that in the gospels refers to twelve disciples selected by Jesus in his historical life. Paul distinguishes "the Twelve" from "the apostles" (cf. 1 Cor 15:5, 7). For him being an apostle rests on two criteria: (1) to have seen the risen Lord and (2) to have been commissioned by him to preach the Gospel and found churches (1 Cor 9:1-5). Thus not all resurrection witnesses are apostles, only those who fulfill both criteria. Paul lists a woman (Junia) as "outstanding among the apostles" (Rom 16:7).

Boasting

For Paul, one "boasts" (*kauchēsis*; *kauchāsthai*) in that on which one relies for security, recognition, justification, or salvation. Such boasting is legitimate or illegitimate according to the basis on which it rests. Boasting has a negative sense when what it relies on is human achievement that is either illusory, misplaced, or unrecognizing of God (cf. 3:27; 4:2; 1 Cor 1:29; 3:21; 4:7; 5:6; 2 Cor 5:12; Gal 6:13). Boasting has a positive sense when it rests on God or the achievement of God's grace in human agents (cf. Rom 5:2, 11; 15:17; 1 Cor 1:31; 15:31; 2 Cor 1:12; 7:4; 11:16-33 [passim]; Gal 6:14; Phil 1:26; 2:16; 3:3; 1 Thess 2:19). Faith, which responds uniquely to God's creative power (cf. Rom 4:17), excludes boasting in the first sense, particularly boasting in "works [of the law]" (3:27).

Body	Paul uses the Greek word *sōma* in a special way to indicate the whole person under the aspect of having the capacity to belong to, be in touch or association or communication with the world of persons, influences, events outside the self. The body is the instrument of communication. Paul places a high value on life in the body and insists that the bodily life of believers here and now has value and dignity because of our destiny to share in the bodily resurrection of Christ (1 Cor 6:12-20; 15:35-58).
Body of Christ	Paul uses "body" in a special way to indicate the union of Christians with Christ. As risen Lord, Christ constitutes a personal, corporate sphere of salvation with whom believers find association through faith and baptism: 1 Corinthians 12:12-13; Romans 12:4-5 (see also "in Christ"). Paul thinks of the believing community as especially the Body of Christ when assembled to celebrate the Eucharist: 1 Corinthians 10:16-17; 11:23-29 (cf. esp. v 29: "without discerning the body").
Church	In secular Greek usage the term *ekklēsia* refers to an assembly of citizens "called out" from their homes (*ek-kalein*) by the civic herald to gather in the assembly to hear a solemn proclamation from the ruler or to make decisions. The early believers saw themselves as called out from the darkness of unbelief to hear in community the Good News of their risen Lord. In each separate locality they constitute "the assembly [*ekklēsia*] of God." Paul usually employs the term with reference to the local communities but this does not mean that he lacks a sense of a total *ekklēsia*, a renewed people of God, made up, on the analogy of Israel, from the spread (*diaspora*) of communities in each place (cf. 1 Cor 1:1-2).

Communion

"Communion" is the translation of the Greek word *koinōnia* that best catches the depth of its usage by Paul. Other translations are "fellowship" or "sharing" or "common participation." *Koinōnia* denotes the union created among a group of people through their sharing some experience together: e.g., the fellowship created when people gather to celebrate a person's birthday, symbolized perhaps by the sharing of a cake. As the allusion to the Eucharist in 1 Corinthians 10:16-17 indicates, Paul thinks of Christian *koinōnia* as having a "vertical" dimension in that it denotes union with Christ and a "horizontal" dimension in that it denotes the union believers have with one another through their common participation in the Body of Christ.

Death

Death (*thanatos*) can refer simply to death in the physical sense that is the lot of all animate beings, humans included. Beyond this, Paul speaks of "death" in a more fundamental eschatological sense involving eternal separation from God. In line with Jewish tradition Paul sees physical death as affecting the human race as a legacy of Adam's sin, ratified in the sinning of all his descendants (Rom 5:12-21; 1 Cor 15:21-22). Sin renders physical death "eternal" death (1 Cor 15:56), whereas the union with Christ enjoyed by believers gives them hope, beyond physical death, of sharing his risen life (Rom 6:3-8; 8:10-11; 1 Cor 15:20-28, 54-56; 2 Cor 5:1-5).

Desire

Desire (*epithymia*) almost always has a negative connotation in Paul (exceptions: Phil 1:23; 1 Thess 2:17). Beyond lust in a sexual sense, "desire" also expresses covetousness in the more general sense of selfish aspiration for what is forbidden or inappropriate for human beings. Paul sees the prohibitions pronounced by the law not only as ineffective in controlling desire but as actually prone to provoke desire for what it forbids (Rom 7:7-8).

Faith   Faith (*pistis*) is that attitude whereby I discern God acting creatively in my personal life and, as a consequence, surrender my life project to that perception in trust and obedience. For Paul faith is specifically focused on God's creative action on behalf of the sinful world in the cross and resurrection of Jesus (Rom 3:21-26; 10:9-10). It is therefore faith in "the one who justifies the ungodly" (Rom 4:5). Paul points to the biblical figure of Abraham as the great exemplar of faith and hope because of his unwavering belief in the divine promise that he would have a son and indeed a vast progeny (Gen 15:6; Rom 4; Gal 3:6-14). In this way Abraham both prefigured and modelled the way in which the nations of the world (Gentiles) would attain justification and salvation through the Messiah Jesus.

Flesh   Flesh (*sarx*) is sometimes used by Paul in a neutral sense to indicate simply the *human* aspect (e.g., the Christ "according to the flesh" [Rom 9:5] = "the Christ according to his human origins"; cf. also Rom 1:3; 4:1 [Abraham]). More characteristically, drawing on biblical (Old Testament) usage, Paul employs "flesh" in a negative sense denoting the human person from the aspect of weakness, proneness to mortality and sin, hostility to God. "Flesh," then, does not simply denote the physical aspect of human beings; "sins of the flesh" can refer to nonphysical vices such as backbiting, false witness, and slander, as much as to sexual impropriety (cf. the list in Gal 5:19-21). Paul does not identify "flesh" with "Sin" (*hamartia*) but "flesh" denotes human nature under the aspect of being vulnerable to the inroads of sin. Flesh gives rise to "desire" (*epithymia*), which in Paul almost always has negative meaning, indicating human aspiring to what is forbidden.

Fellowship   See "Communion."

Freedom

In a social context where slavery was common, freedom (*eleuthēria*) was highly prized. Paul chiefly speaks of freedom in connection with freedom from sin (which he basically thinks of as enslavement to the force of radical selfishness), freedom from death, and freedom from the law (of Moses). As a believer in Christ, Paul came to see the law as performing the task of a harsh schoolmaster that God employed to bring home to Jews their sinfulness and need for redemption (cf. Gal 3:21-25). This was not—and is not—the way most Jews experience(d) the law, but it became Paul's conviction in light of his understanding of the meaning of the cross of Christ. Paul is particularly concerned in Galatians to insist that the community stand fast in the freedom (from law) that Christ has won for them. Freedom, however, does not mean license to do whatever one wants. Freedom is above all displayed in the love (for the neighbor) that is the fulfillment of the law (Gal 5:14).

Gentiles

"Gentiles" (*ethnē*) is the Jewish way of referring to all the non-Jewish people and nations of the world. For stylistic reasons Paul sometimes uses "Greek(s)" as a substitute for "Gentile(s)" (e.g., Rom 1:16). Paul polemically sees Abraham as the archetypal Gentile and model of the way in which God has planned to bring the nations of the world to salvation (Rom 4; Gal 3): through grace and faith in Christ rather than taking on "the works of the law."

Glory

Glory (*doxa*) in biblical thought denotes the presence and power of the unseen God. Human beings cannot see God but they can discern the divine presence and power from the things God has made and the saving events God works on behalf of Israel. Human beings, created in the image and likeness of God, particularly reflect the divine glory, the basis of their authority in the universe

(Ps 8:6-9)— though this reflection is tarnished by sin. For Paul "glory" chiefly has an eschatological reference in that it refers to the final state of human beings when the completion of God's saving work in Christ will have restored them to the image and likeness of God, intended by the Creator from the beginning. In his glory as risen Lord, Christ is the model and exemplar of humanity fully arrived (2 Cor 3:17-18; Rom 8:29-30).

Gospel   "Gospel" has a biblical (Old Testament) background in the prophecies of (Second) Isaiah (Isa 40–66), who used it with reference to "telling the good news" of the liberation of those taken captive to Babylon at the time of the exile (Isa 40:9; 52:7; 61:1). It later became a more or less technical expression for the liberation longed for in the messianic age. For the early believers in Jesus the adoption of the Greek noun *euangelion* brought new resonances to "gospel" associated with the sense of a new reign or a new era dawning. In Paul "Gospel" refers to the Good News of the installation of Jesus, the crucified and risen One (1 Cor 15:3-5), at the right hand of God as Messiah and Son of God in power (Rom 1:3-4), bringing freedom from sin and inaugurating through the Spirit the reign of God (1 Cor 15:22-28). In a later generation the Evangelists (beginning presumably with Mark) joined the core message seen as above in Paul to the oral traditions about what Jesus said and did in his historical life. They thereby created the literary genre "gospel," a quasi-biography of Jesus, as an effective instrument for proclaiming "the Gospel."

Grace   The Greek word *charis* most basically denotes the charm or attractiveness of a person who spontaneously wins the favor of others. Reciprocally, then, it denotes the favor and goodwill created in the other person through such charm. More concretely *charis* can refer to a gift bestowed on a person as an expression of such favor. In biblical usage the Greek term picks up the Hebrew term *hēn* in much the same sense, especially in respect to the favor of God bestowed on human beings, with or without their doing anything to merit it. In the New Testament the sense of unmerited divine favor predominates. Paul sees the entire sending and work of Christ as the spear point of an immense wave of God's grace flowing over a sinful world, seeking to reconcile that world to its Creator (2 Cor 5:18–6:2; Rom 5:15). Paul understands his conversion on the Damascus road as a radical experience of being grasped by God's grace, so that henceforth his entire life and energy becomes an instrument of that grace to the wider world (cf. 1 Cor 15:10). His apostolic calling is a gift (*charis*) in the sense of a specific concrete expression of God's grace toward him personally (Rom 1:5; 15:15; 1 Cor 3:10; Gal 2:9).

Hope

Faith shades into hope (*elpis*) since faith in God is always faith in God's promise of salvation, which as yet is only partially fulfilled (through justification) and will be completed when the bodily lives of believers, now mortal and prone to suffering and weakness, find full salvation through conformity to the risen life of Christ (1 Cor 15; Rom 5:1-11; 8:23-25, 28-39). For Paul, hope that God will faithfully complete the process of salvation derives particularly from consideration of the immense love God has already shown in the giving up of the Son to die for sinful human beings (Rom 5:6-10; 8:32). The engendering of hope in believers is one of the key effects of the gift of the Spirit (Rom 5:5; 8:23; 2 Cor 1:22; 5:5).

"In Christ"

This distinctive Pauline phrase expresses the union believers have with Christ and with one another because of their existence, brought about by faith and baptism, in the person of the risen Lord as a corporate "sphere of salvation." This is why Paul speaks of being baptized "into" Christ and, correlatively, of life "in Christ" and of Christ's life "in" us. Paul conceives of life "in Christ" not simply in a static way but as a dynamic insertion into the total "career" of Christ: his death, burial, and (in due course) resurrection (Rom 6:1-11). Beyond this, believers are inserted into the "mind" of Christ, his disposition at all stages of his existence to empty himself out in an obedience of unselfish love (Phil 2:6-11). Thus because of their existence "in Christ" believers should feel and give expression in their lives to the love of Christ welling up within them in this sense through the Spirit (Phil 2:5; Rom 15:1-3).

Justification

Justification (*dikaiōsis, dikaiousthai*), originally a legal term referring to the verdict of acquittal given by a judge, is closely aligned to "righteousness" in Paul and refers to the divine declaration that persons are righteous in God's sight and to the status of right relationship with God ("justified") that flows therefrom. While in conventional Jewish expectation justification is something that the righteous might hope to receive from God at the last judgment on the basis of their law-righteousness, for Paul, through the death and resurrection of Christ, God has brought forward the verdict of justification for believers, enabling them to enjoy, while still on the way to full salvation, the final relationship with God (divine filiation ["sons and daughters of God"]), attested by the Spirit (Rom 8:15-17; Gal 4:4-7).

Koinōnia

See "Communion."

Law

For Paul "law" (*nomos*) almost always refers to the Jewish law of Moses. The law is good in itself and enshrines the moral values by which all should live. Paul's problem with the law lies in its incapacity to address human sinfulness at sufficiently radical depth. This is because it simply issues commands and prohibitions from outside, in contrast to Christ, who, in his costly obedience on the cross, entered right into the sinful human situation (2 Cor 5:21) and released the Spirit as the truly effective remedy for sin (Rom 8:1-4). Paul's negative comments about the law stem particularly from his strong opposition to its imposition on converts from the Gentile world on the grounds that adherence to it, especially in regard to its ritual requirements—"works of the law" (circumcision; Sabbath observance; food regulations)—are necessary for justification (see entry for "Works of the Law" below). For Paul this restricts salvation to Jews only and rebuffs the costly action of God in the person of the Son upon the cross (Gal 2:20-21).

Life   Life (*zōē*) can refer simply to ordinary life. In line with other New Testament writers Paul will also use it in an eschatological sense to refer to the share in God's "eternal life" that is the destiny of believers on the basis of justification (cf. Rom 8:10: "the Spirit means life because of righteousness"). Arrival at the fullness of salvation will mean attainment of "life" in this sense.

Love   Paul speaks of love (*agapē*) in the sense of God's (or Christ's) love (Rom 5:5-10; 8:31-39), believers' love for God (Rom 8:28; 1 Cor 2:9), and the love believers ought have for each other. The Spirit is the felt experience of God's love (Rom 5:5). The faith of believers finds expression in love (Gal 5:6). Love is especially the fruit of the Spirit (Gal 5:22), which is essentially the impact of the ongoing love of Christ as risen Lord (1 Cor 15:45; 2 Cor 5:14). For Paul love is the "fulfillment" (*plērōma*) of the law (Rom 13:8-10; Gal 5:13-14). In 1 Corinthians 13 Paul cites at length a "hymn to love" (cf. also 1 Thess 3:12; 4:9-10).

Mystery	Mystery (*mystērion*) refers in Paul to knowledge of heavenly matters and especially of God's eternal saving plan, accessible to human beings only through revelation. Paul uses the term specifically in regard to what is destined to occur at the end of time (Rom 11:25; 16:25; 1 Cor 15:51). In the (deutero-Pauline) letters Ephesians and Colossians "mystery" refers to God's plan to unite Jews and Gentiles in one body, the church.
Promise	Paul uses "promise" (*epangelia*) with reference to God's promise to Abraham that, despite his advanced age and the barrenness of his wife Sarah, he would have a son (Isaac) and indeed an immense progeny (Gen 15:1-6; 18:1-15; etc.). In one particular descendant ("seed"), Christ, all the nations of the earth would be blessed. This blessing, which in fact is the gift of the Spirit, will come to the nations of the world insofar as they become "seed"/"descendants" of Abraham by imitating his faith (Rom 4:16-25; Gal 3:14). For Paul this promise to Abraham includes all the blessings of salvation. It catches up and restores the original divine bequest to human beings (to "inherit the world" [Rom 4:13; 1 Cor 3:21-23; cf. Gen 1:26-28]), frustrated by human sin. The Sinai covenant, with its promulgation of the law to Israel, cannot annul or disturb the focus of the blessing on Christ as "seed of Abraham" (Gal 3:15-17) and on all who through faith and baptism come to be "in" him (Gal 3:26-29).
Reconciliation	Reconciliation (*katallagē*) is a significant image Paul employs to describe God's saving work for the world in Christ. The presupposition is that, prior to that saving work, the human world is alienated and at enmity with God. The impulse toward reconciliation comes entirely from God, the injured party, so to speak. In Christ, specifically in Christ-crucified, God is reaching out to

that alienated world, graciously and unconditionally offering reconciliation and peace. The relevant passages are Romans 5:10-11 and especially 2 Corinthians 5:18–6:2 (also Rom 11:15; cf. Col 1:20, 22; Eph 2:16). Within the overall image of reconciliation Paul presents himself and his fellow workers as "ambassadors" of God, appealing to human beings to be reconciled to God (2 Cor 5:19-20).

Redemption   In the ancient world those taken prisoner in war were routinely sold into slavery by their captors. The only way to secure their freedom was for relatives or friends to "redeem" them through payment of a price. Thus "redemption" (*apolytrō-sis*) has the sense of liberation achieved at a cost. Used metaphorically by Paul in relation to God's saving act in Christ (Rom 3:24; 1 Cor 1:30; cf. Col 1:14; Eph 1:7), redemption conveys the sense of freedom from the slavery of sin achieved through his costly death on the cross—but without any connotation of his "paying" a price to any agent (the Devil; Sin personified; etc.).

Righteousness   Righteousness (*dikaiosynē*; translated "justice" in older Catholic Bibles) is a biblical concept that refers to the status I have in the eyes of another with whom I am in relationship because I have acted faithfully in accordance with that relationship. The best shorthand synonym for "righteousness" is "faithfulness"—with the connotation of faithfulness within the requirements of a relationship. Paul speaks of "righteousness" with respect both to God and to human beings. God's righteousness ("the righteousness of God") refers to the divine faithfulness to the covenant with Israel and also to God's faithfulness, as Creator, to the rest of the world. Paul sees God's action in Christ as the culminating exercise of the divine righteousness—for Israel and for the world (Rom 3:21-26). Within the covenant relationship between God and Israel "righteousness" is required also of human beings, specifically a righteousness measured and determined by fulfilling the requirements of the Mosaic law ("law-righteousness"). For Paul the cross of Christ has shown that there is no righteousness on the human side, whether on the part of Israel or of the world in general (Rom 1:18–3:20; 3:23). By the same token, Paul sees and proclaims the cross of Christ as the free and gracious communication of divine righteousness to believers, bringing about their justification and setting them on the path to salvation.

Salvation

Paul speaks of salvation (*sōtēria*) in reference to rescue from the destruction destined to fall on the unbelieving world at the time of the judgment (Gal 1:4; 1 Thess 1:10). The term almost always has this future reference in Paul. Believers live in the time "between" justification (which is behind them [Rom 5:1]) and salvation (which is still outstanding and a matter of hope). Believers are therefore "on the way" to salvation; they are "being saved" (*sōzomenoi*). Negatively, salvation means rescue from the ills of the present age (suffering, temptation, death); positively, it means entrance into the blessings associated with the final establishment of the rule of God and the arrival of that fullness of humanity that was the Creator's intent for human beings from the start—the fullness of humanity ("glory") "modelled" by the risen Christ (2 Cor 3:17–4:6; Rom 8:29). The aspect of salvation that believers already have is the renewed relationship with God (justification), attested by the gift of the Spirit. Bodily, however, they are still anchored in the present age and await in this sense "the redemption of our bodies" (Rom 8:23).

Scripture

Paul reads Scripture (*graphē*), that is, the Old Testament, entirely from the perspective of his experience of Christ. What God has done—for Israel and for the world as a whole—is the fulfillment of the salvation promised in the Scriptures. Hence Scripture functions as "promise" or as foreshadowing the way salvation was to run in the messianic age, which for Paul has now dawned in Christ. Paul clinches arguments from experience (e.g., the experience of the Spirit [Gal 3:1-13]) by showing from Scripture that this was how God indicated that things would run in the messianic age. While Paul's use of Scripture may seem arbitrary to us today, his methods of interpretation are usually in line with Jewish practice of the time.

Sin

Paul speaks of sin (*hamartia*) almost always in the singular ("Sin"). He rarely speaks of "sins" (plural), which he regards as merely "symptoms" of the deeper-seated "virus" denoted by the singular usage. Paul images sin in Romans 5–8 as a kind of tyrant power that, apart from the redemptive action of Christ, has got all human beings in its enslaving grip. Sin in this sense refers to a radical selfishness that poisons relationships in all directions: to God, to one's fellow human beings, to one's body, and to the wider nonhuman world (Rom 8:19-22). In this sense sin is more than the sum total of the sinning of individuals. There is a solidarity in sinning that affects human beings universally—a universality that Paul, drawing on a Jewish tradition, sees flowing to all human beings as a legacy of the ("original") sin of Adam, which all subsequent human sinning ratifies (Rom 5:12). In the face of this deep-seated problem the law is impotent, indeed counterproductive (5:20; 7:6, 13). But the grace of Christ, the embodiment of divine unselfish love displayed in his obedience on the cross (Rom 5:19; Phil 2:8), is more than sufficient to match the sum total of human sinning and so bring hope to the world (Rom 5:12-21).

Spirit

In biblical thought generally, "spirit" (Hebrew *ruach*; Greek *pneuma*) denotes the impact of God's power as it is felt or perceived in the world. In the

New Testament the Spirit is closely linked to the person of Christ. For Paul the Spirit is the felt experience of God's love (Rom 5:5; 8:15), especially as it is communicated through the impact of the risen Lord, whom he describes as "life-giving Spirit" (1 Cor 15:45). The Spirit replaces the law as the regulator and energizing force of the moral life of believers (Rom 8:1-11); it is the sure witness to the reality for believers that they are "justified" in God's sight (Gal 3:1-9; 4:6-7) and is the pledge or "down payment" (2 Cor 1:22) or "firstfruits" (Rom 8:23) of the full gift of salvation to come. Paul occasionally speaks of the human "spirit" (Rom 8:16; 1 Cor 2:11). In this sense "spirit" is the positive counterpart to "flesh," denoting that aspect of the human person that is open to God, receptive of (eternal) life, capable of being transformed into divine likeness (2 Cor 3:17-18).

"Works of the Law"   This phrase is now seen as technical expression denoting the ritual requirements of the Jewish law—circumcision for males, Sabbath observance, food laws—that served in a particular way to identify and mark off Jews from other peoples ("identity markers"). Paul uses the phrase in contexts where he is countering attempts to force converts from the non-Jewish (Gentile) world to become Jews first, by submitting to these practices, on the grounds that without such identity they cannot find inclusion in the community of salvation (Rom 3:20-30; 4:4-5; Gal 2:16). More traditionally, the phrase has been interpreted as referring to any human attempt to gain right standing in God's eyes ("righteousness") through obedience to the precepts of law in a more general ethical sense. Pauline scholarship remains divided over which of these interpretations is more true to Paul.

Wrath   This disturbing biblical concept does not so much refer to an emotion in God as to the destructive force of God's judgment falling on the powers that oppress Israel; in this way the divine wrath actually operates salvifically for Israel. In the apocalyptic worldview of the New Testament, including Paul, "wrath" (*orgē*) refers to the final destruction that will fall on the world that has remained hostile to God and unresponsive to the Gospel. As in the case of Israel, it is something that the faithful may hope to be delivered from rather than something that might fall on them (Gal 1:4; 1 Thess 1:10; Rom 5:9 [where there is *no* reference to "God," despite the customary translations "wrath (anger) of God," "divine wrath"]).

Further Reading

Paul in General

Harrington, Daniel J. *Meeting St. Paul Today: Understanding the Man, His Mission, and His Message*. Chicago: Loyola Press, 2008.

Horrell, David G. *An Introduction to the Study of Paul*. 2nd ed. London and New York: T & T Clark, 2006.

Galatians

Hays, Richard B. "Galatians," in *The New Interpreter's Bible*, edited by L. E. Keck. Vol. 11, 181–348. Nashville, TN: Abingdon, 2000.

Matera, Frank J. *Galatians*. Sacra Pagina 9. Collegeville, MN: Liturgical Press, 1992.

Romans

Byrne, Brendan. *Romans*. Sacra Pagina 6. Collegeville, MN: Liturgical Press, 1996.

Johnson, Luke Timothy. *Romans: A Literary and Theological Commentary*. Macon, GA: Smyth & Helwys, 2001.